DIGITAL MONSTERS DIGIMON TAMERS™

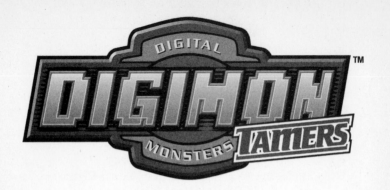

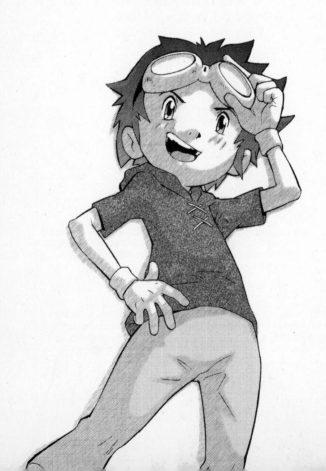

Translator - Stephanie Sheh
English Adaptation - Lianne Sentar
Retouch and Lettering - Jackie Medel
Cover Layout - Patrick Hook
Graphic Designer - Deron Bennett

Editor - Paul Morrissey
Digital Imaging Manager - Chris Buford
Pre-Press Manager - Antonio DePietro
Production Managers - Jennifer Miller and Mutsumi Miyazaki
Art Director - Matt Alford
Managing Editor - Jill Freshney
VP of Production - Ron Klamert
President & C.O.O. - John Parker
Publisher & C.E.O. - Stuart Levy

Email: info@TOKYOPOP.com
Come visit us online at www.TOKYOPOP.com

A  Manga

TOKYOPOP Inc.
5900 Wilshire Blvd. Suite 2000
Los Angeles, CA 90036

Digimon Tamers Vol. 1

ISBN: 1-59182-821-X

First TOKYOPOP printing: April 2004

10 9 8 7 6 5 4 3 2 1
Printed in the USA

DIGITAL

DIGIMON™

TAMERS

MONSTERS

VOLUME 1

YUEN WONG YU

TOKYOPOP®

LOS ANGELES • TOKYO • LONDON

HENRY WONG

A cool-headed Tamer who fiercely opposes violence. He's half-Chinese and highly intelligent.

TERRIERMON

Quite possibly the cutest Digimon ever. He may look like a bunny, but he's actually...well, not that different from a bunny.

GARGOMON

Terriermon's Champion form. He's a bit trigger happy with those gun hands of his.

DIGI KNOW THESE GUYS?

CALUMON

A mysterious digimon who loves to play. No, really--loves.

IMPMON

A mysterious digimon who loves to cause mischief. What's his true goal?

OUR STORY

Takato Matsuki, a hardcore fan of the Digimon game and TV show, one day finds Guilmon--a Digimon he designed, and in the real world! Despite Takato's excitement, he soon finds out being a real Digimon Tamer is far less simple than playing a video game...

HIROKAZU "KAZU" SHIODA

KENTA KITAGAWA

Takato's friends. They play the digimon game, but don't believe

CHARACTER DATA

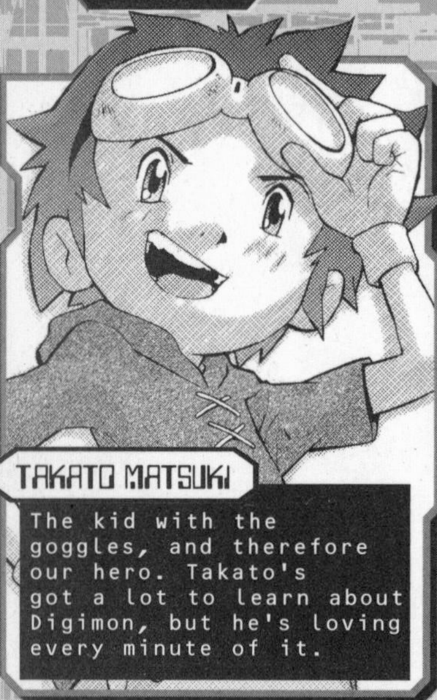

TAKATO MATSUKI

The kid with the goggles, and therefore our hero. Takato's got a lot to learn about Digimon, but he's loving every minute of it.

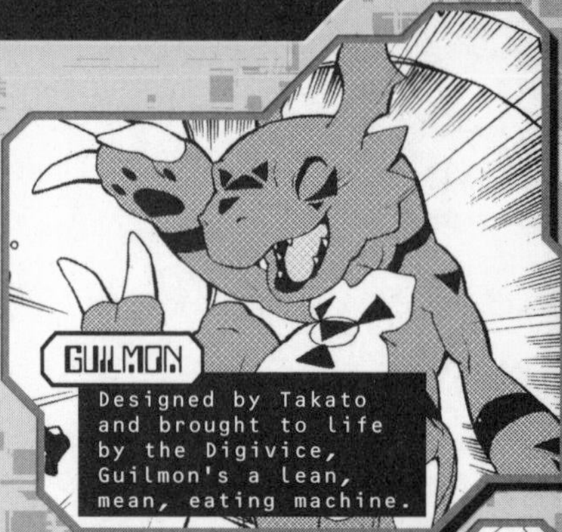

GUILMON

Designed by Takato and brought to life by the Digivice, Guilmon's a lean, mean, eating machine.

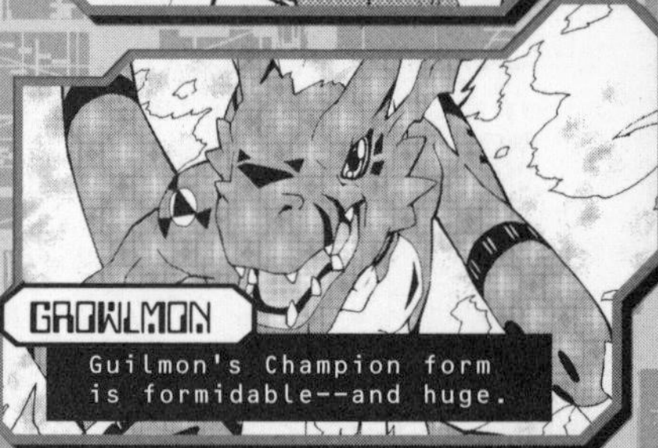

GROWLMON

Guilmon's Champion form is formidable--and huge.

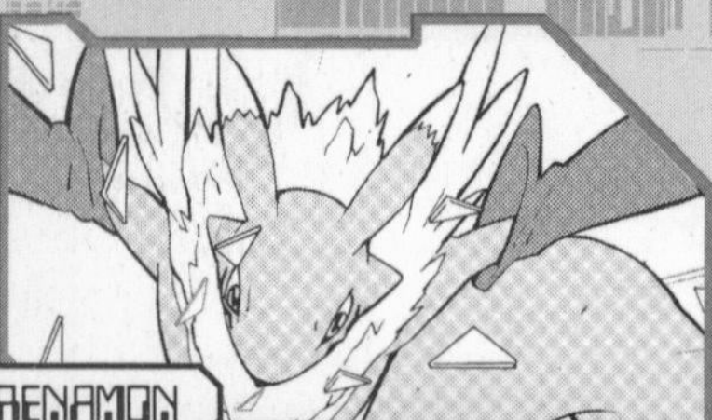

RENAMON

A fierce warrior with surprising intelligence. Renamon may not show it, but she cares deeply for Rika.

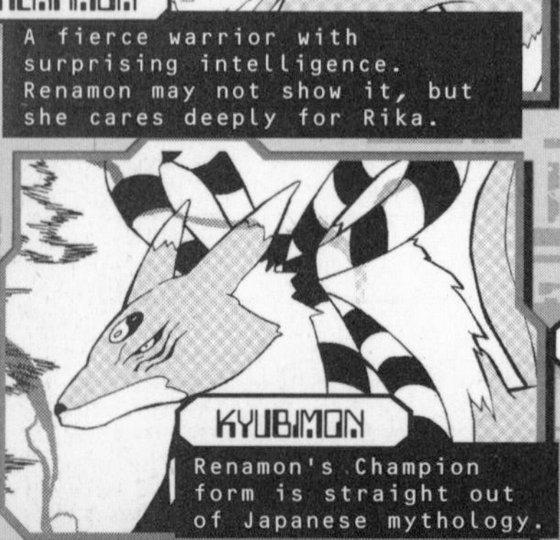

KYUBIMON

Renamon's Champion form is straight out of Japanese mythology.

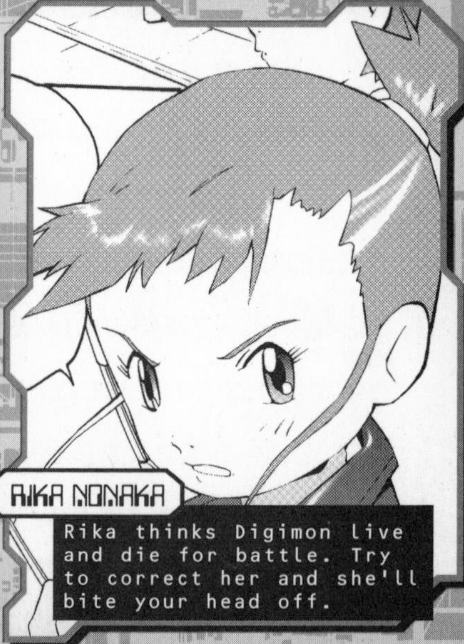

RIKA NONAKA

Rika thinks Digimon live and die for battle. Try to correct her and she'll bite your head off.

CONTENTS

1

CHAPTER 01: THE ART OF MAKING A FRIEND 10

CHAPTER 02: FAR CUTER DIGIMON 32

CHAPTER 03: DANGEROUS DEVELOPMENTS 55

CHAPTER 04: SECRETS AND ANGER MANAGEMENT 73

CHAPTER 05: BIG TROUBLE IN LITTLE TOKYO 93

CHAPTER 06: DAZED AND CONFUSED 115

CHAPTER 7 : FREEING THE DIGIVOLUTION CONVOLUTION...............................137

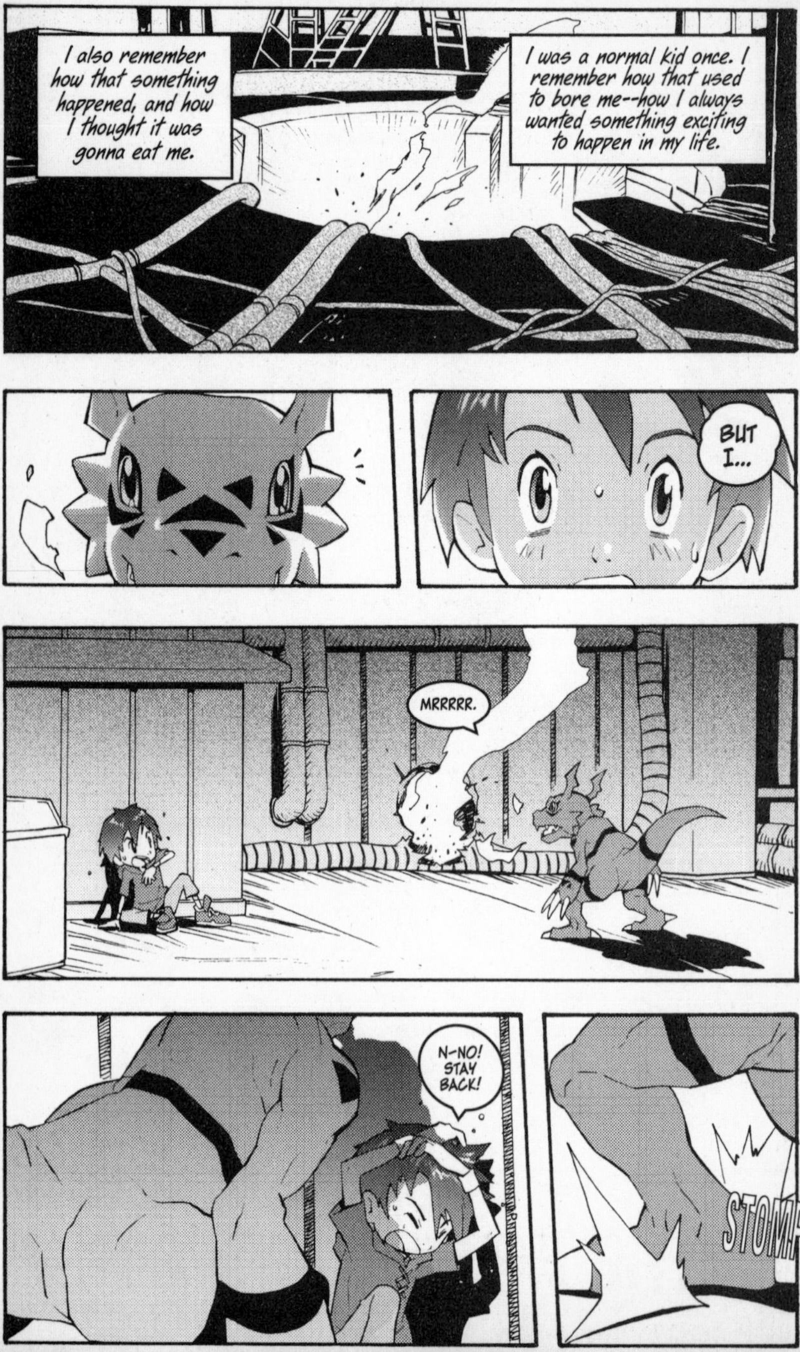
I was a normal kid once. I remember how that used to bore me--how I always wanted something exciting to happen in my life.
I also remember how that something happened, and how I thought it was gonna eat me.
BUT I...
MRRRRR.
STOMP
N-NO! STAY BACK!

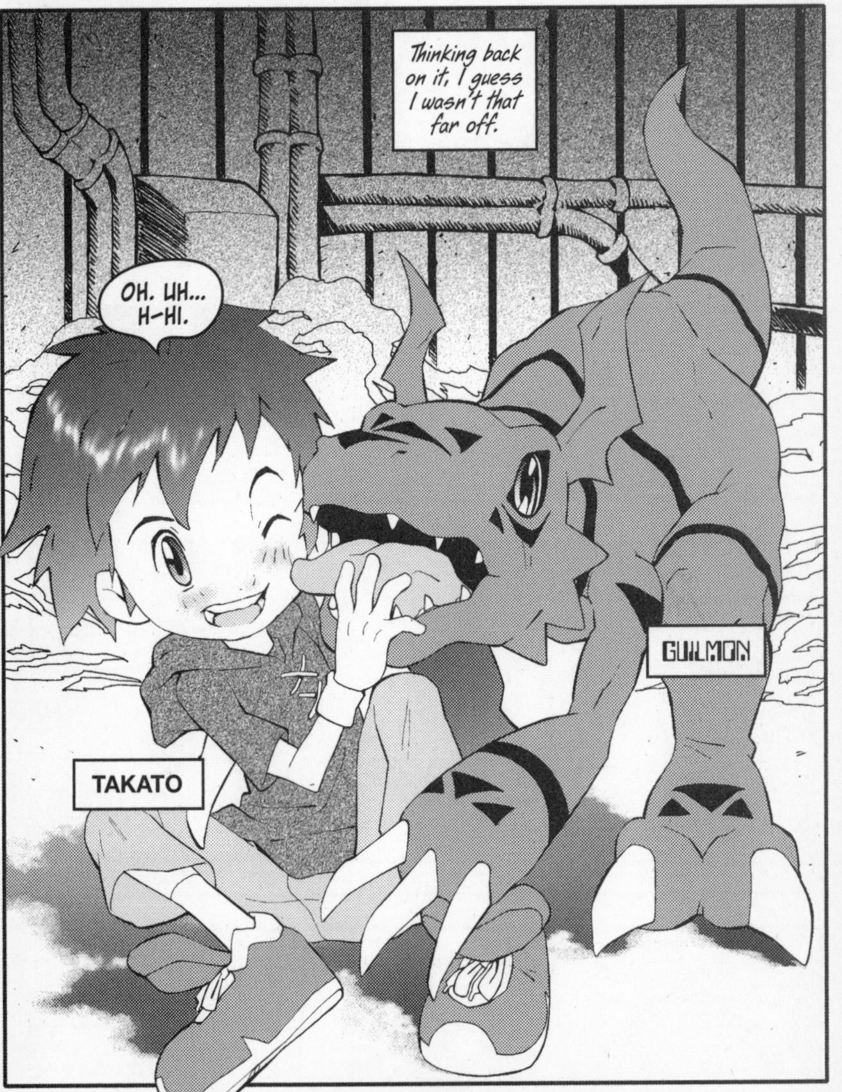
Thinking back on it, I guess I wasn't that far off.
OH. UH... H-HI.
GUILMON
TAKATO

CHAPTER 1:

THE ART OF MAKING A FRIEND

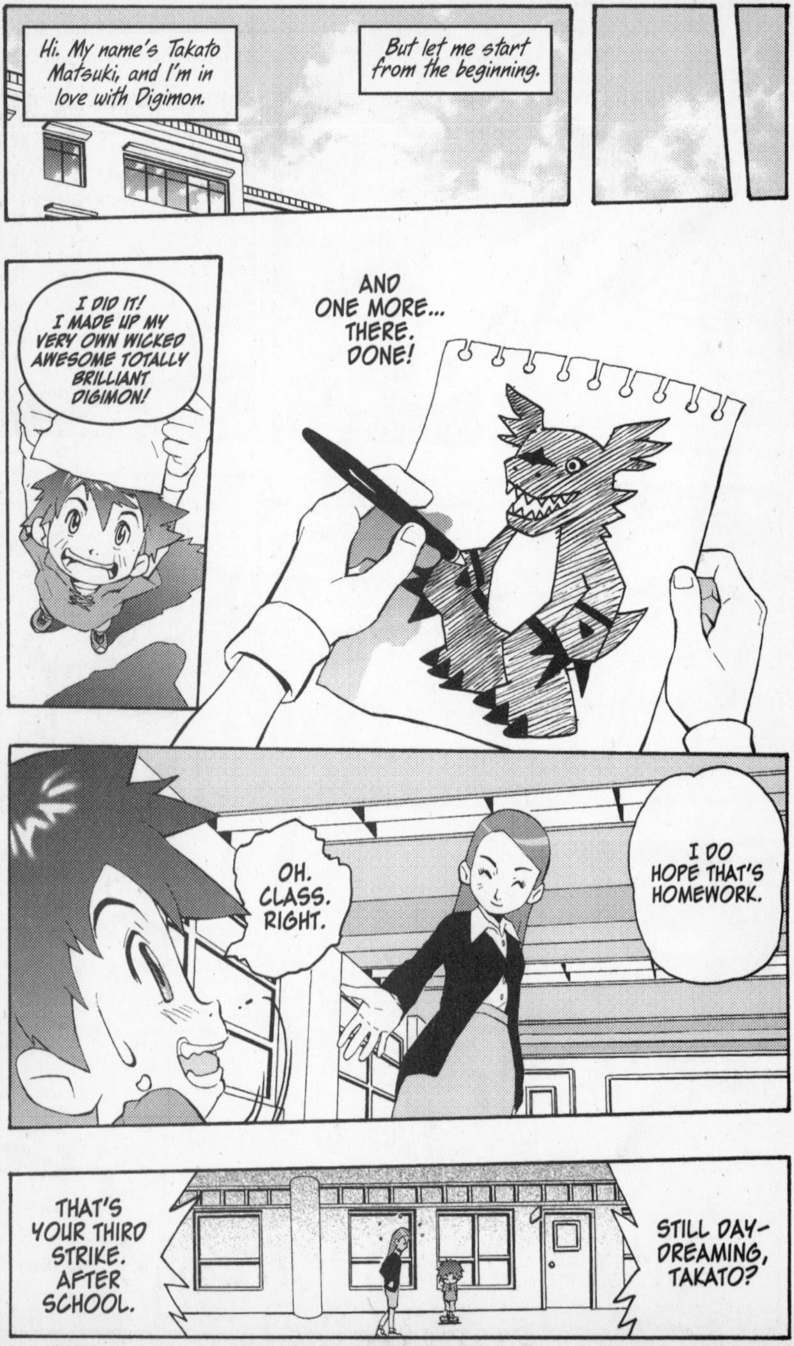
Hi. My name's Takato Matsuki, and I'm in love with Digimon.
But let me start from the beginning.
AND ONE MORE... THERE. DONE!
I DID IT! I MADE UP MY VERY OWN WICKED AWESOME TOTALLY BRILLIANT DIGIMON!
I DO HOPE THAT'S HOMEWORK.
OH. CLASS. RIGHT.
STILL DAY-DREAMING, TAKATO?
THAT'S YOUR THIRD STRIKE. AFTER SCHOOL.

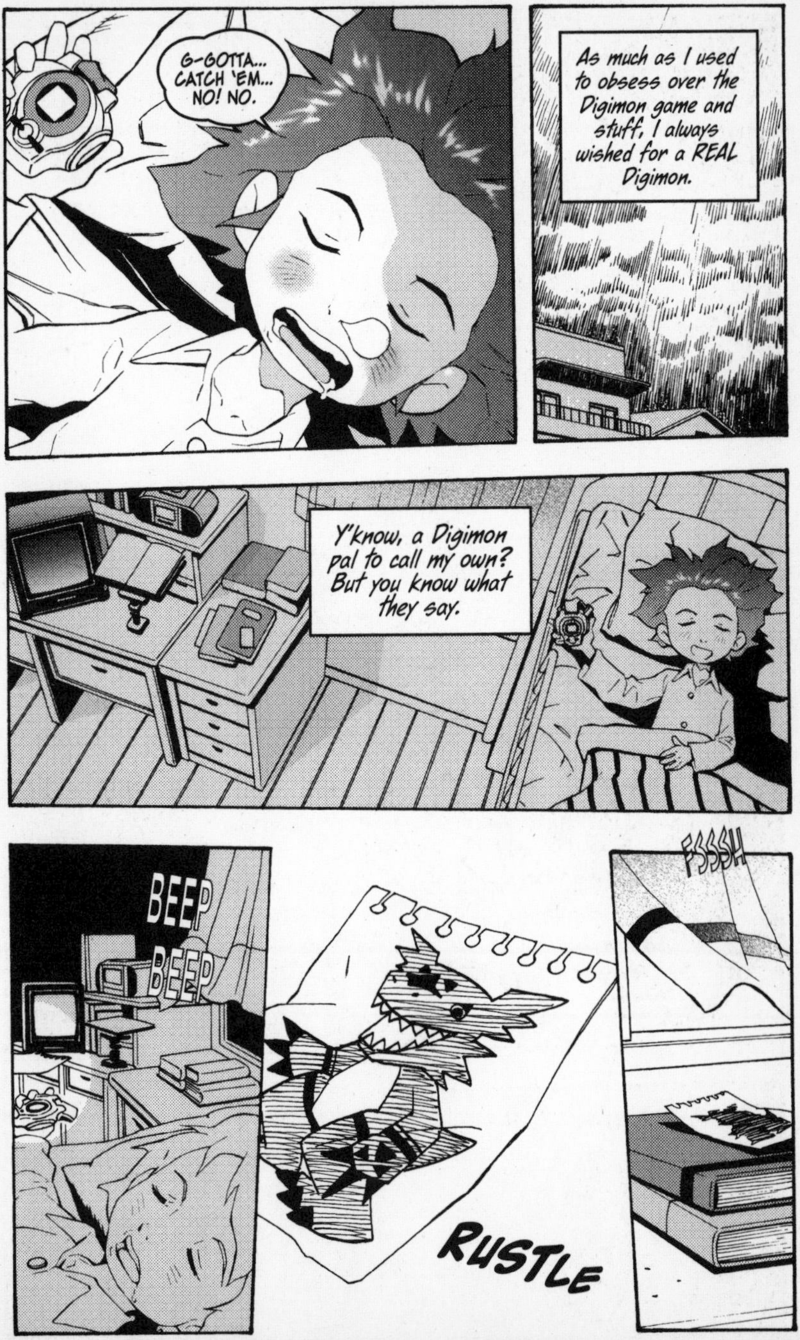
As much as I used to obsess over the Digimon game and stuff, I always wished for a REAL Digimon.
G-GOTTA... CATCH 'EM... NO! NO.
Y'know, a Digimon pal to call my own? But you know what they say.
FSSSH
RUSTLE
BEEP
BEEP

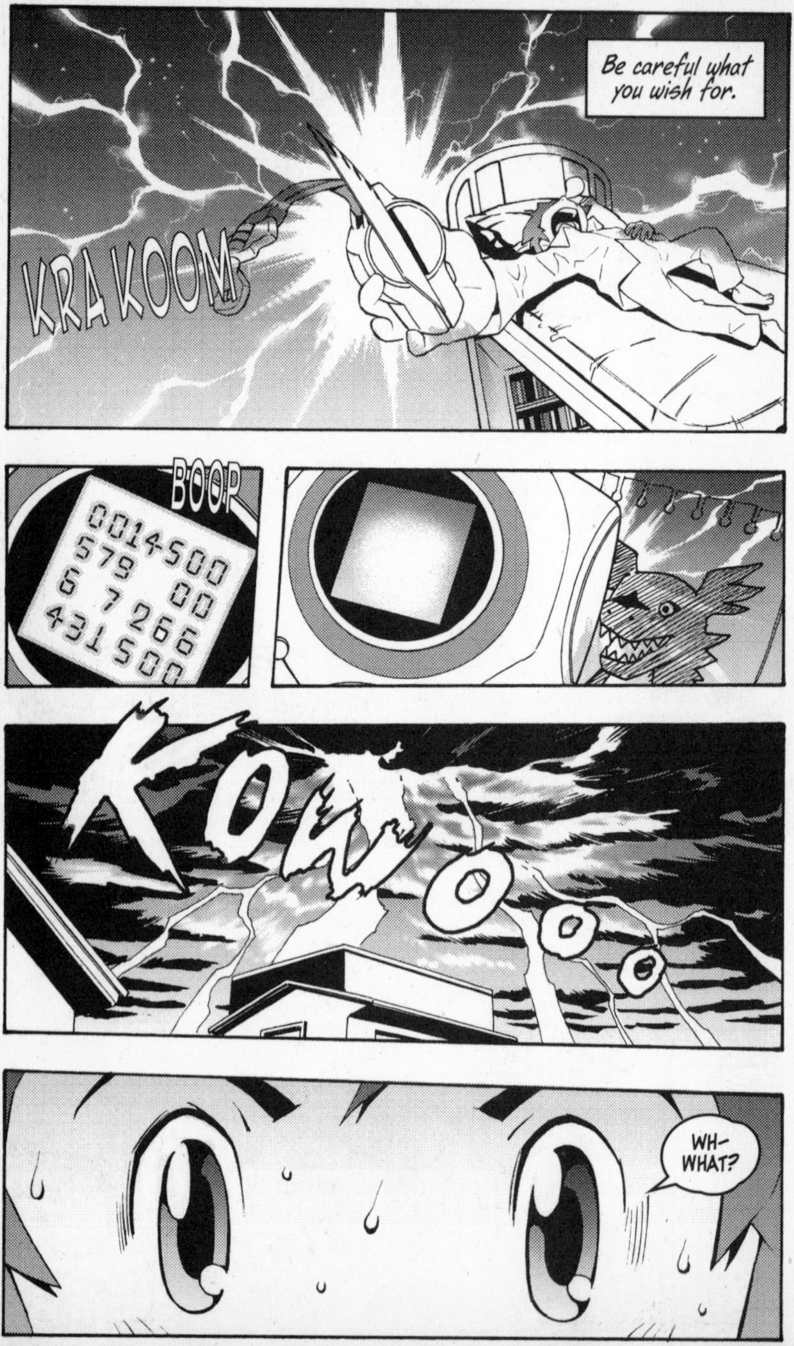
Be careful what you wish for.
KRA KOOM
BOOP
0014500
579
6 7 266
431500
KOWOOOO
WH-
WHAT?

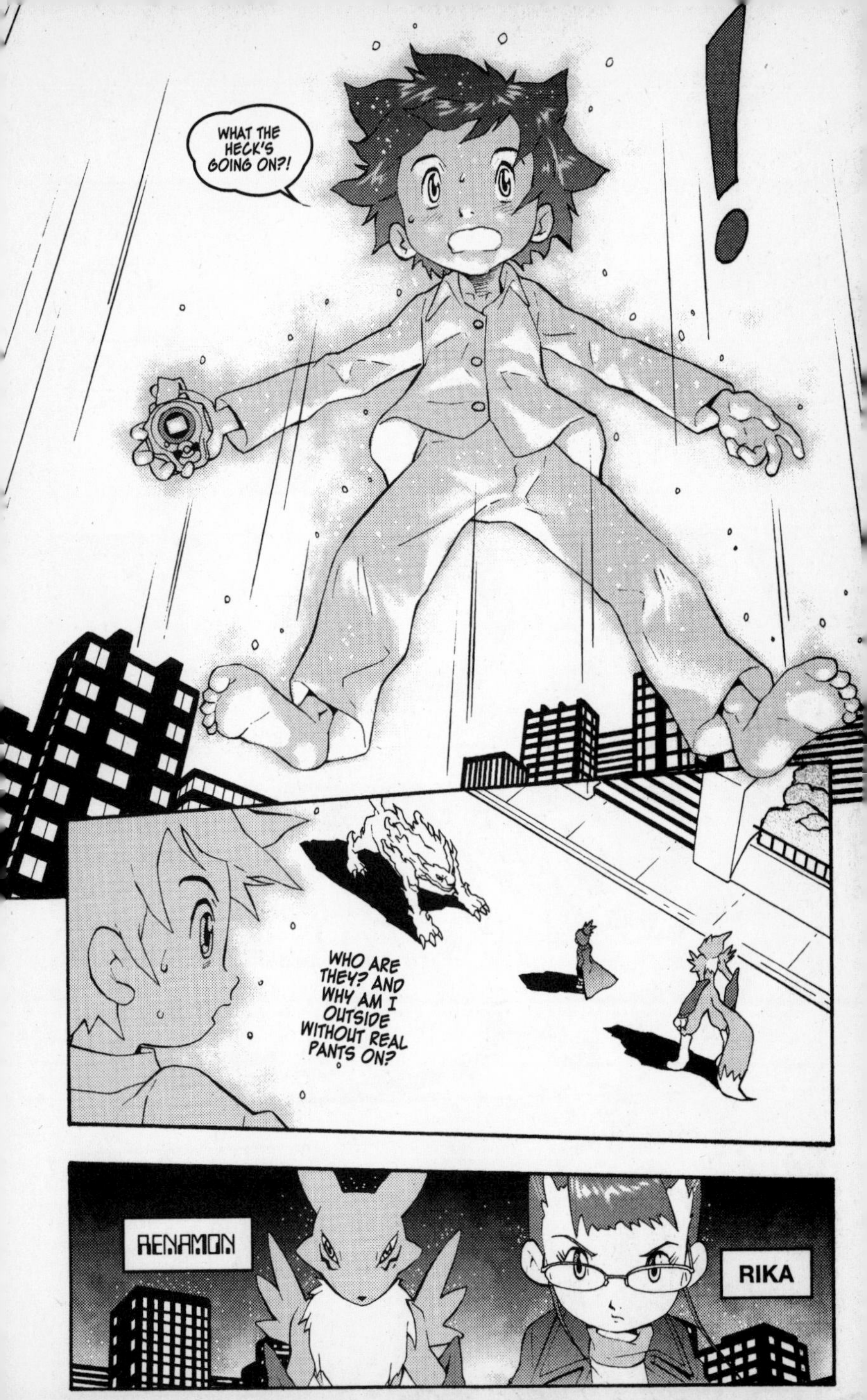
!
WHAT THE HECK'S GOING ON?!
WHO ARE THEY? AND WHY AM I OUTSIDE WITHOUT REAL PANTS ON?
RIKA
RENAMON

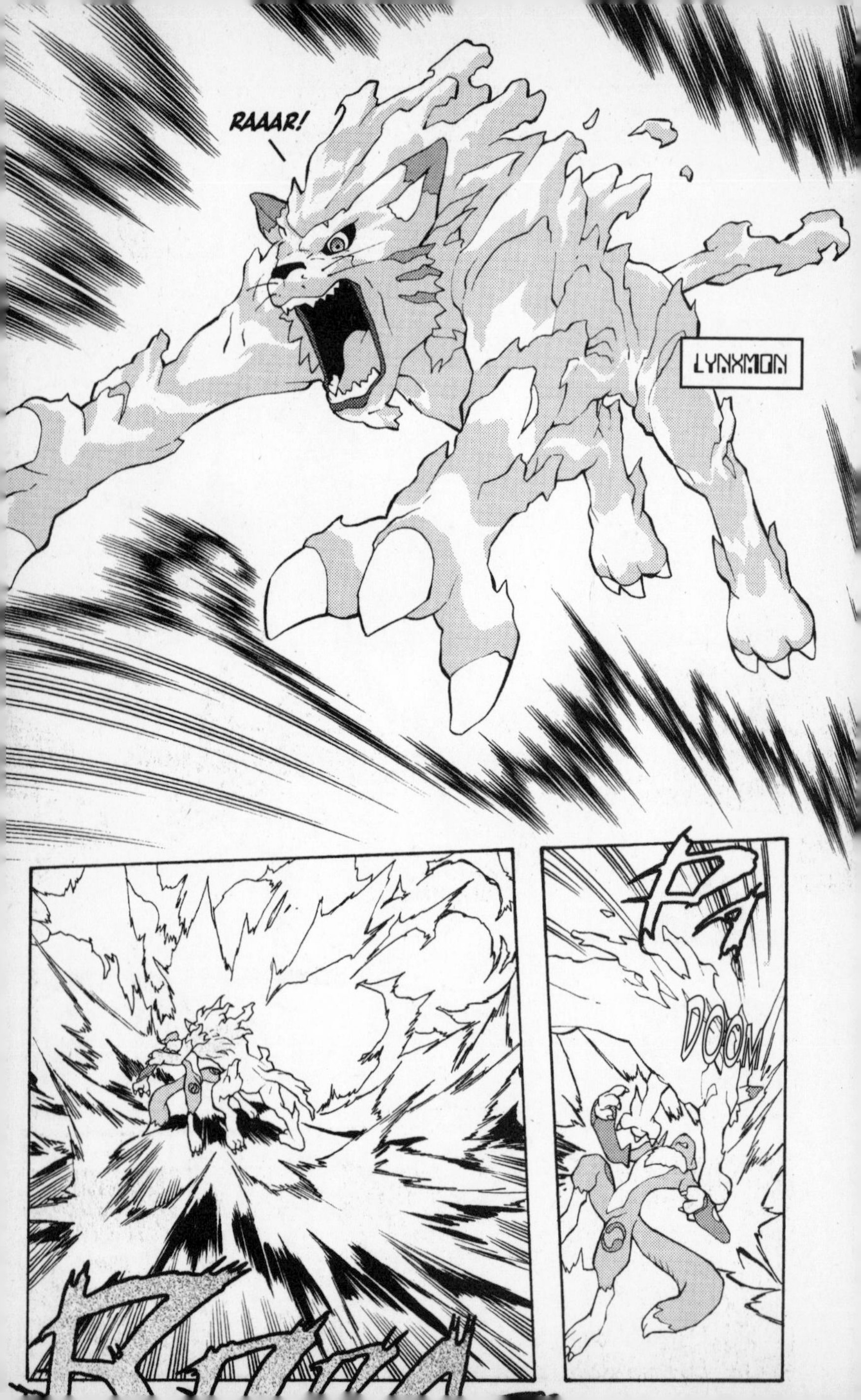
RAAAR!
LYNXMON
DOOM

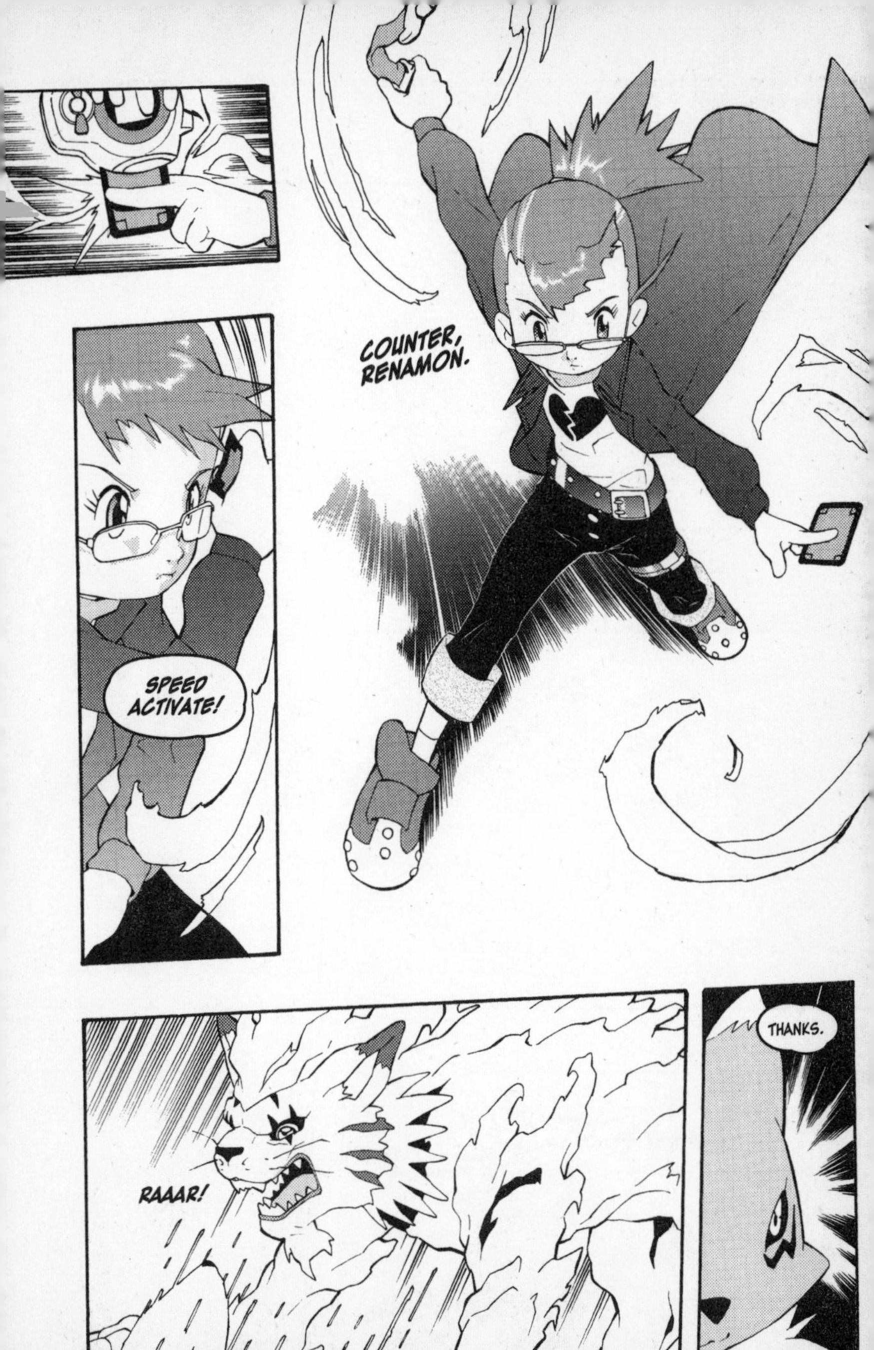
COUNTER, RENAMON.
SPEED ACTIVATE!
THANKS.
RAAAR!

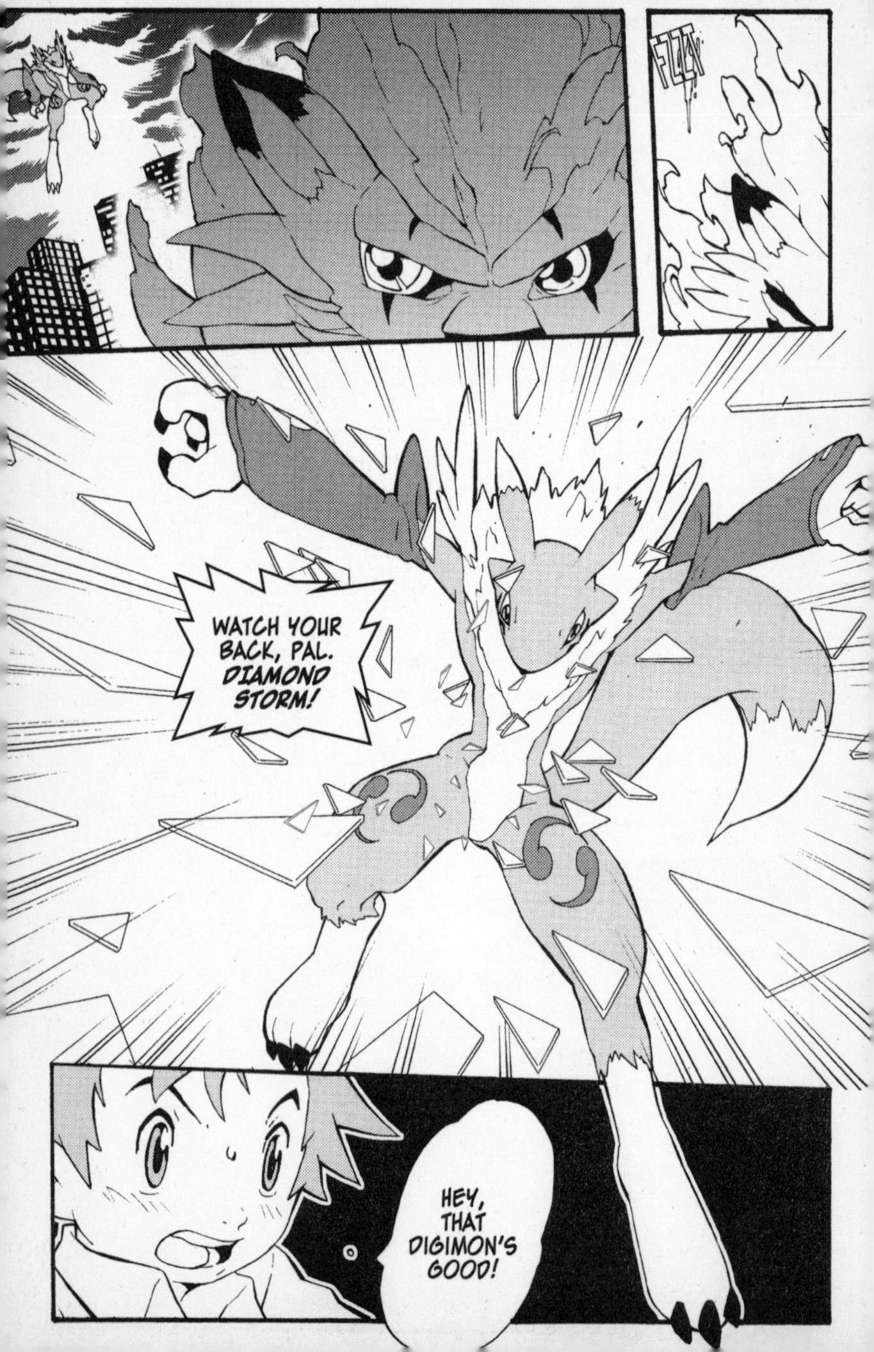
FZZT
WATCH YOUR BACK, PAL. DIAMOND STORM!
HEY, THAT DIGIMON'S GOOD!

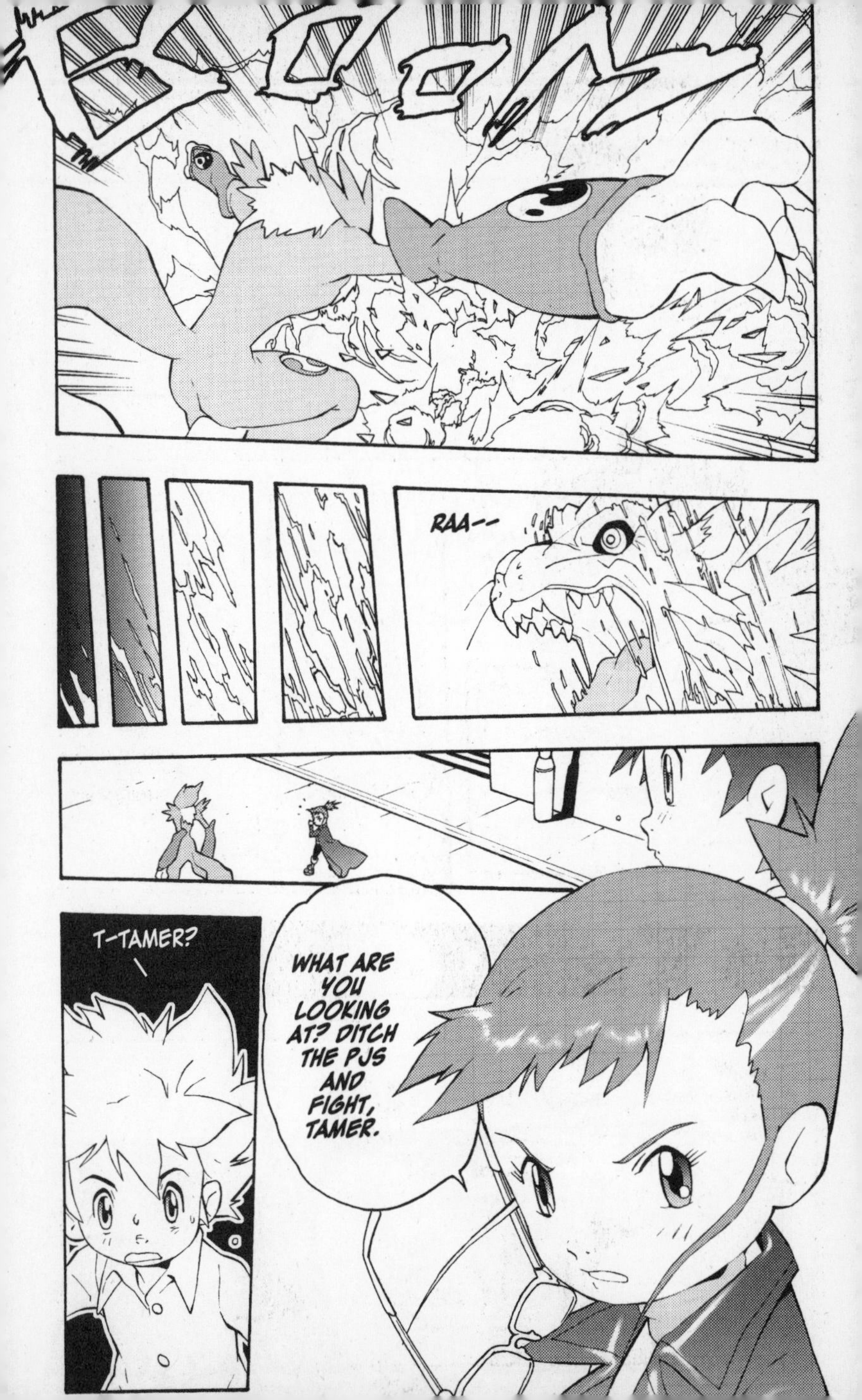
RAA--
WHAT ARE YOU LOOKING AT? DITCH THE PJS AND FIGHT, TAMER.
T-TAMER?

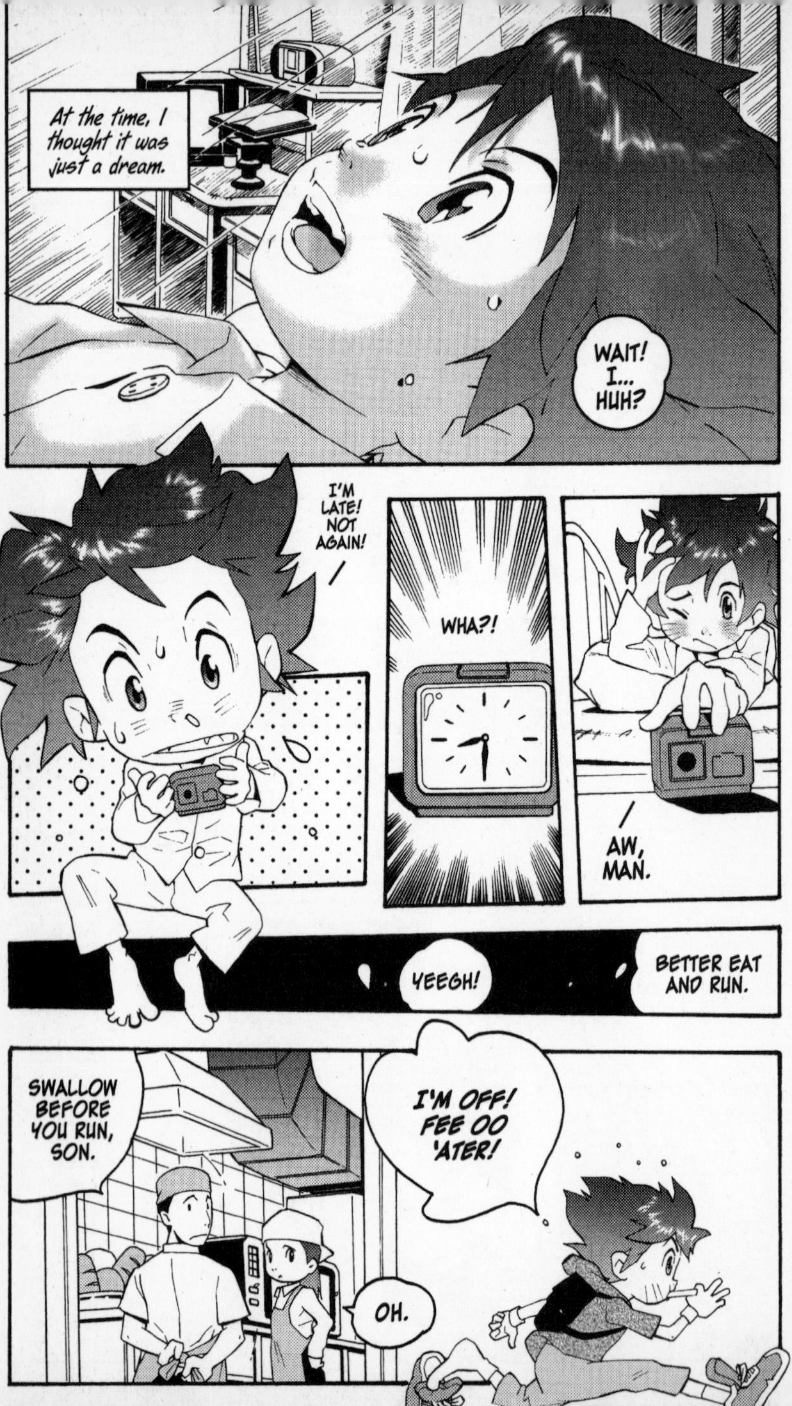
At the time, I thought it was just a dream.
WAIT! I... HUH?
AW, MAN.
WHA?!
I'M LATE! NOT AGAIN!
BETTER EAT AND RUN.
YEEGH!
I'M OFF! FEE OO 'ATER!
SWALLOW BEFORE YOU RUN, SON.
OH.

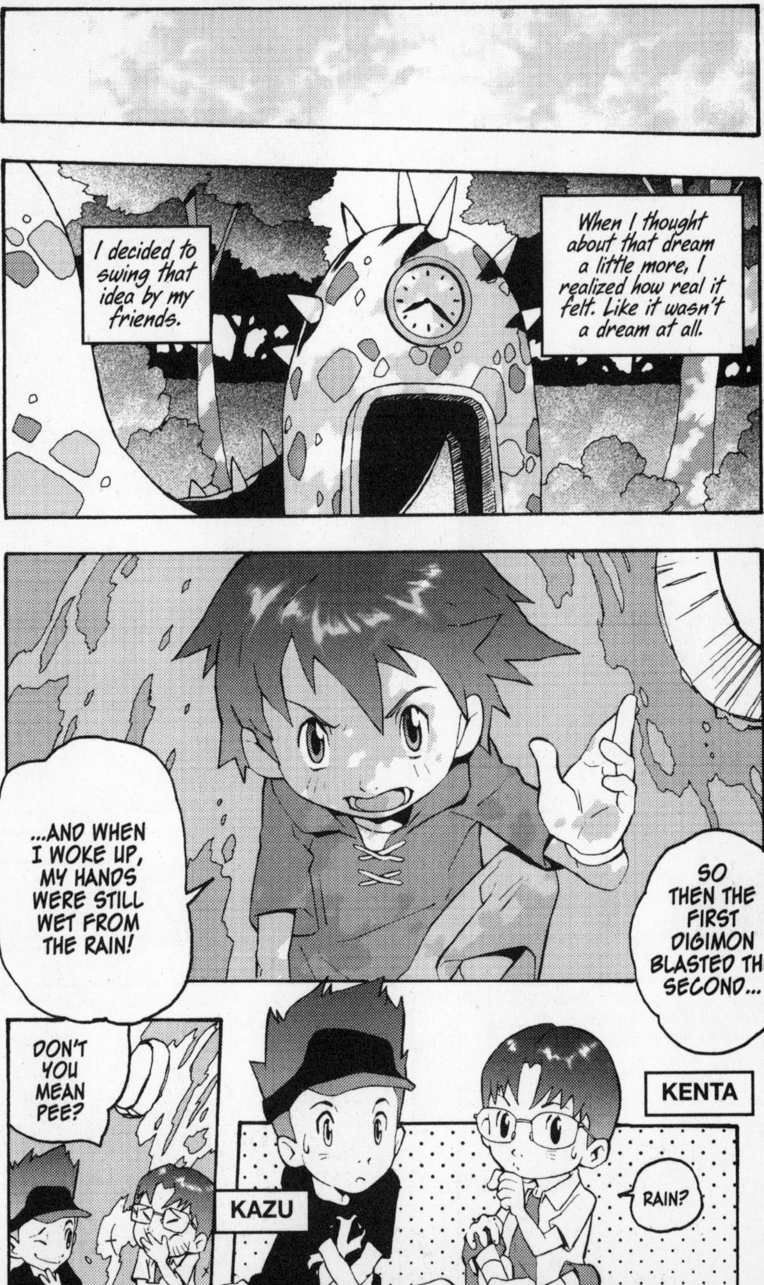
When I thought about that dream a little more, I realized how real it felt. Like it wasn't a dream at all.
I decided to swing that idea by my friends.
SO THEN THE FIRST DIGIMON BLASTED THE SECOND...
...AND WHEN I WOKE UP, MY HANDS WERE STILL WET FROM THE RAIN!
KENTA
RAIN?
KAZU
DON'T YOU MEAN PEE?

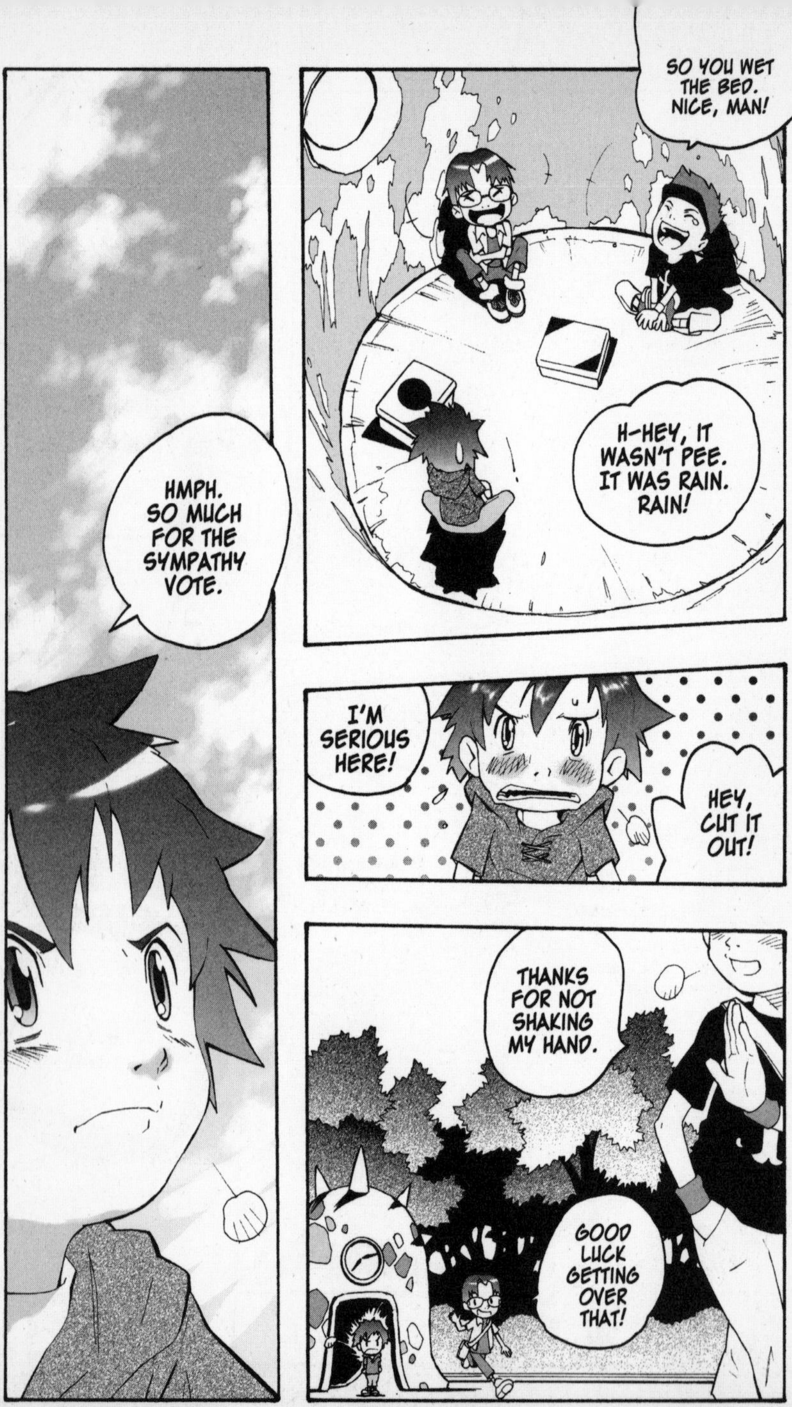
SO YOU WET THE BED. NICE, MAN!
H-HEY, IT WASN'T PEE. IT WAS RAIN. RAIN!
HEY, CUT IT OUT!
I'M SERIOUS HERE!
THANKS FOR NOT SHAKING MY HAND.
GOOD LUCK GETTING OVER THAT!
HMPH. SO MUCH FOR THE SYMPATHY VOTE.

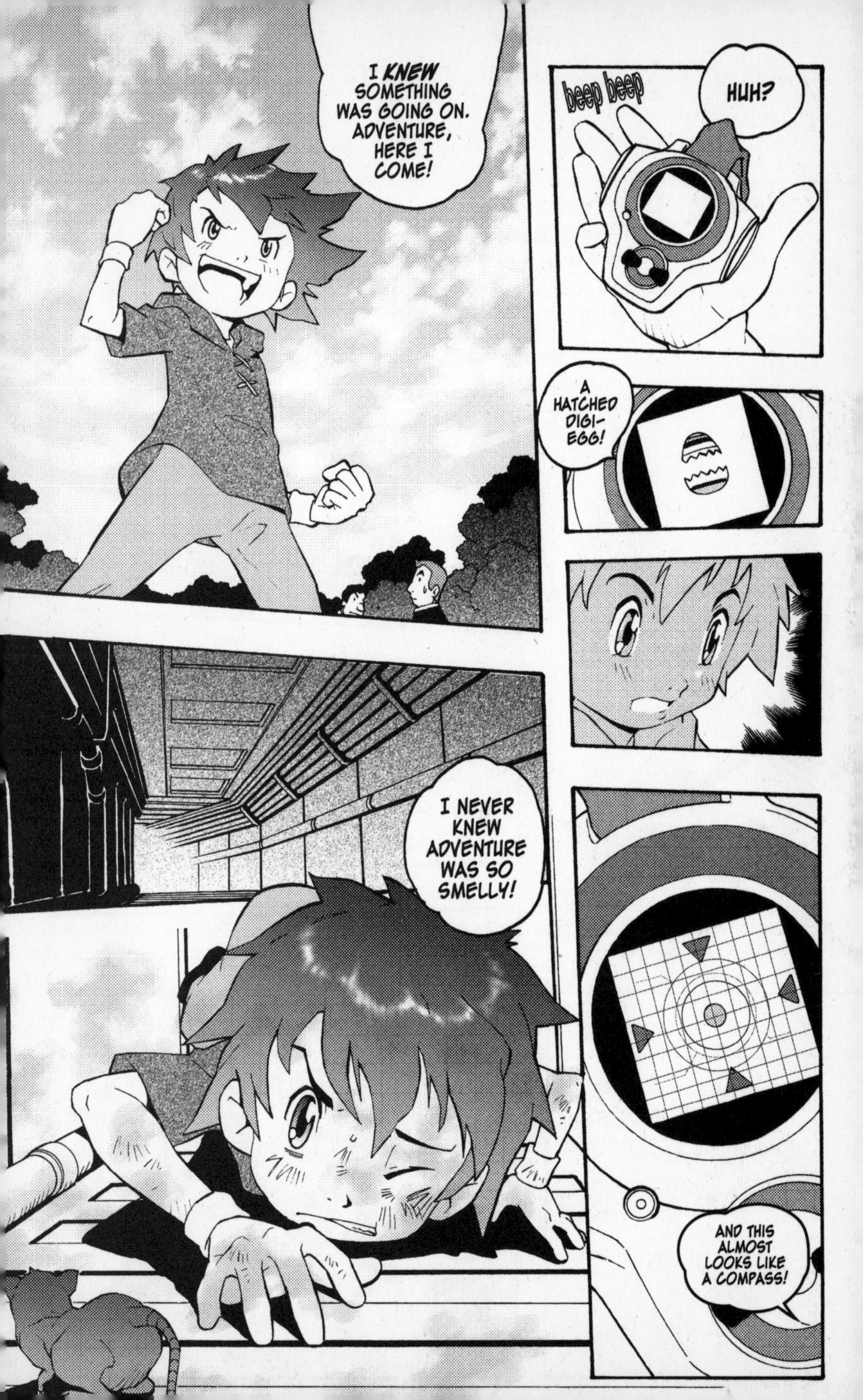
beep beep
HUH?
A HATCHED DIGI-EGG!
AND THIS ALMOST LOOKS LIKE A COMPASS!
I KNEW SOMETHING WAS GOING ON. ADVENTURE, HERE I COME!
I NEVER KNEW ADVENTURE WAS SO SMELLY!

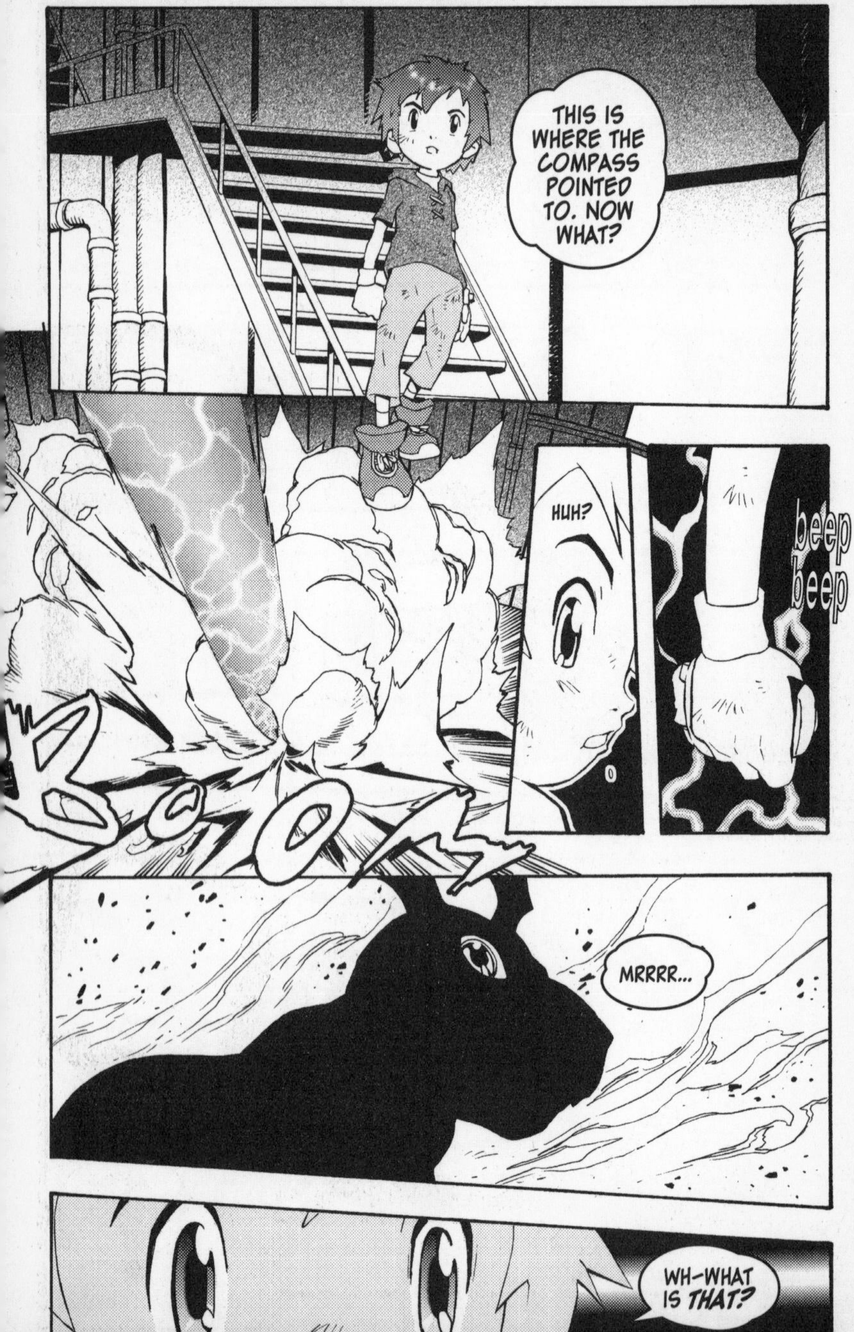
THIS IS WHERE THE COMPASS POINTED TO. NOW WHAT?
beep beep
HUH?
BOOOM
MRRRR...
WH-WHAT IS *THAT?*

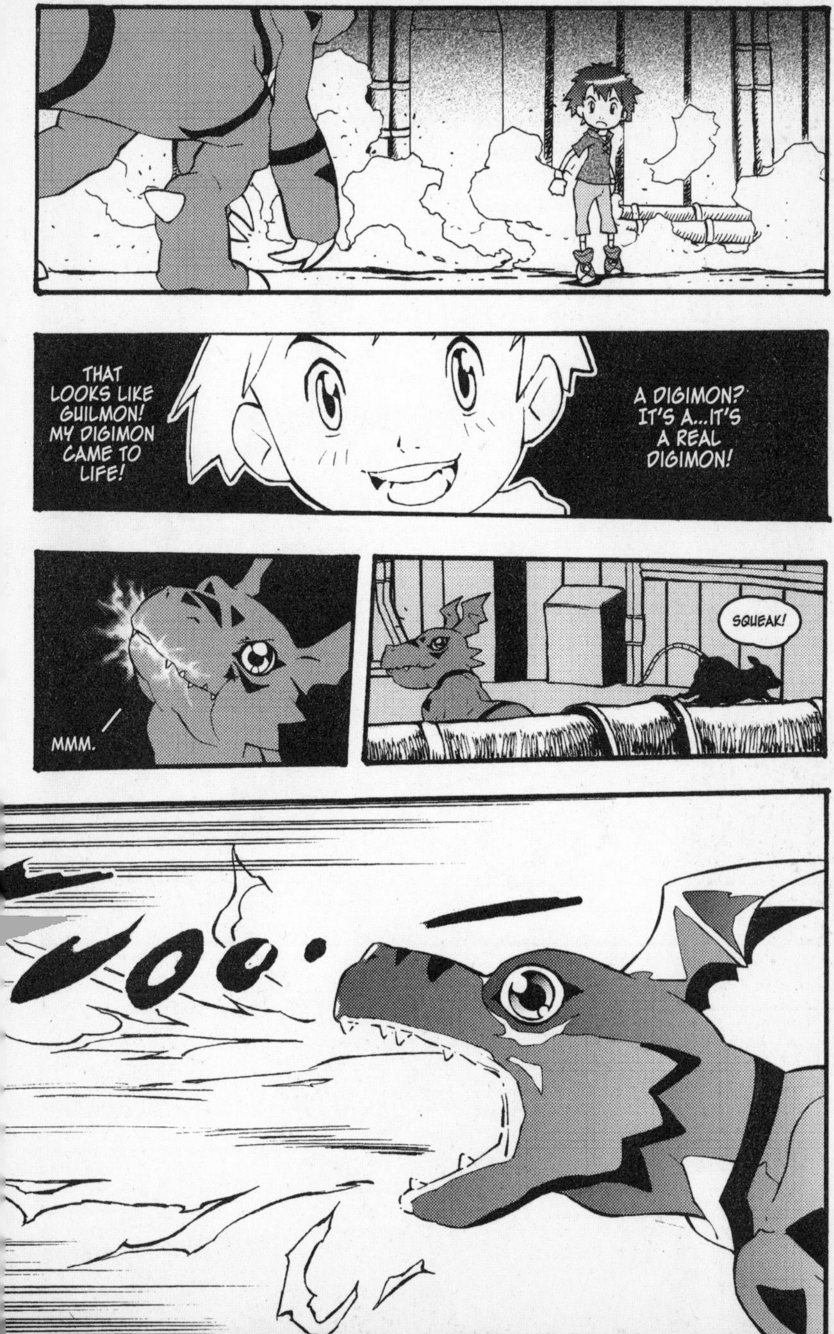
A DIGIMON? IT'S A...IT'S A REAL DIGIMON!
THAT LOOKS LIKE GUILMON! MY DIGIMON CAME TO LIFE!
SQUEAK!
MMM.

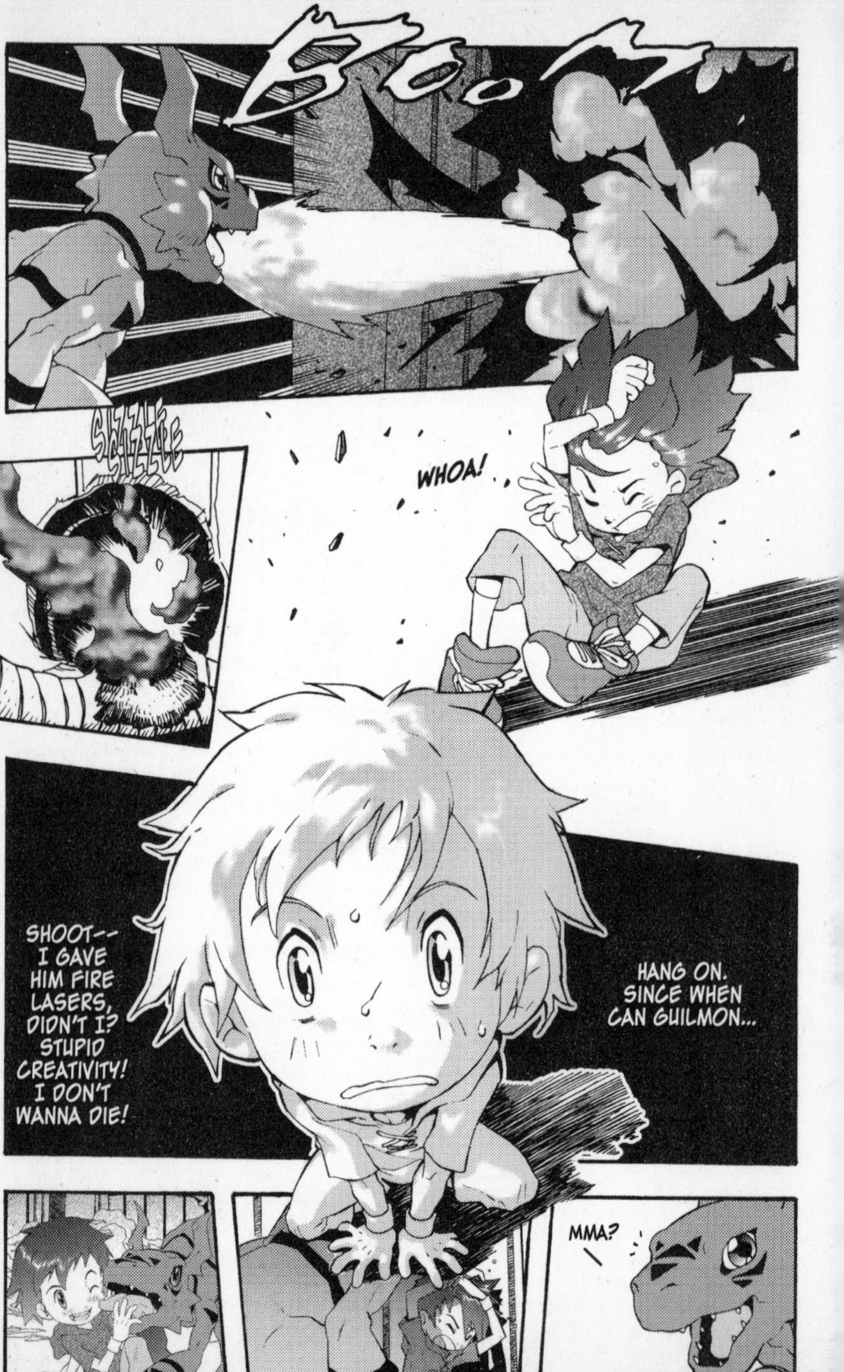
BOOM
WHOA!
SIZZZZLE
HANG ON. SINCE WHEN CAN GUILMON...
SHOOT-- I GAVE HIM FIRE LASERS, DIDN'T I? STUPID CREATIVITY! I DON'T WANNA DIE!
MMA?

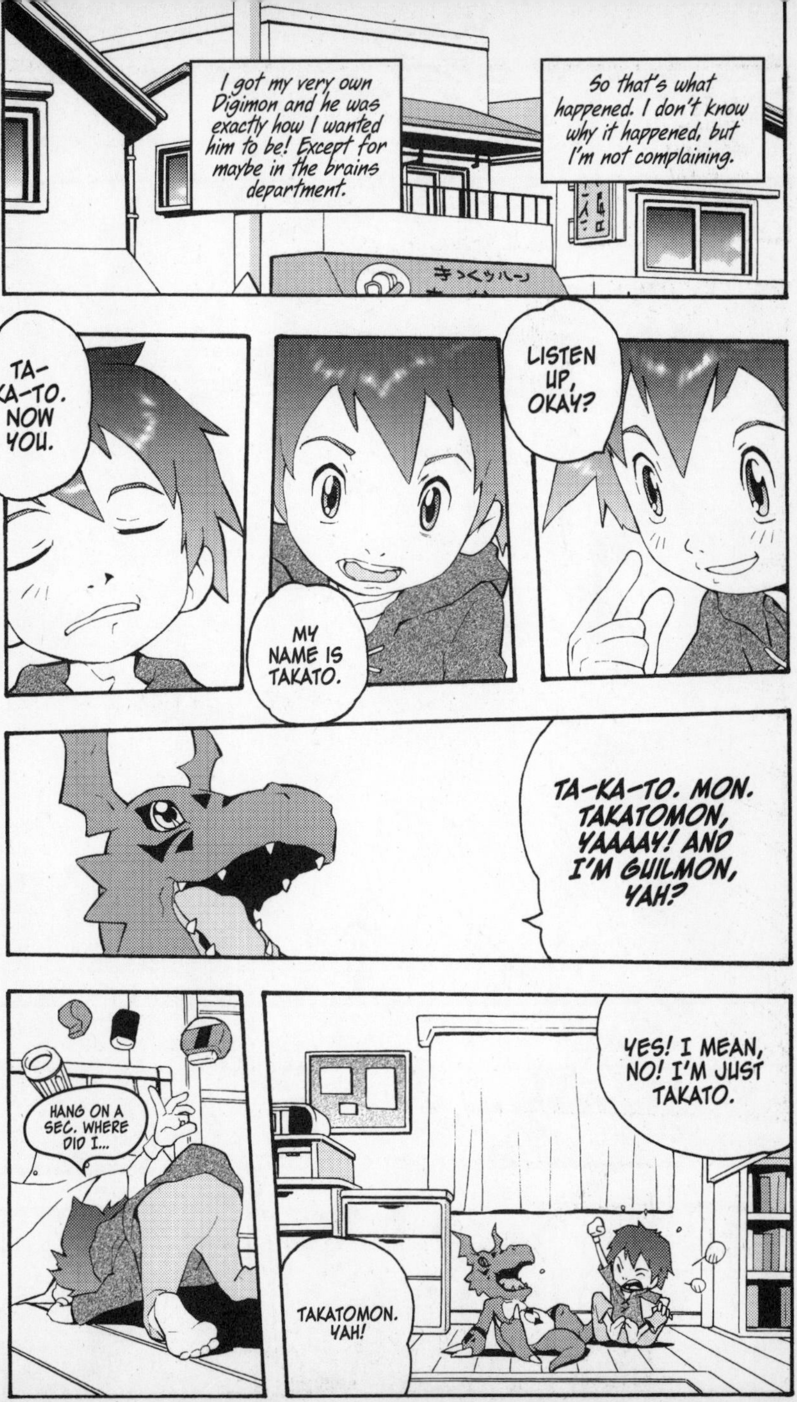
So that's what happened. I don't know why it happened, but I'm not complaining.
I got my very own Digimon and he was exactly how I wanted him to be! Except for maybe in the brains department.
LISTEN UP, OKAY?
MY NAME IS TAKATO.
TA-KA-TO. NOW YOU.
TA-KA-TO. MON. TAKATOMON, YAAAAY! AND I'M GUILMON, YAH?
YES! I MEAN, NO! I'M JUST TAKATO.
TAKATOMON. YAH!
HANG ON A SEC. WHERE DID I...

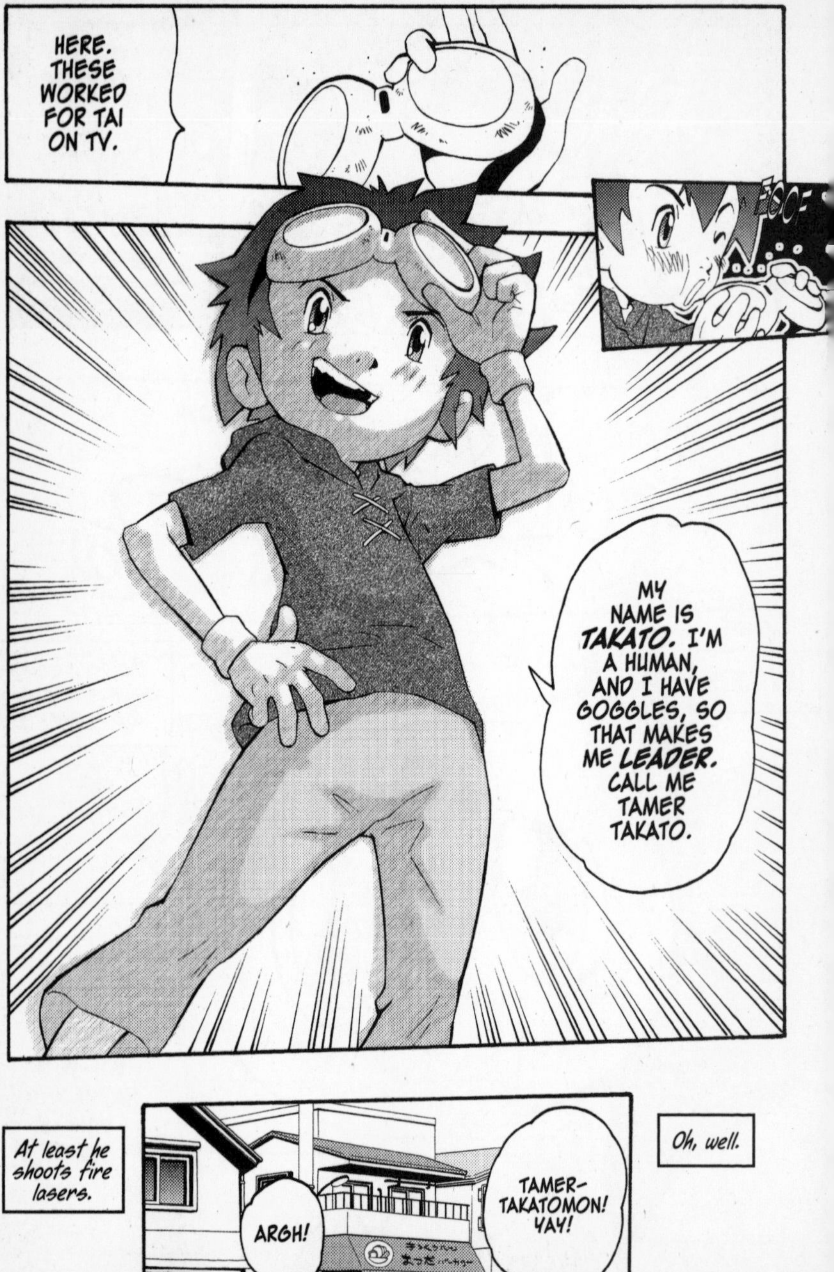
HERE. THESE WORKED FOR TAI ON TV.
FOOF
MY NAME IS TAKATO. I'M A HUMAN, AND I HAVE GOGGLES, SO THAT MAKES ME LEADER. CALL ME TAMER TAKATO.
Oh, well.
TAMER-TAKATOMON! YAY!
ARGH!
At least he shoots fire lasers.

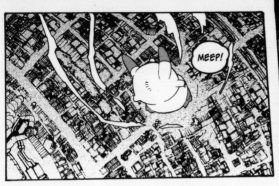

MEEP!

ROOM

SA

— OW.

PO

CALUMON

But my finding Guilmon was only the beginning.

WH-WHAT HAPPENED? WHERE AM I?

And my being a Tamer was WAY harder than on TV.

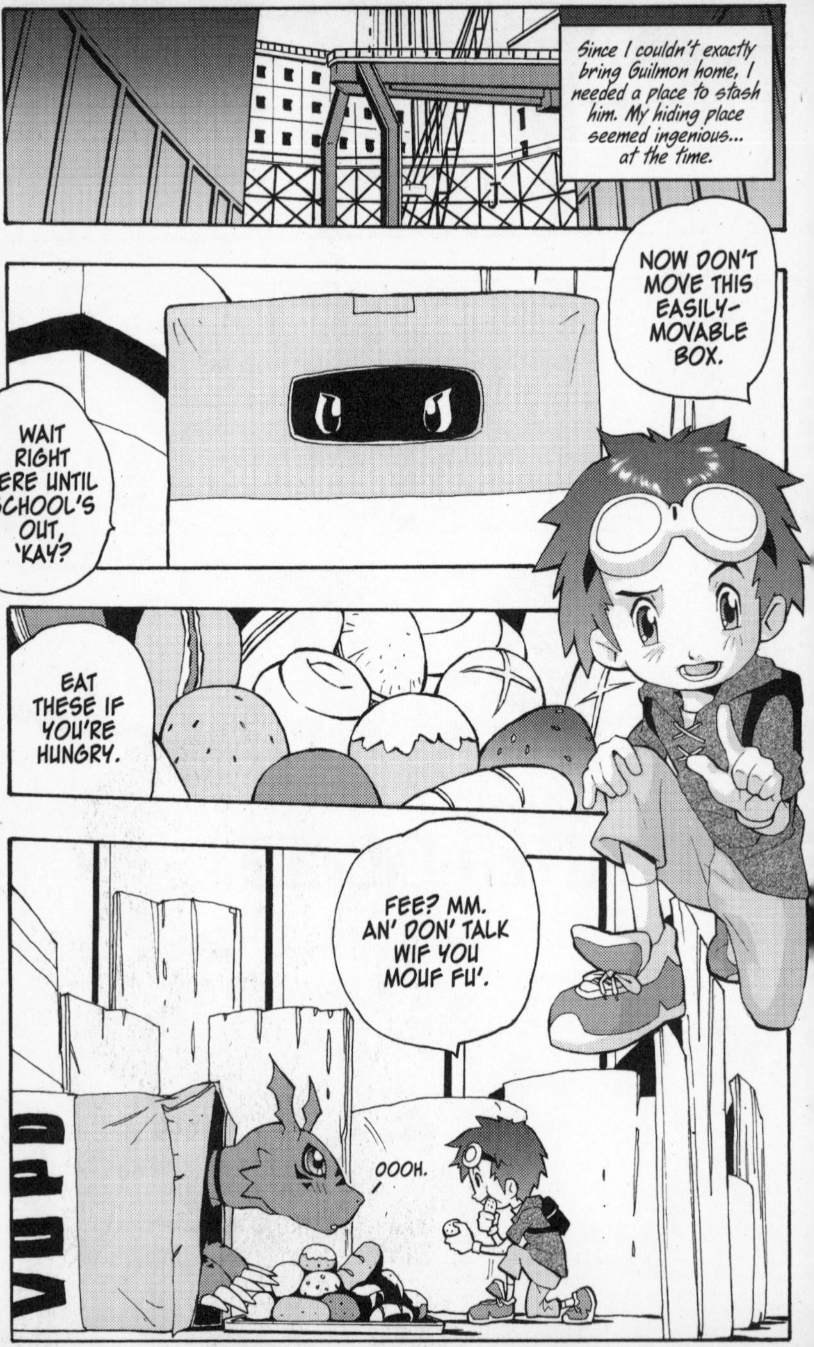
Since I couldn't exactly bring Guilmon home, I needed a place to stash him. My hiding place seemed ingenious... at the time.
NOW DON'T MOVE THIS EASILY-MOVABLE BOX.
WAIT RIGHT HERE UNTIL SCHOOL'S OUT, 'KAY?
EAT THESE IF YOU'RE HUNGRY.
FEE? MM. AN' DON' TALK WIF YOU MOUF FU'.
OOOH.

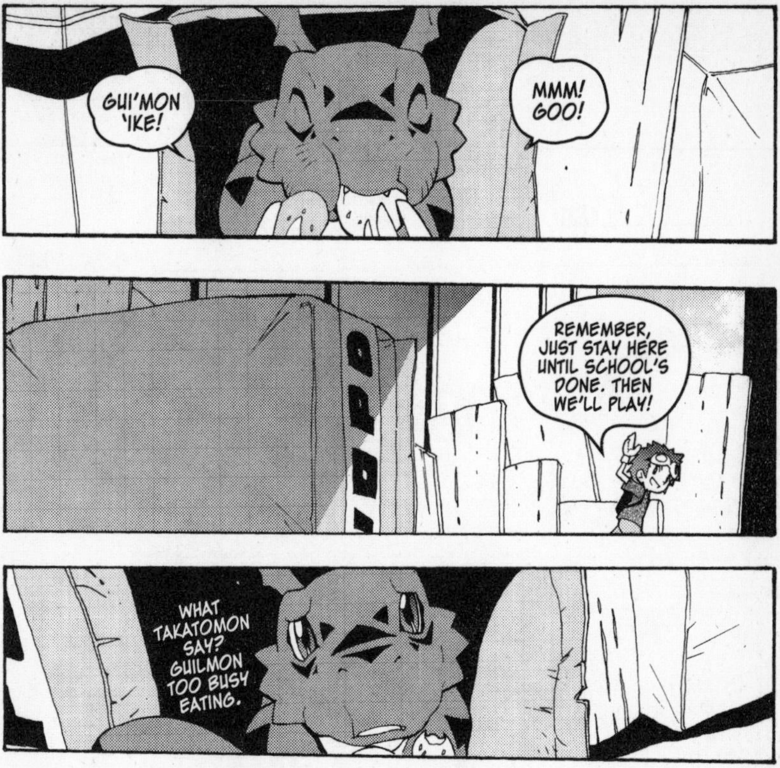
MMM! GOO!
GUI'MON 'IKE!
REMEMBER, JUST STAY HERE UNTIL SCHOOL'S DONE. THEN WE'LL PLAY!
WHAT TAKATOMON SAY? GUILMON TOO BUSY EATING.

CHAPTER 2:
FAR CUTER DIGIMON

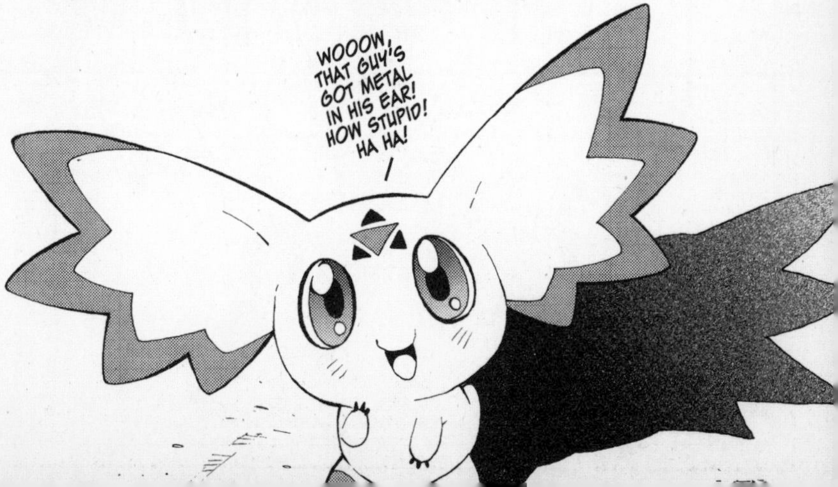
WOOOW, THAT GUY'S GOT METAL IN HIS EAR! HOW STUPID! HA HA!

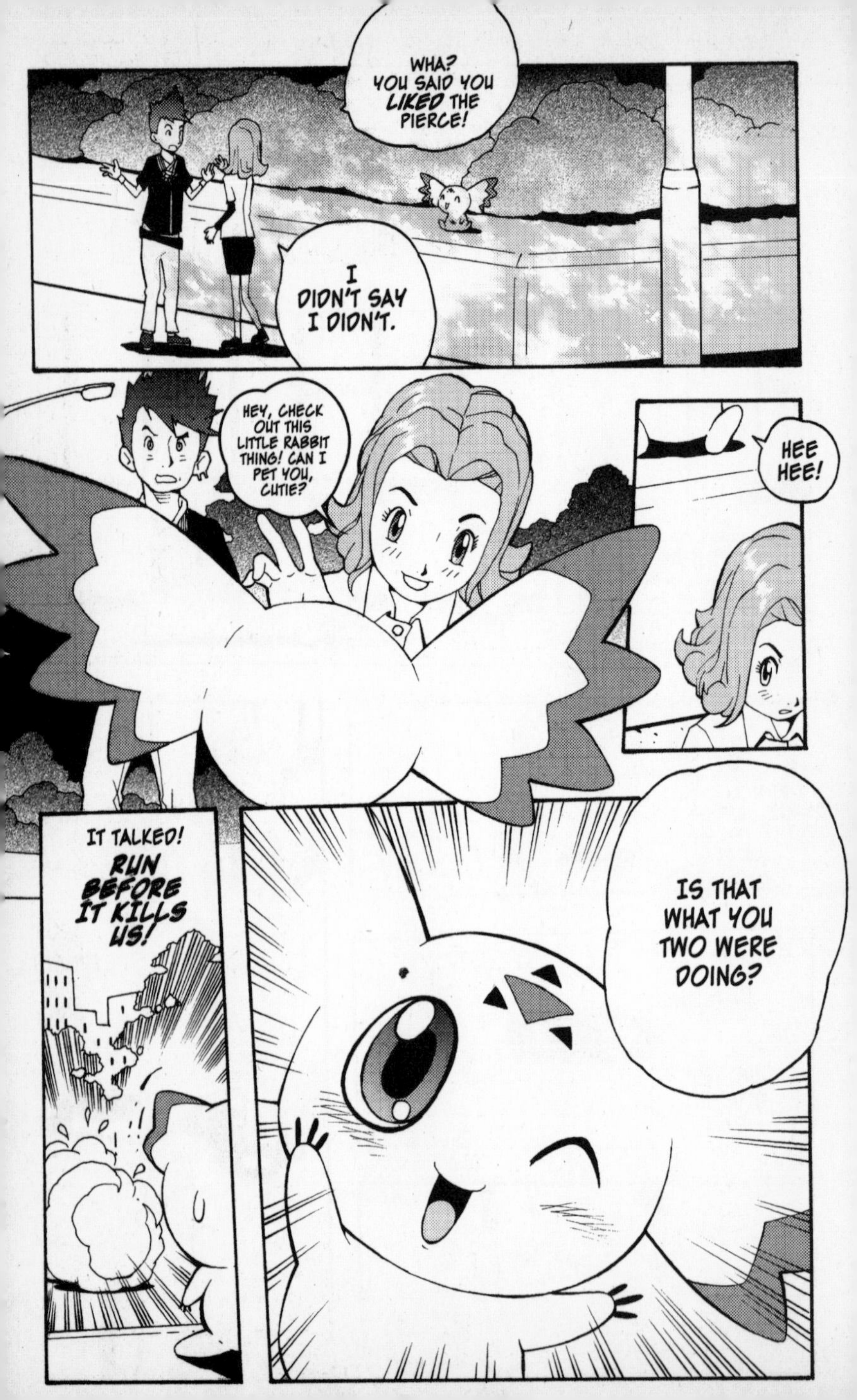
WHA? YOU SAID YOU LIKED THE PIERCE!
I DIDN'T SAY I DIDN'T.
HEE HEE!
HEY, CHECK OUT THIS LITTLE RABBIT THING! CAN I PET YOU, CUTIE?
IS THAT WHAT YOU TWO WERE DOING?
IT TALKED! RUN BEFORE IT KILLS US!

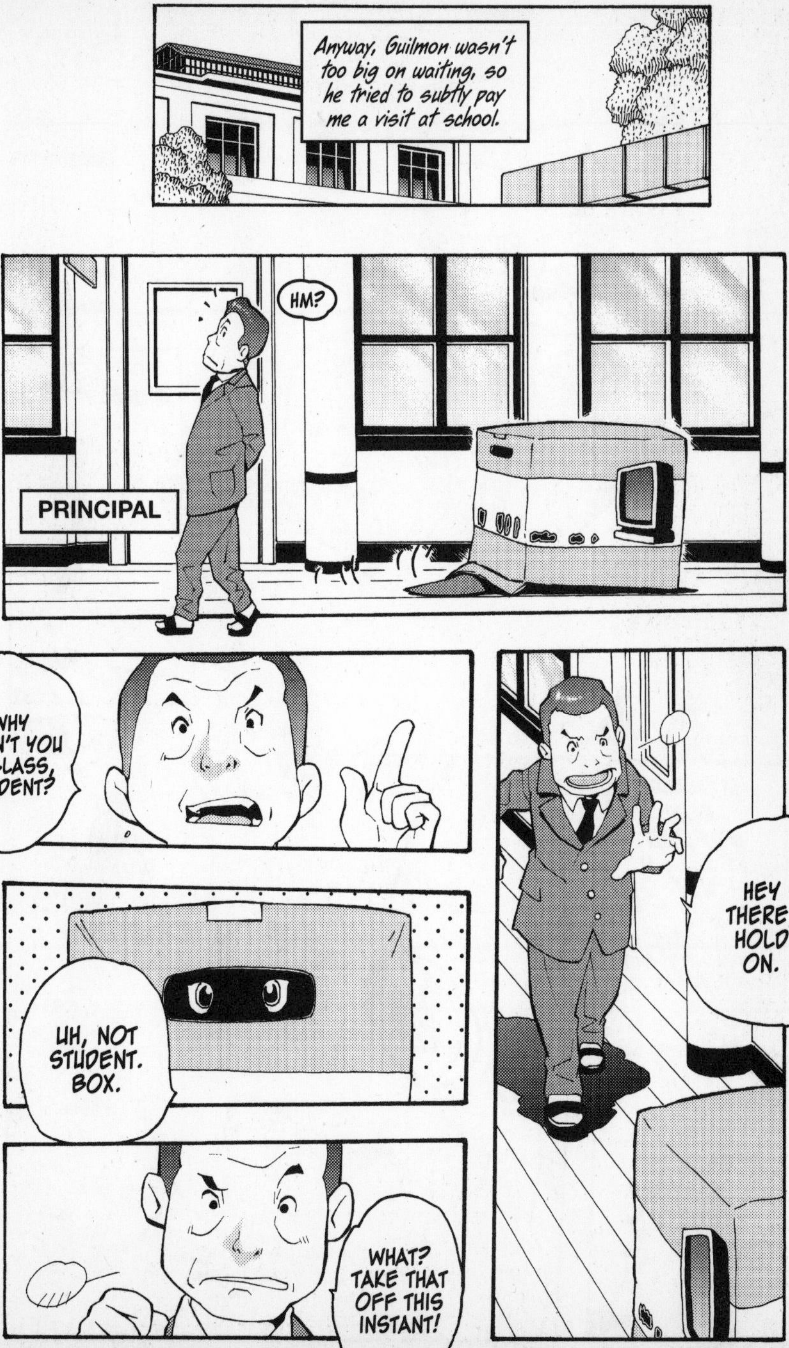
Anyway, Guilmon wasn't too big on waiting, so he tried to subtly pay me a visit at school.
HM?
PRINCIPAL
HEY THERE, HOLD ON.
WHY AREN'T YOU IN CLASS, STUDENT?
UH, NOT STUDENT. BOX.
WHAT? TAKE THAT OFF THIS INSTANT!

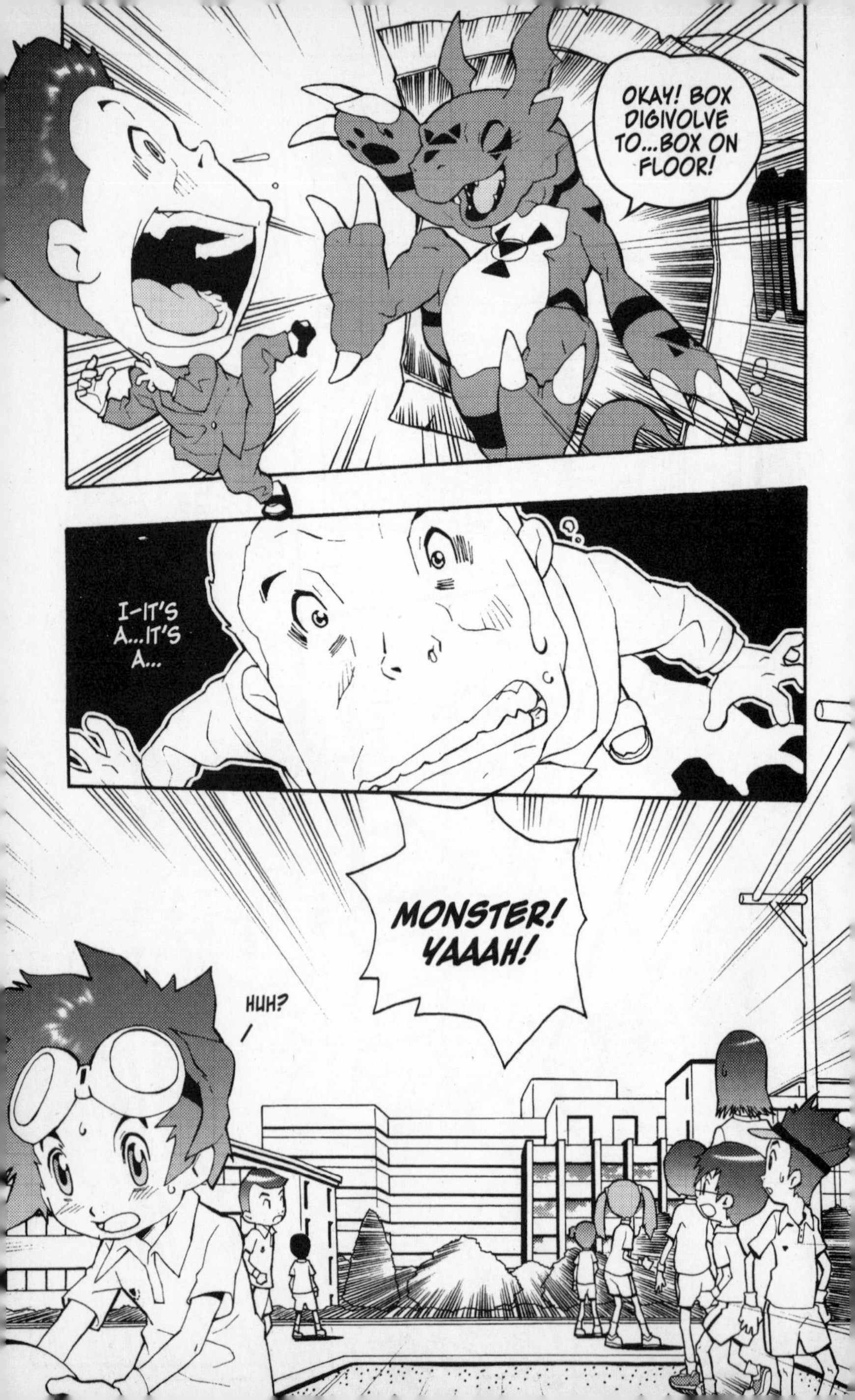
OKAY! BOX DIGIVOLVE TO...BOX ON FLOOR!
I-IT'S A...IT'S A...
MONSTER! YAAAH!
HUH?

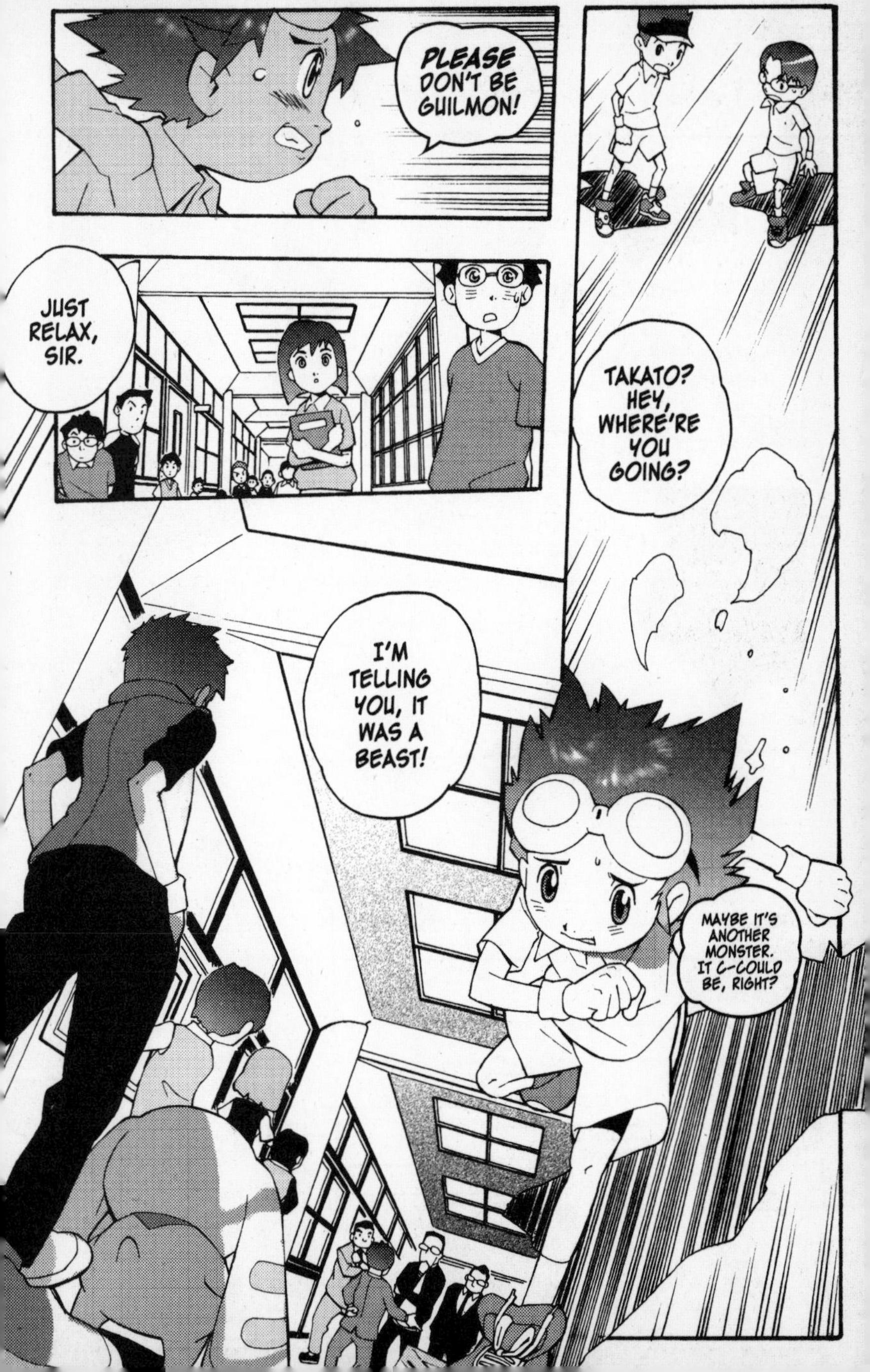
TAKATO? HEY, WHERE'RE YOU GOING?
PLEASE DON'T BE GUILMON!
JUST RELAX, SIR.
I'M TELLING YOU, IT WAS A BEAST!
MAYBE IT'S ANOTHER MONSTER. IT C-COULD BE, RIGHT?

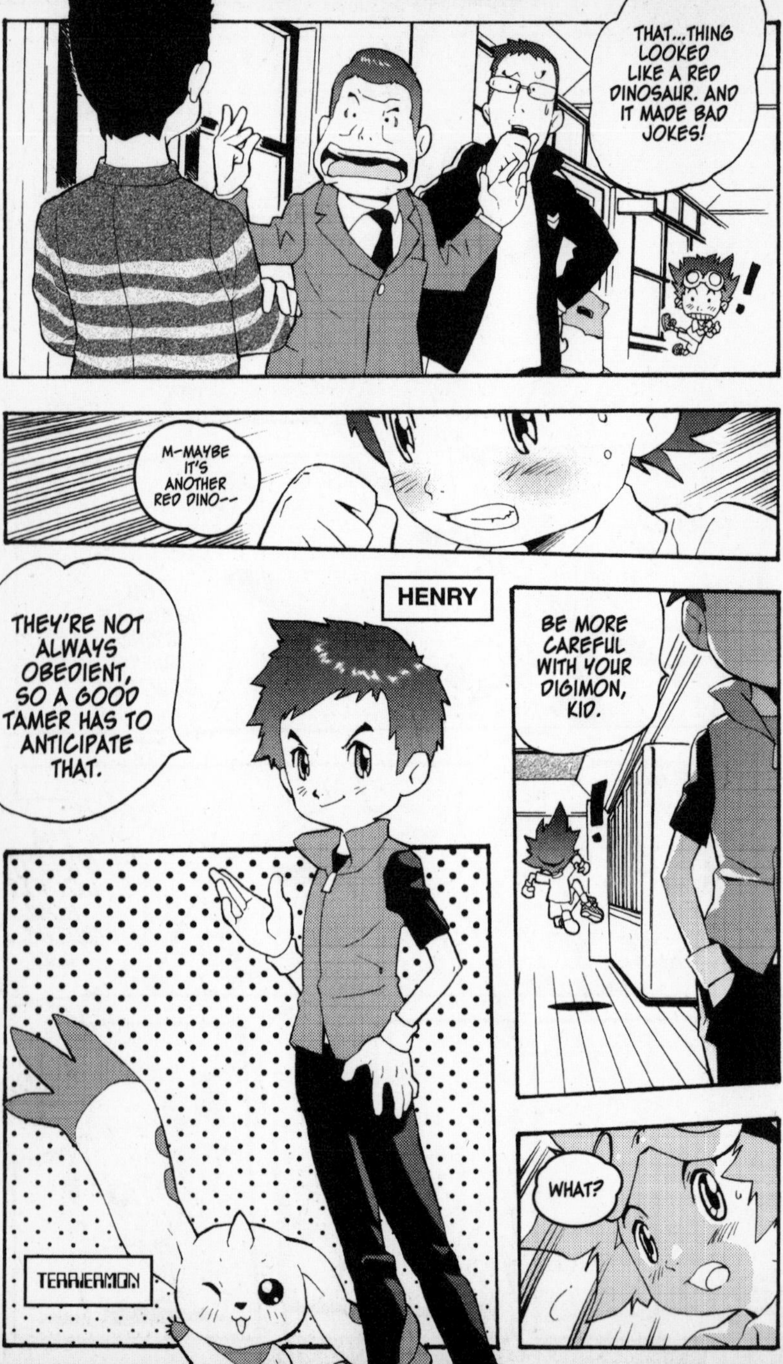
THAT...THING LOOKED LIKE A RED DINOSAUR. AND IT MADE BAD JOKES!
!
M-MAYBE IT'S ANOTHER RED DINO--
BE MORE CAREFUL WITH YOUR DIGIMON, KID.
!
WHAT?
HENRY
THEY'RE NOT ALWAYS OBEDIENT, SO A GOOD TAMER HAS TO ANTICIPATE THAT.
TERRIERMON

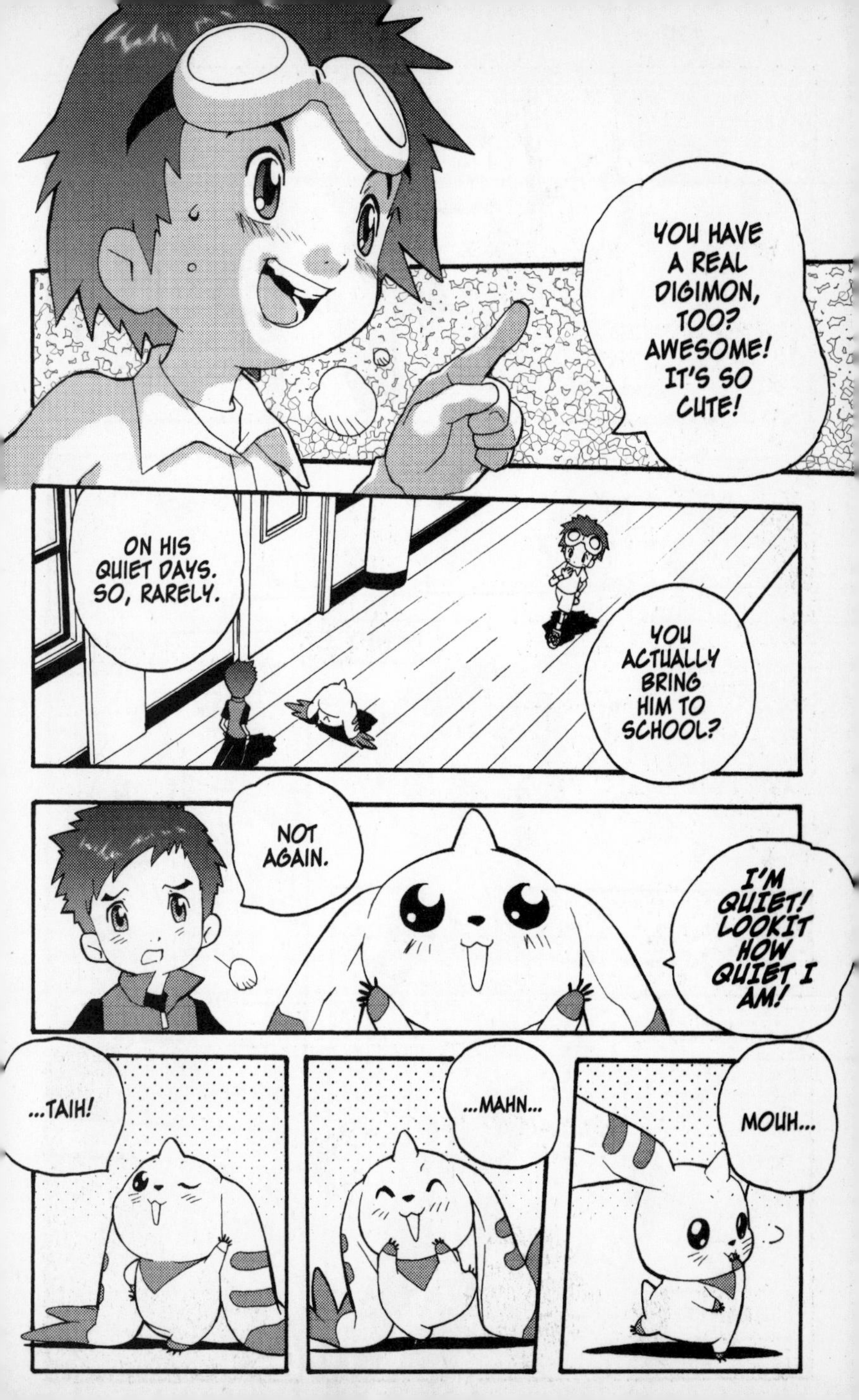
YOU HAVE A REAL DIGIMON, TOO? AWESOME! IT'S SO CUTE!
YOU ACTUALLY BRING HIM TO SCHOOL?
ON HIS QUIET DAYS. SO, RARELY.
I'M QUIET! LOOKIT HOW QUIET I AM!
NOT AGAIN.
MOUH...
...MAHN...
...TAIH!

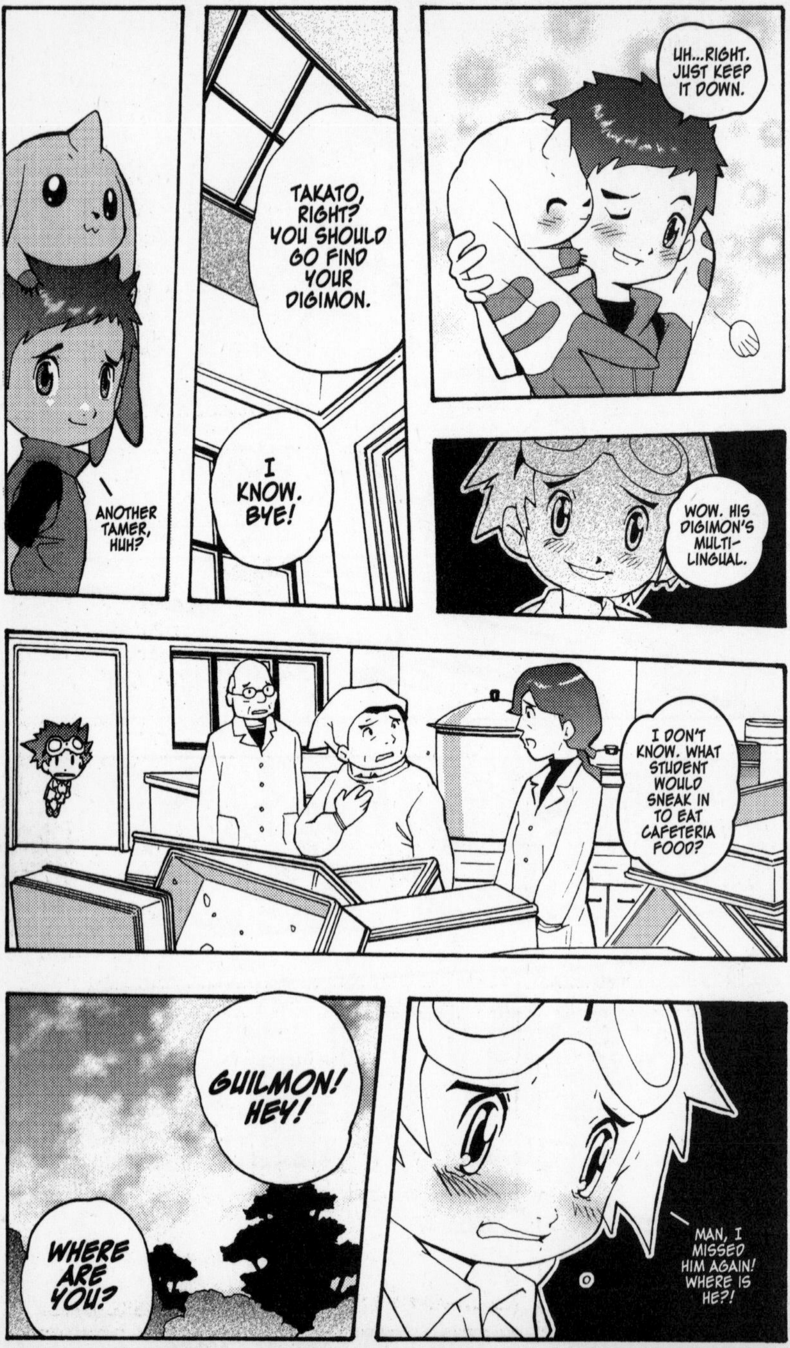
UH...RIGHT. JUST KEEP IT DOWN.
WOW. HIS DIGIMON'S MULTI-LINGUAL.
TAKATO, RIGHT? YOU SHOULD GO FIND YOUR DIGIMON.
I KNOW. BYE!
ANOTHER TAMER, HUH?
I DON'T KNOW. WHAT STUDENT WOULD SNEAK IN TO EAT CAFETERIA FOOD?
MAN, I MISSED HIM AGAIN! WHERE IS HE?!
GUILMON! HEY!
WHERE ARE YOU?

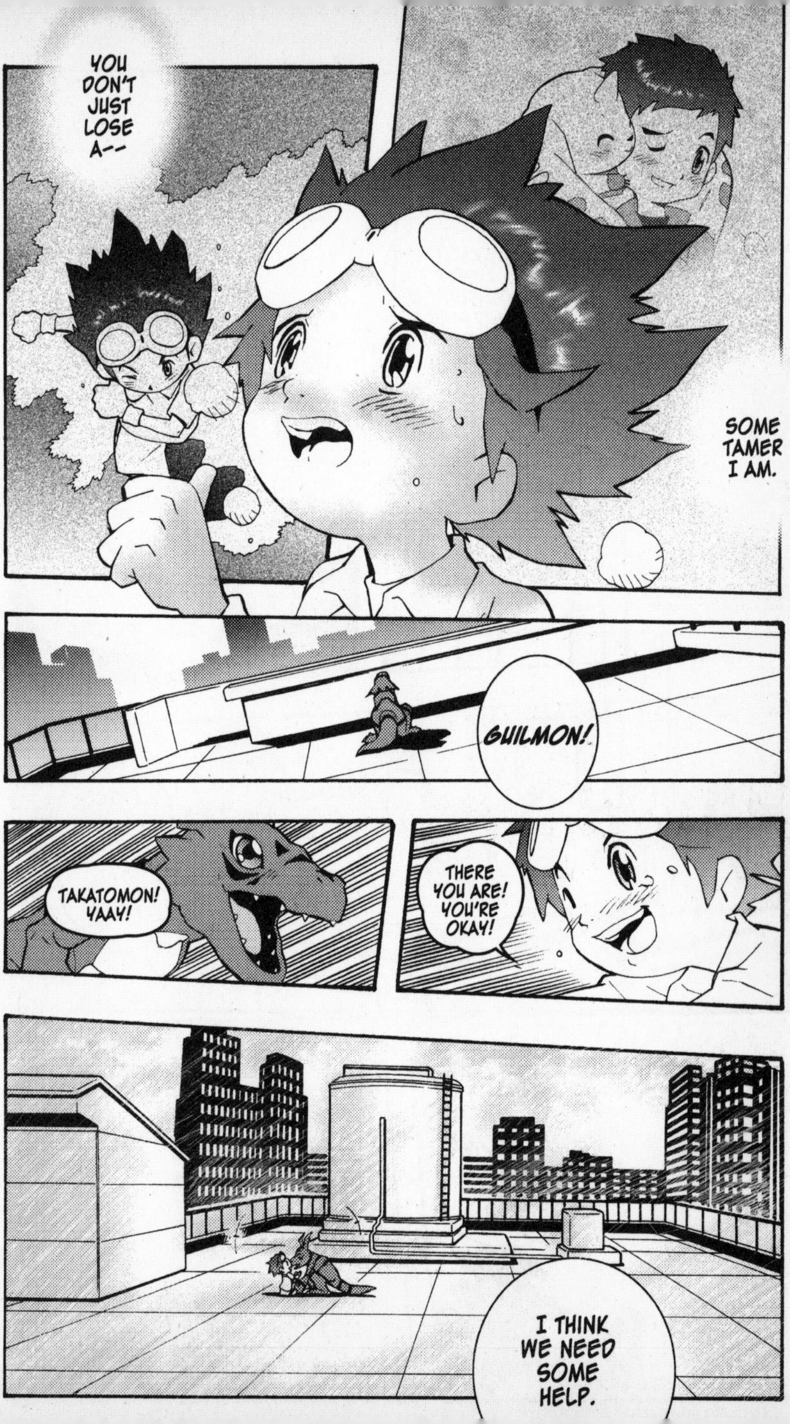
SOME TAMER I AM.
YOU DON'T JUST LOSE A--
GUILMON!
THERE YOU ARE! YOU'RE OKAY!
TAKATOMON! YAAY!
I THINK WE NEED SOME HELP.

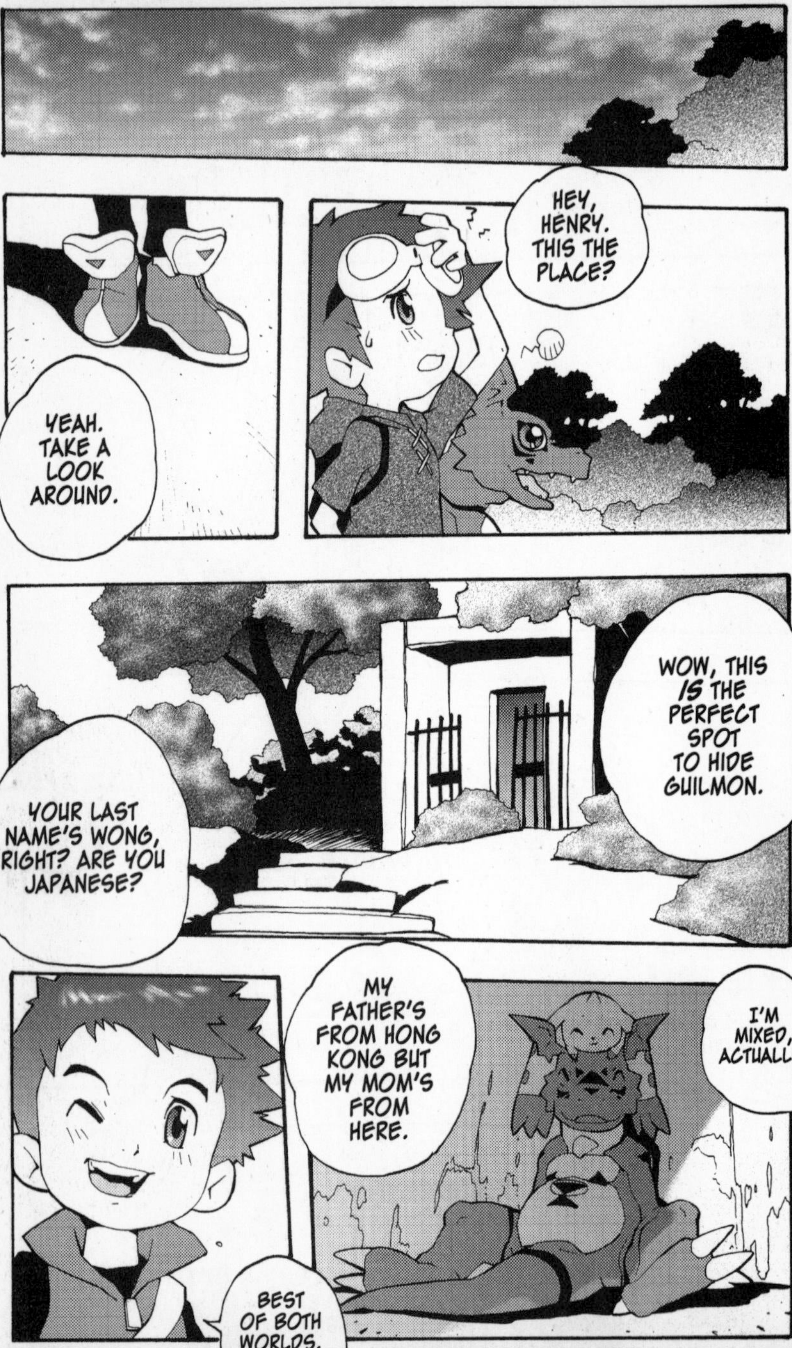
HEY, HENRY. THIS THE PLACE?
YEAH. TAKE A LOOK AROUND.
WOW, THIS *IS* THE PERFECT SPOT TO HIDE GUILMON.
YOUR LAST NAME'S WONG, RIGHT? ARE YOU JAPANESE?
I'M MIXED, ACTUALLY.
MY FATHER'S FROM HONG KONG BUT MY MOM'S FROM HERE.
BEST OF BOTH WORLDS.

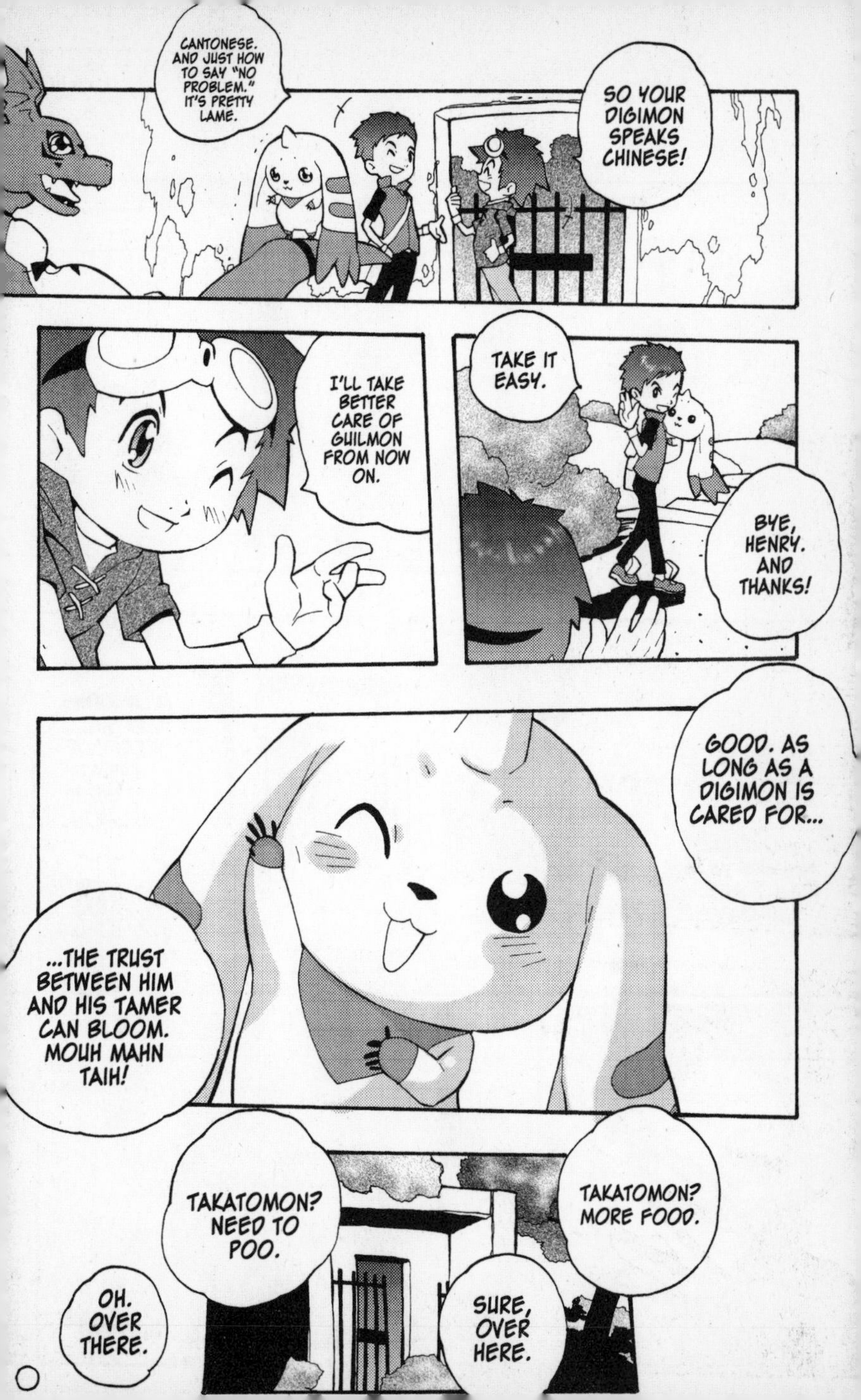
SO YOUR DIGIMON SPEAKS CHINESE!
CANTONESE. AND JUST HOW TO SAY "NO PROBLEM." IT'S PRETTY LAME.
TAKE IT EASY.
BYE, HENRY. AND THANKS!
I'LL TAKE BETTER CARE OF GUILMON FROM NOW ON.
GOOD. AS LONG AS A DIGIMON IS CARED FOR...
...THE TRUST BETWEEN HIM AND HIS TAMER CAN BLOOM. MOUH MAHN TAIH!
TAKATOMON? MORE FOOD.
TAKATOMON? NEED TO POO.
SURE, OVER HERE.
OH. OVER THERE.

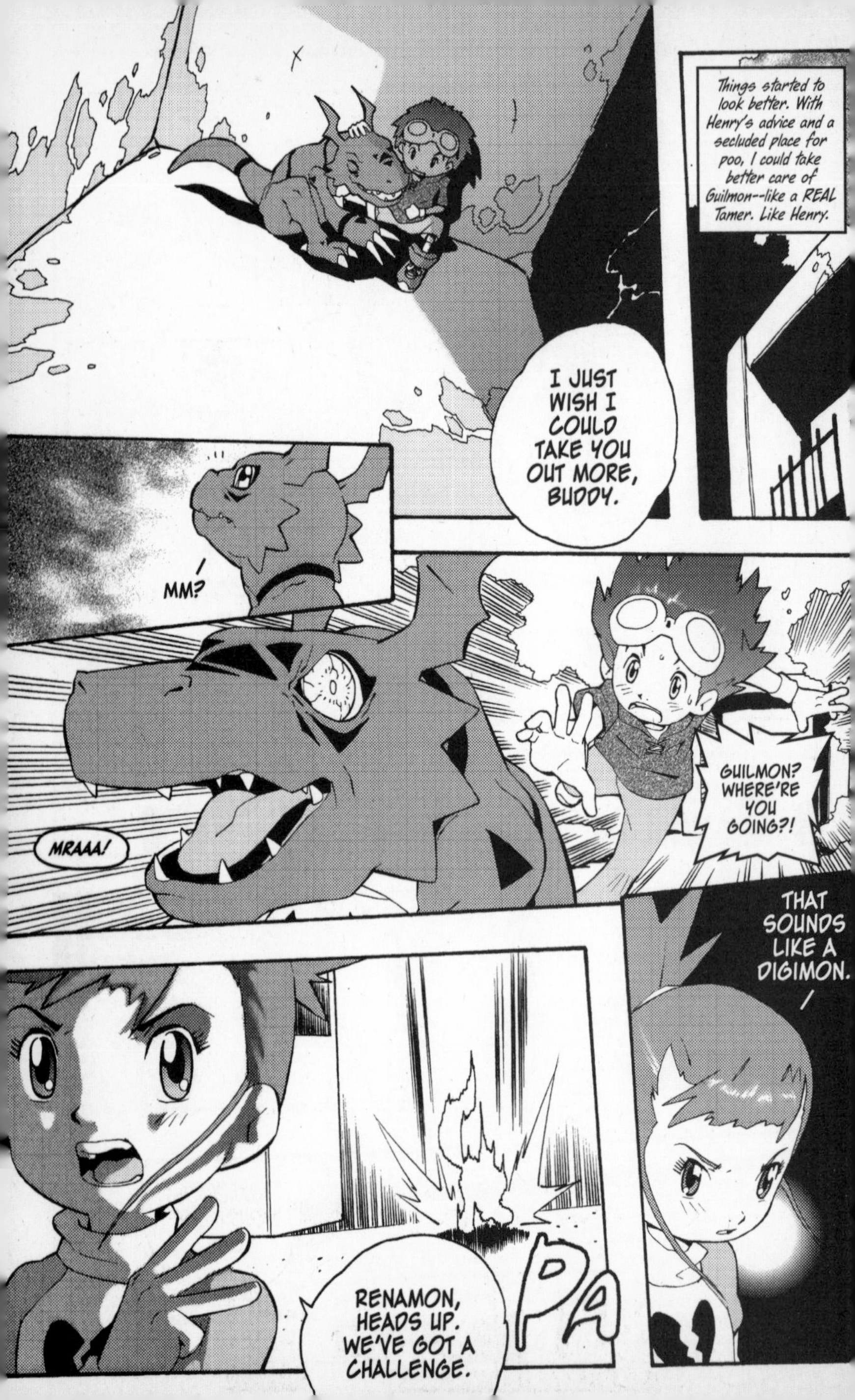
Things started to look better. With Henry's advice and a secluded place for poo, I could take better care of Guilmon--like a REAL Tamer. Like Henry.
I JUST WISH I COULD TAKE YOU OUT MORE, BUDDY.
MM?
GUILMON? WHERE'RE YOU GOING?!
MRAAA!
THAT SOUNDS LIKE A DIGIMON.
PA
RENAMON, HEADS UP. WE'VE GOT A CHALLENGE.

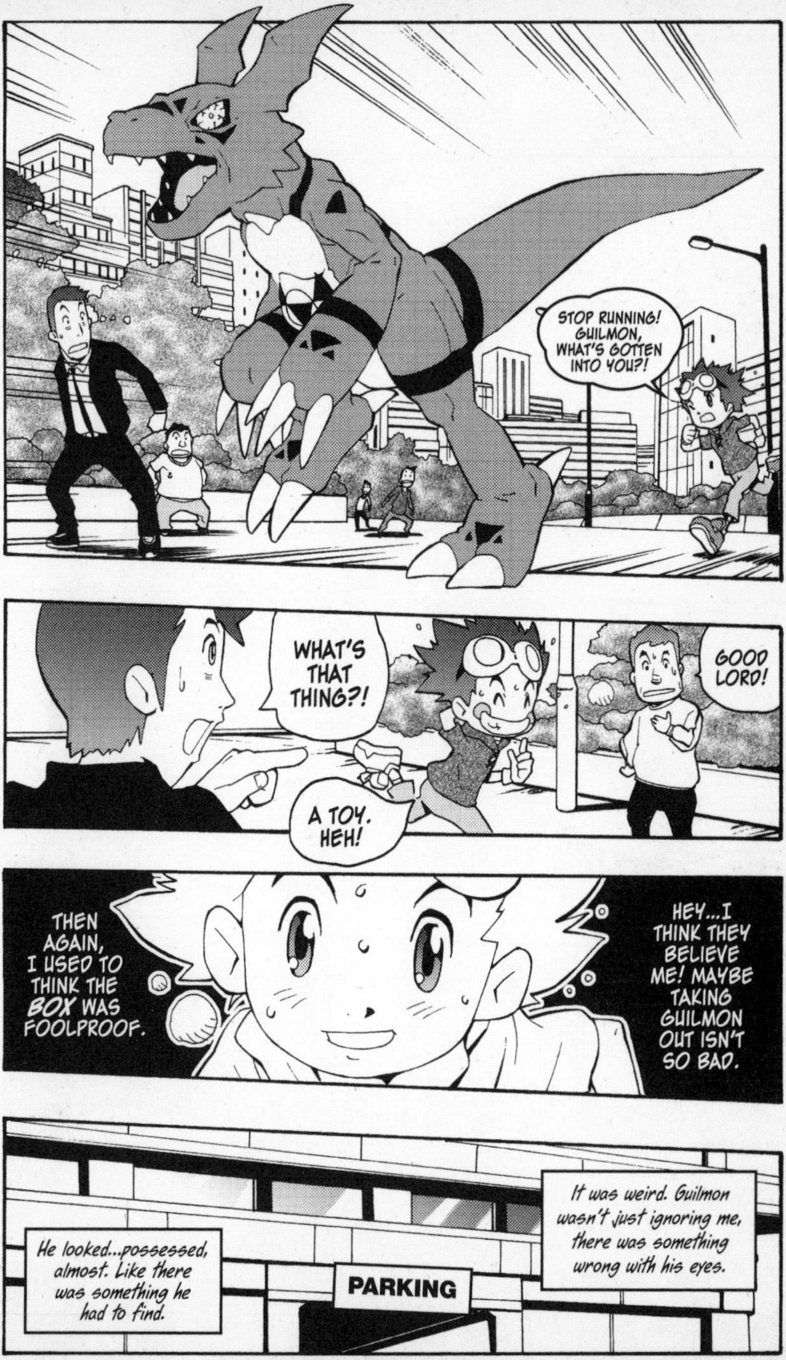
STOP RUNNING! GUILMON, WHAT'S GOTTEN INTO YOU?!
GOOD LORD!
WHAT'S THAT THING?!
A TOY. HEH!
HEY...I THINK THEY BELIEVE ME! MAYBE TAKING GUILMON OUT ISN'T SO BAD.
THEN AGAIN, I USED TO THINK THE *BOX* WAS FOOLPROOF.
It was weird. Guilmon wasn't just ignoring me, there was something wrong with his eyes.
PARKING
He looked...possessed, almost. Like there was something he had to find.

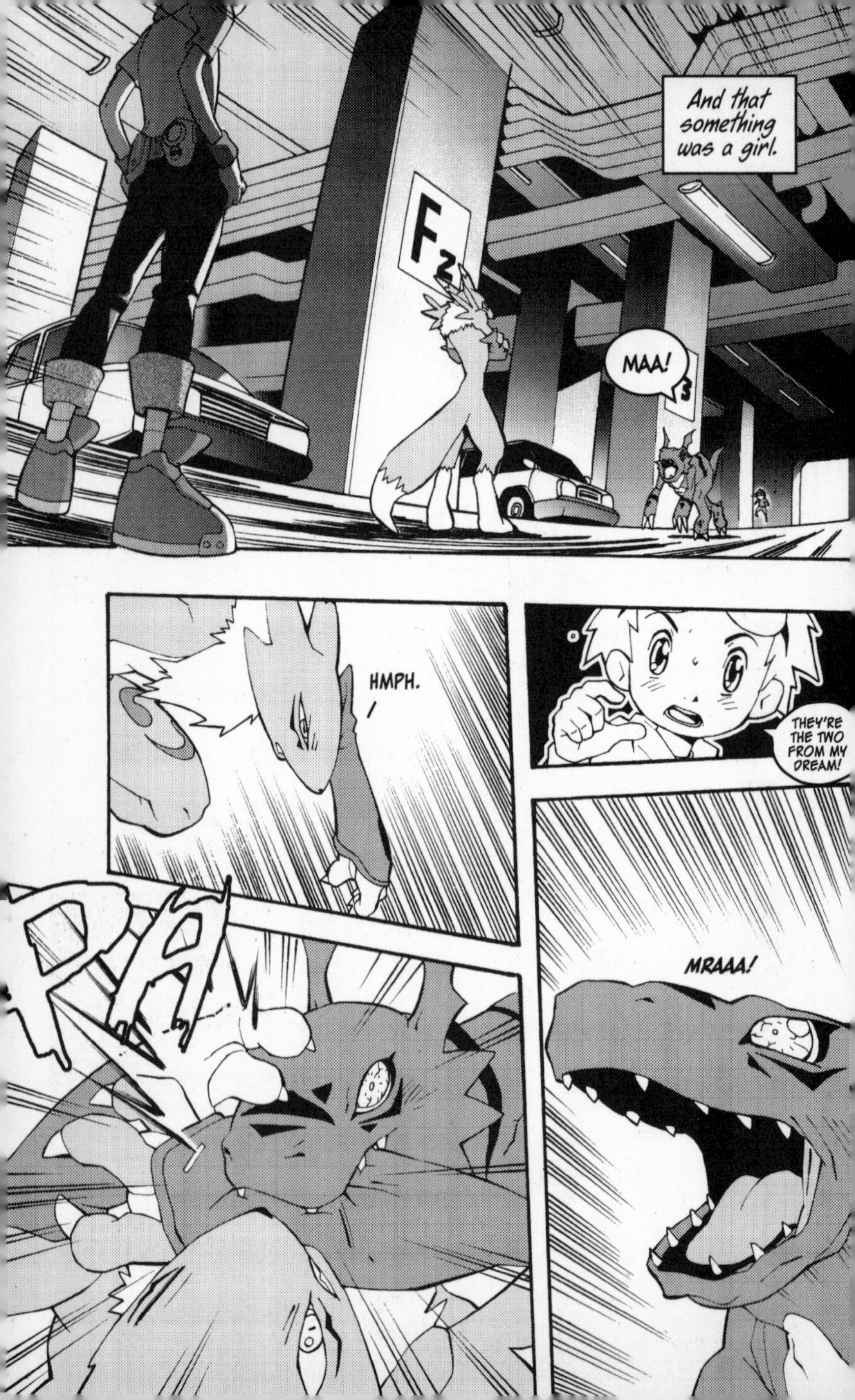

And that something was a girl.
MAA!
THEY'RE THE TWO FROM MY DREAM!
HMPH.
MRAAA!

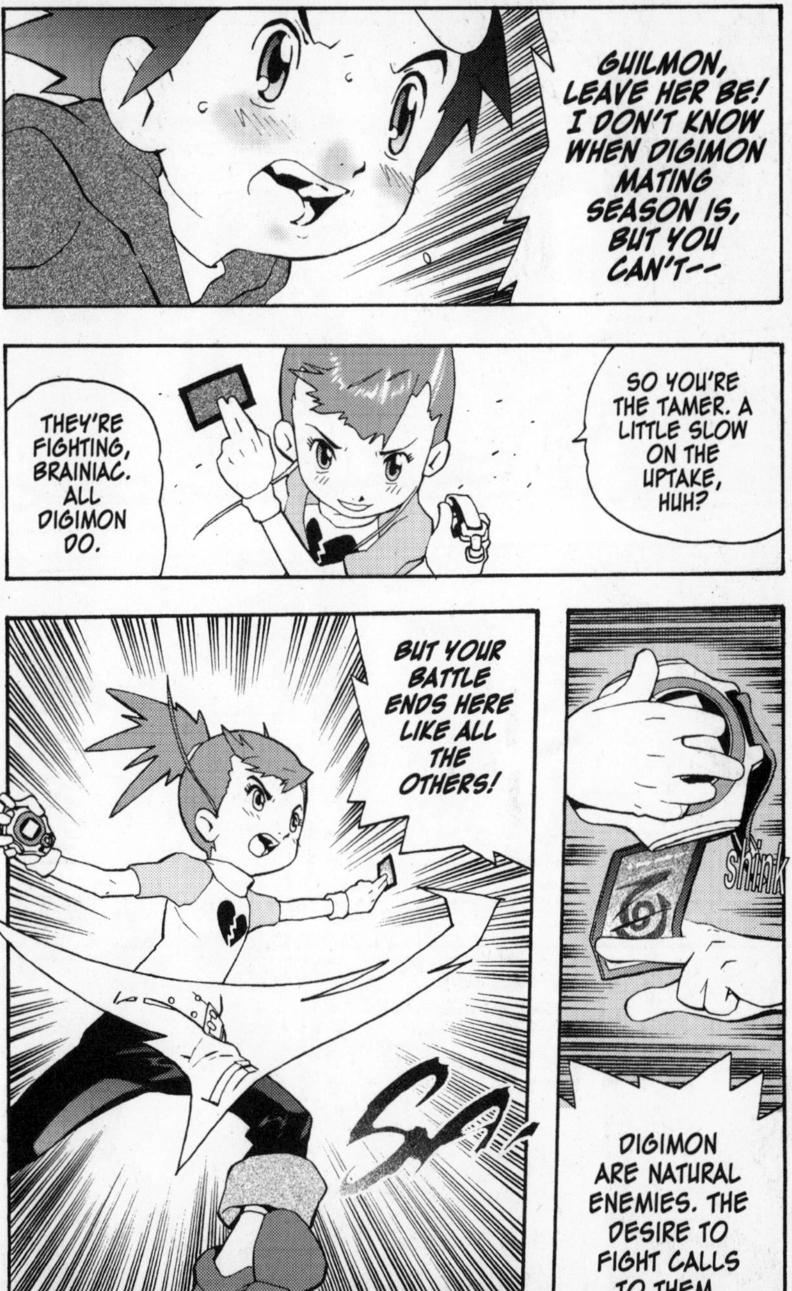
GUILMON, LEAVE HER BE! I DON'T KNOW WHEN DIGIMON MATING SEASON IS, BUT YOU CAN'T--
SO YOU'RE THE TAMER. A LITTLE SLOW ON THE UPTAKE, HUH?
THEY'RE FIGHTING, BRAINIAC. ALL DIGIMON DO.
shink
DIGIMON ARE NATURAL ENEMIES. THE DESIRE TO FIGHT CALLS TO THEM.
BUT YOUR BATTLE ENDS HERE LIKE ALL THE OTHERS!

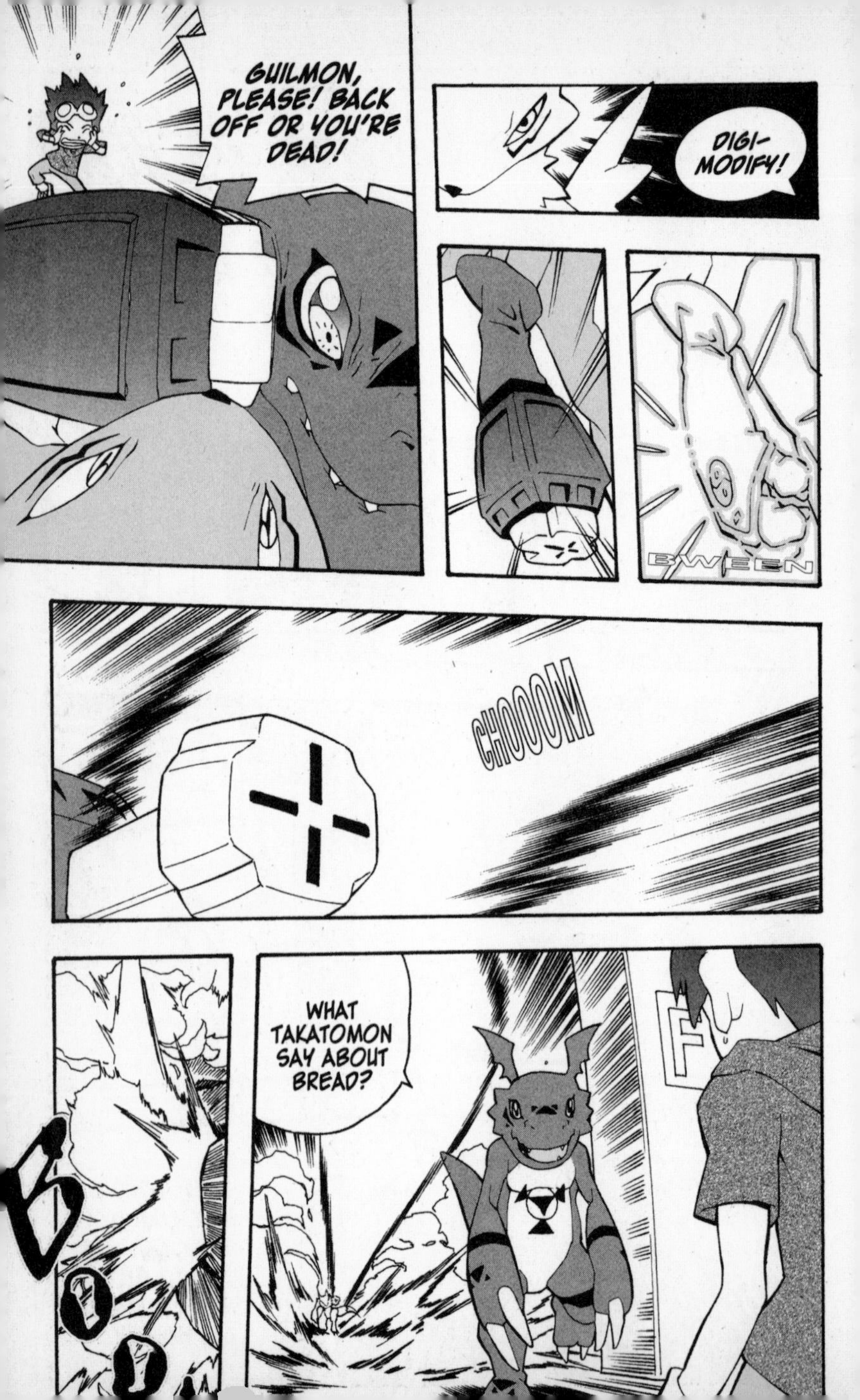

DIGI-MODIFY!
BWEEN
GUILMON, PLEASE! BACK OFF OR YOU'RE DEAD!
CHOOOM
WHAT TAKATOMON SAY ABOUT BREAD?

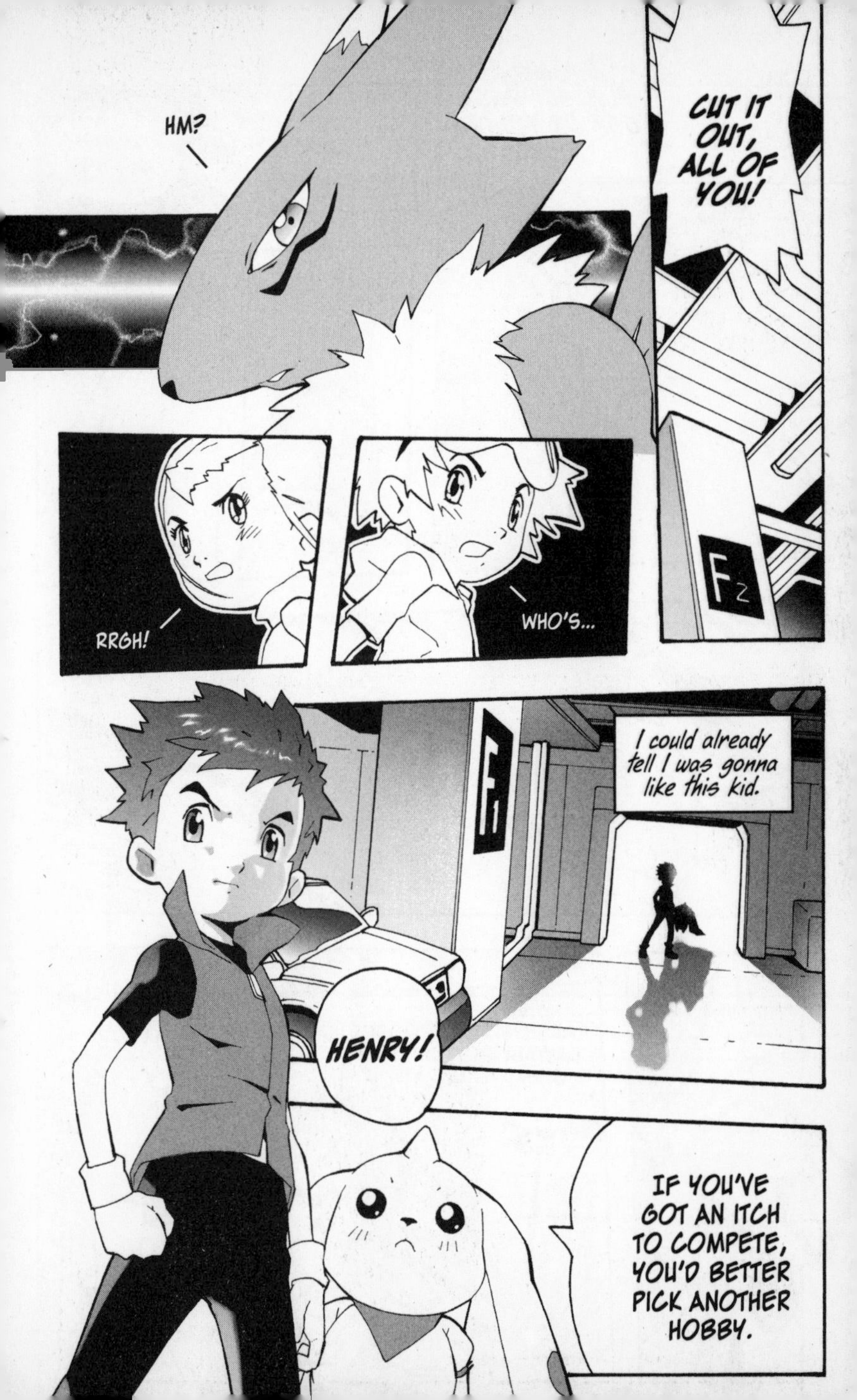
CUT IT OUT, ALL OF YOU!
HM?
WHO'S...
RRGH!
I could already tell I was gonna like this kid.
HENRY!
IF YOU'VE GOT AN ITCH TO COMPETE, YOU'D BETTER PICK ANOTHER HOBBY.

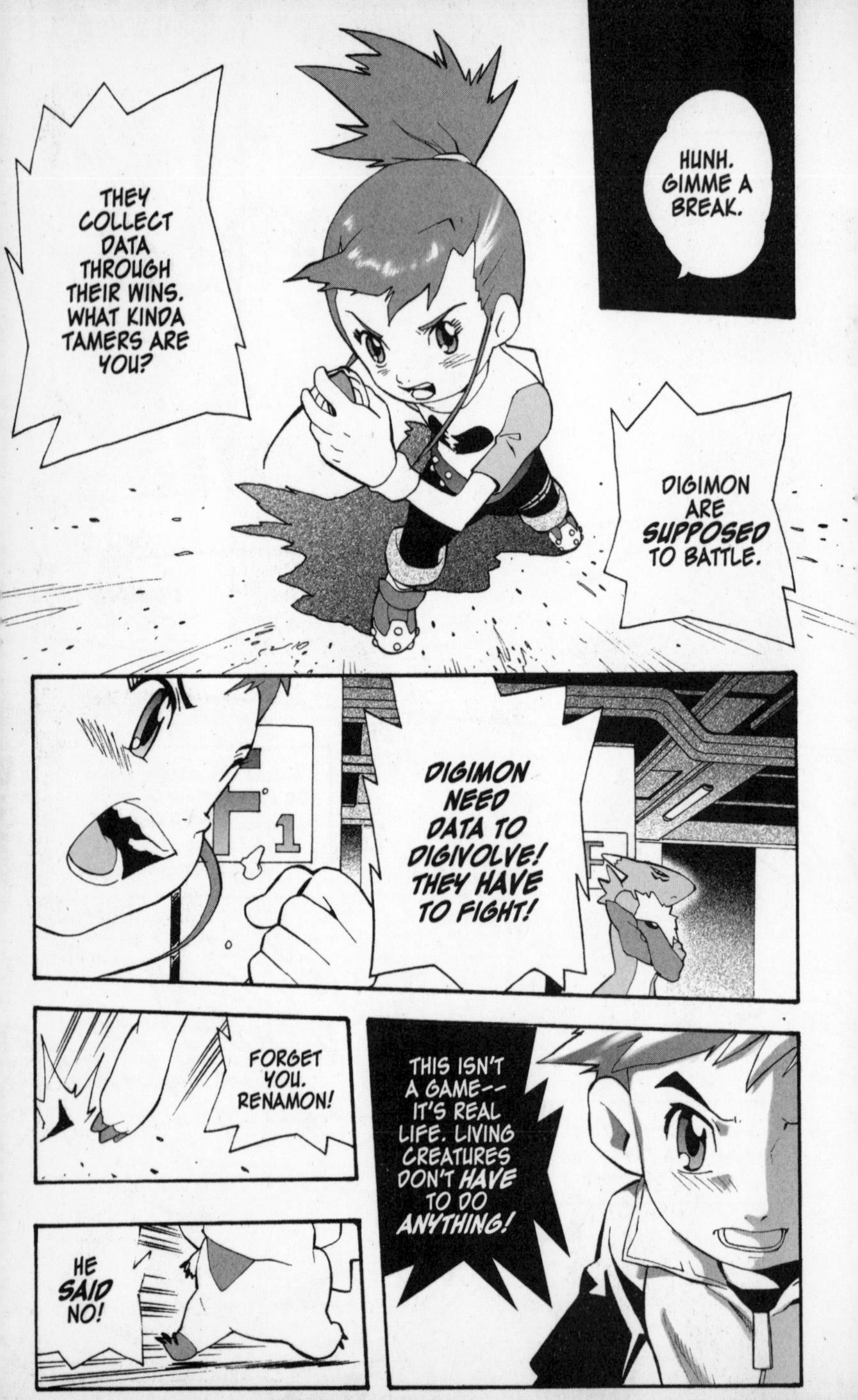
HUNH. GIMME A BREAK.
DIGIMON ARE SUPPOSED TO BATTLE.
THEY COLLECT DATA THROUGH THEIR WINS. WHAT KINDA TAMERS ARE YOU?
DIGIMON NEED DATA TO DIGIVOLVE! THEY HAVE TO FIGHT!
THIS ISN'T A GAME-- IT'S REAL LIFE. LIVING CREATURES DON'T HAVE TO DO ANYTHING!
FORGET YOU. RENAMON!
HE SAID NO!

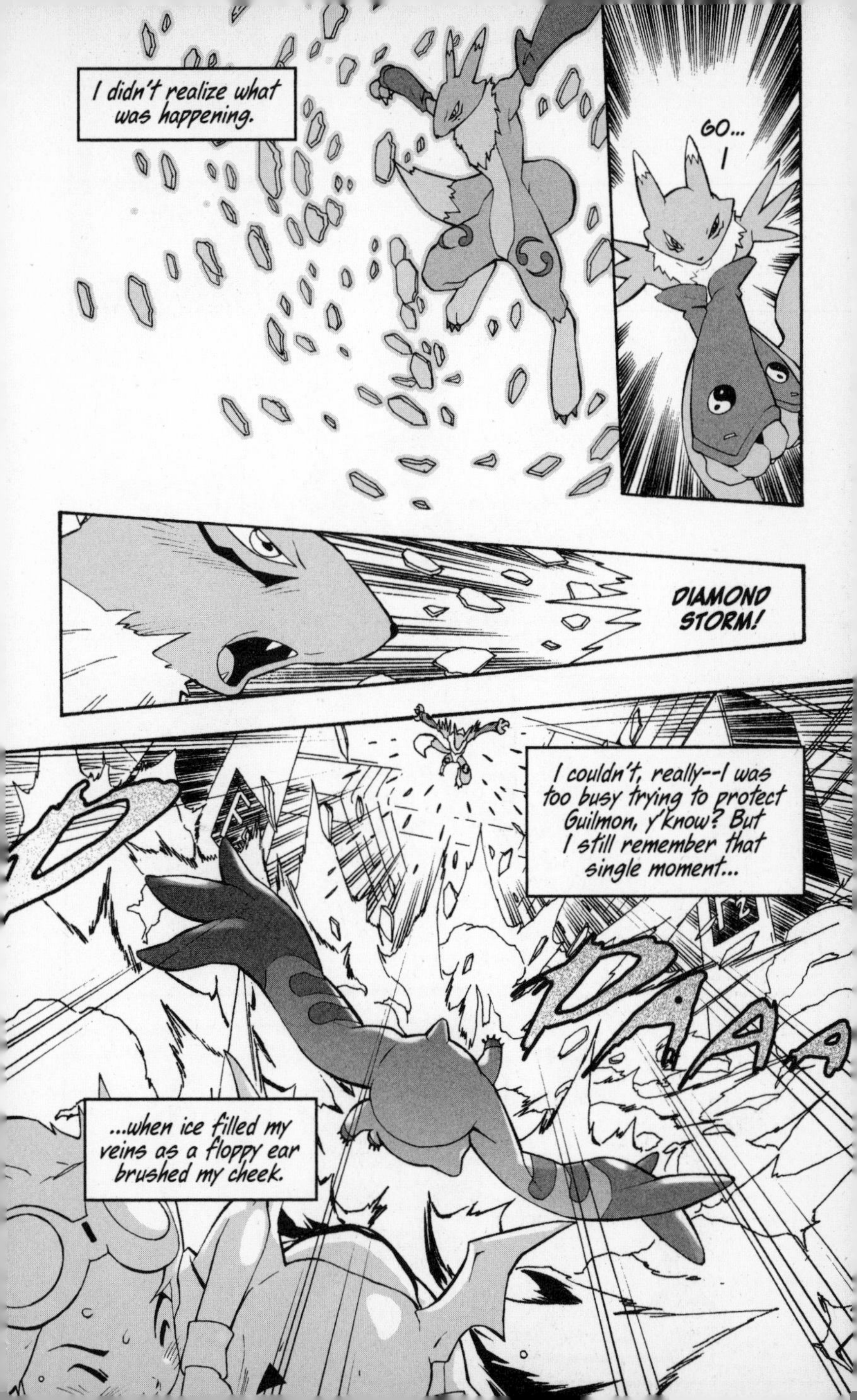
GO... I
I didn't realize what was happening.
DIAMOND STORM!
I couldn't, really--I was too busy trying to protect Guilmon, y'know? But I still remember that single moment...
DAAA
...when ice filled my veins as a floppy ear brushed my cheek.

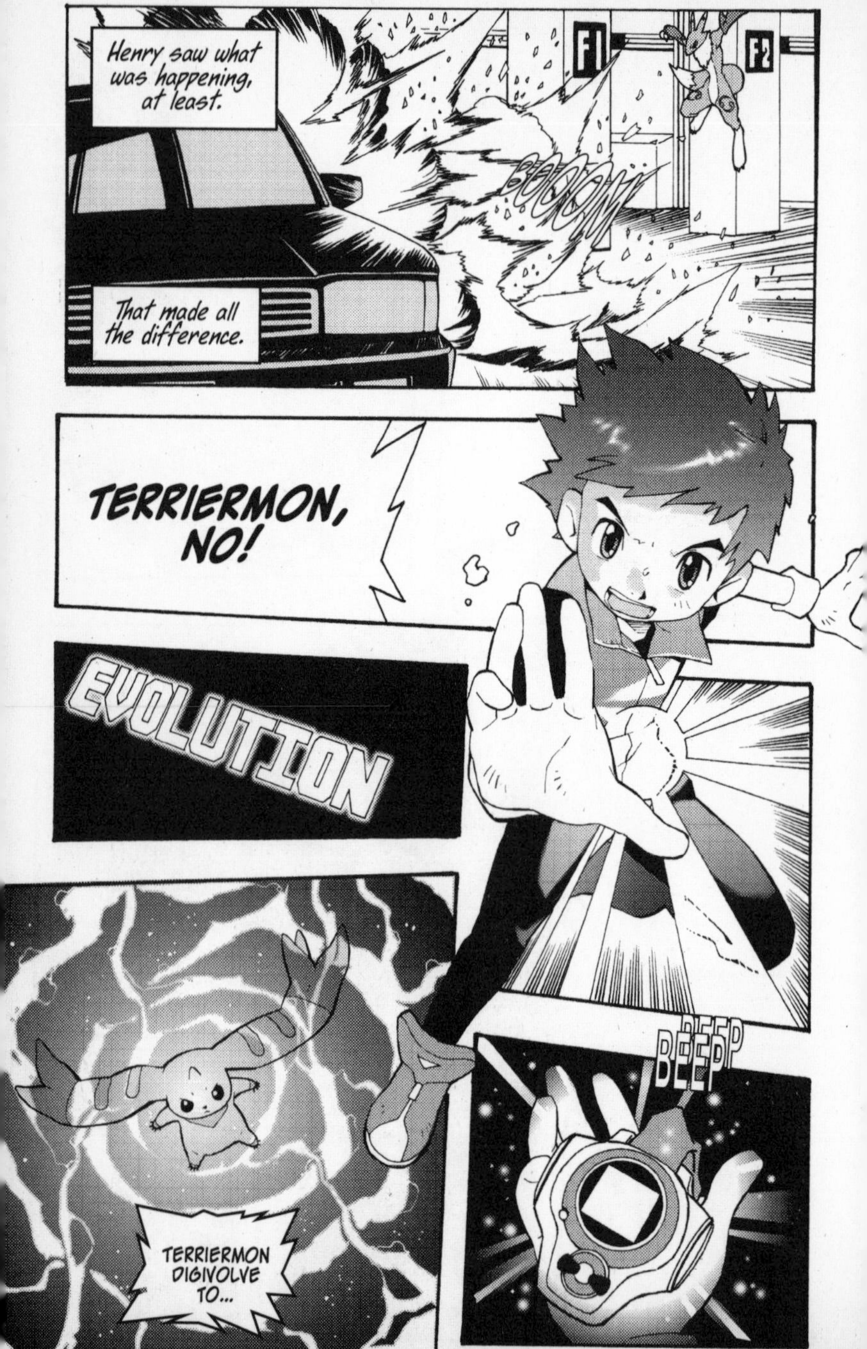

Henry saw what was happening, at least.
BOOOM
That made all the difference.
TERRIERMON, NO!
EVOLUTION
BEEP
BEEP
TERRIERMON DIGIVOLVE TO...

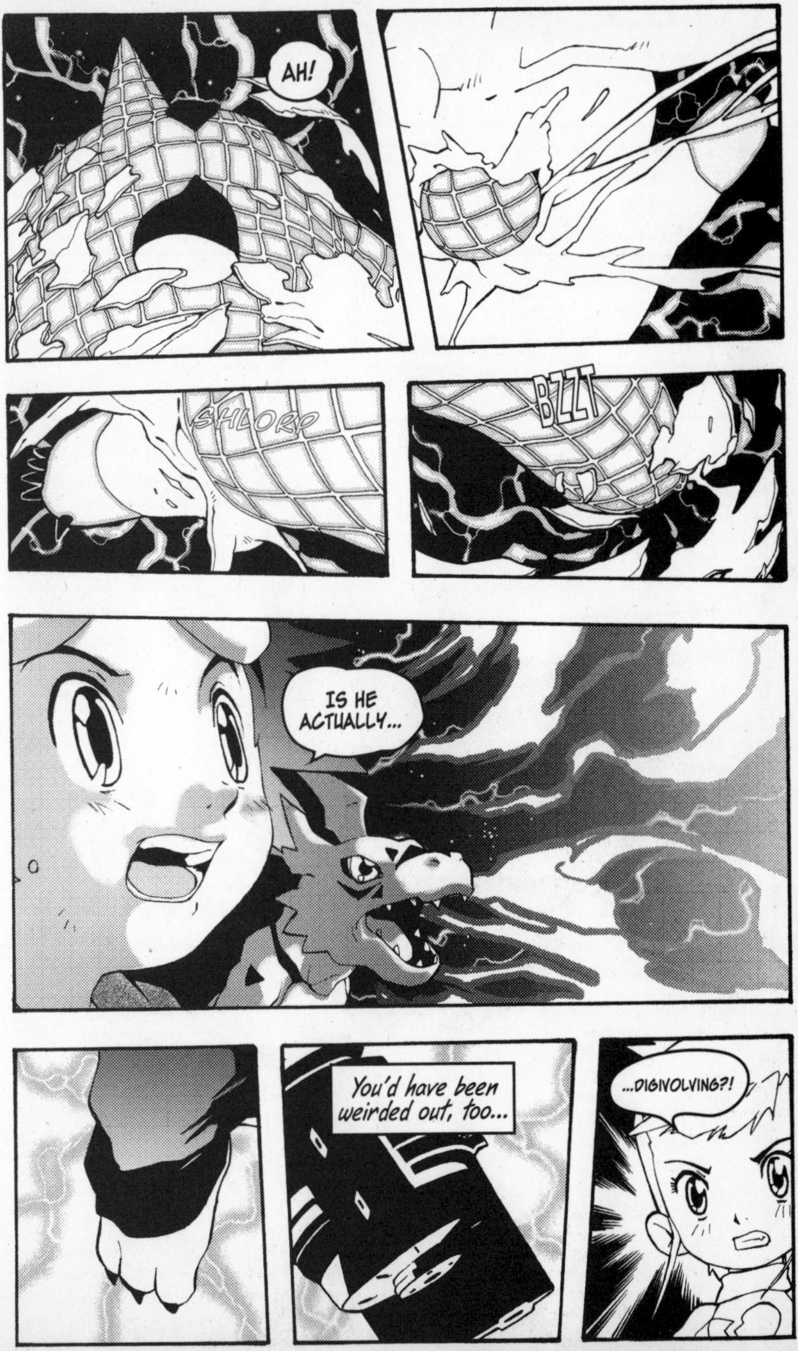
AH!
BZZT
SHLORP
IS HE ACTUALLY...
...DIGIVOLVING?!
You'd have been weirded out, too...

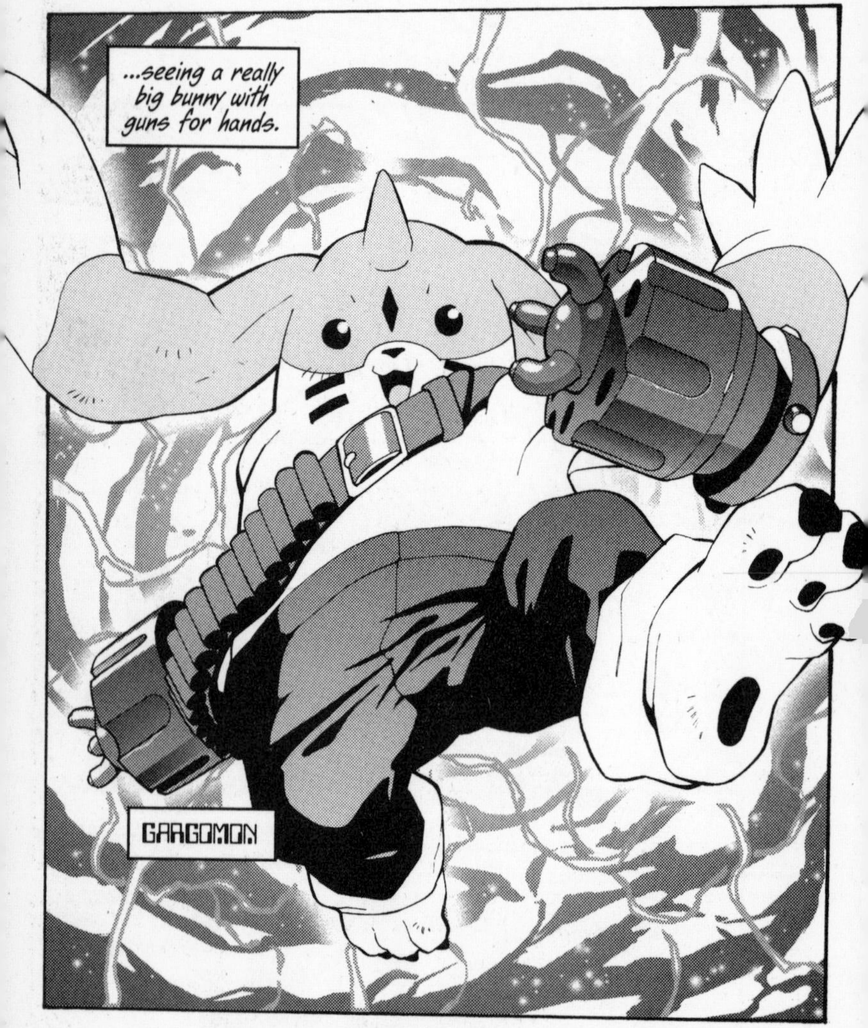
...seeing a really big bunny with guns for hands.
GARGOMON

CHAPTER 3:
DANGEROUS DEVELOPMENTS

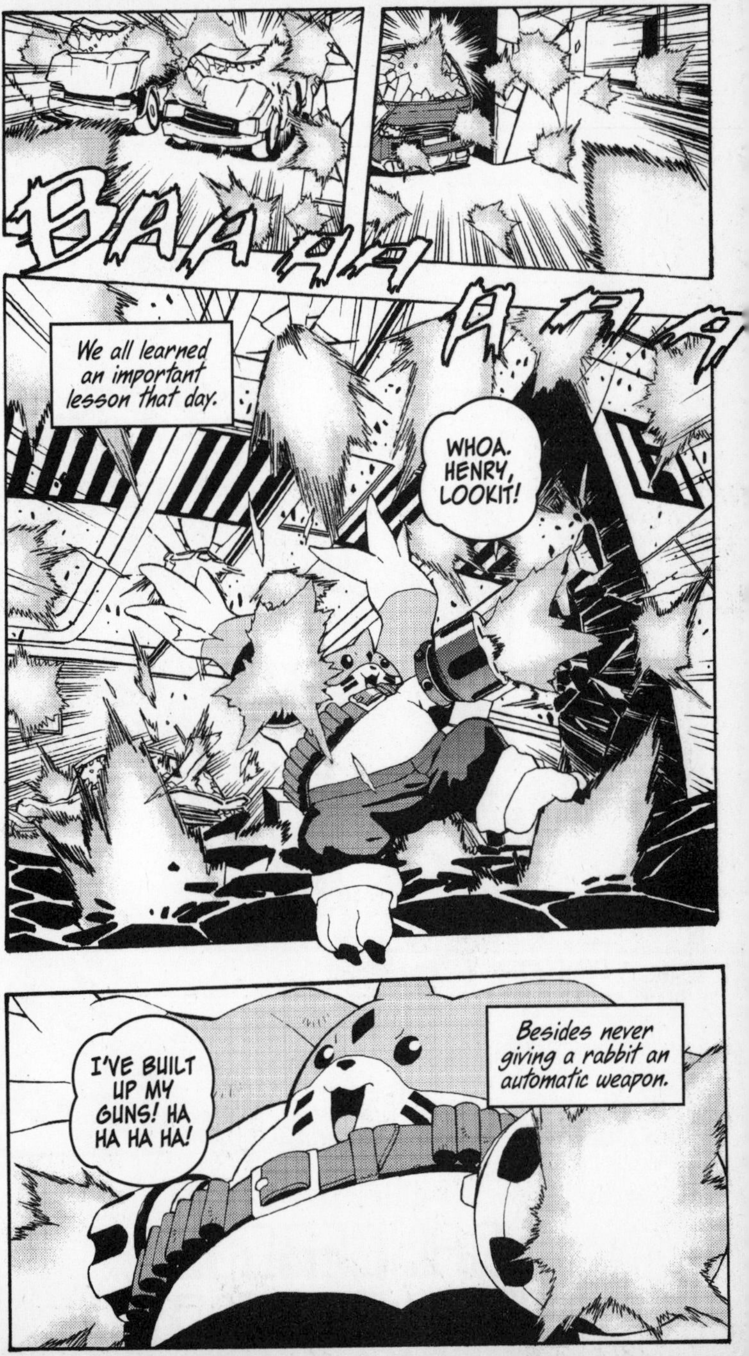
BAAAAAAAAA
WHOA. HENRY, LOOKIT!
We all learned an important lesson that day.
Besides never giving a rabbit an automatic weapon.
I'VE BUILT UP MY GUNS! HA HA HA HA!

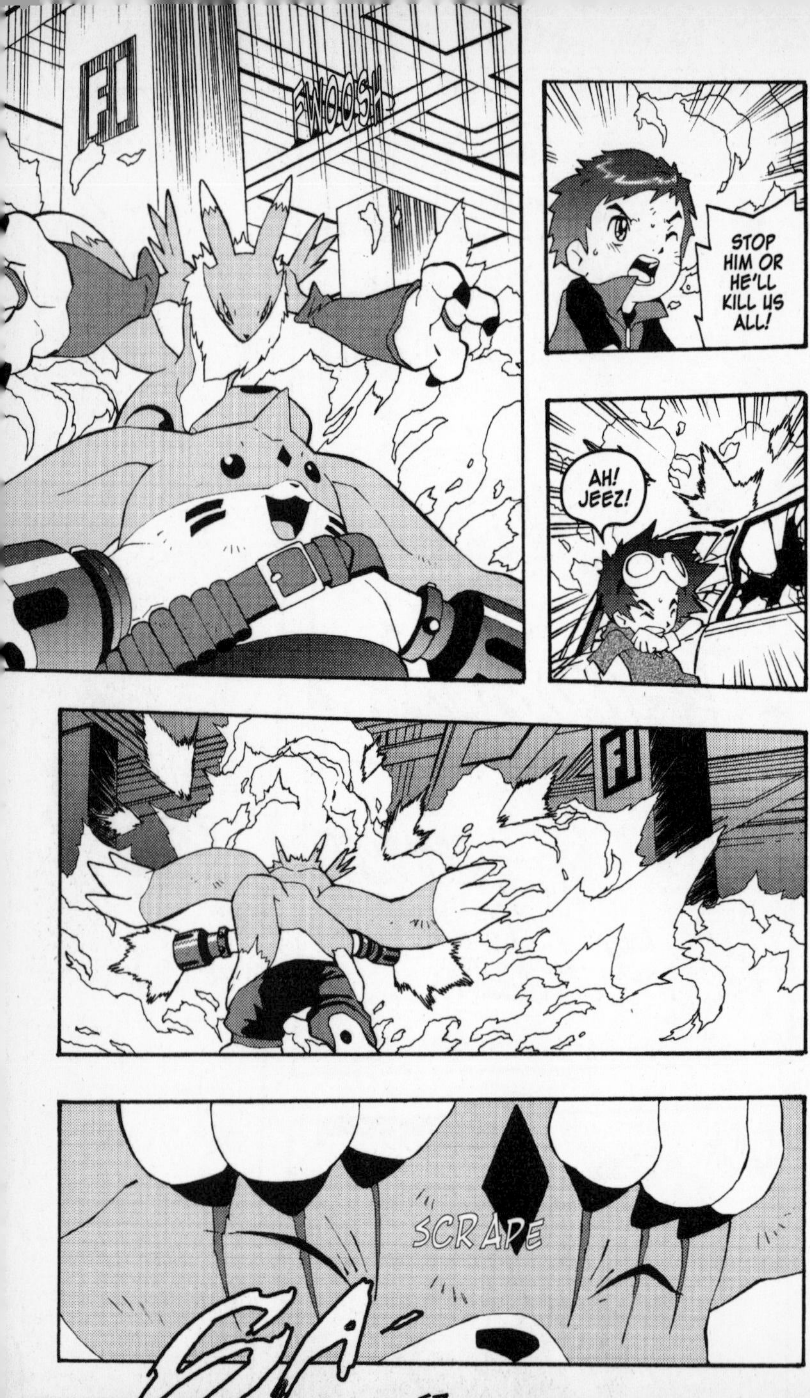
STOP HIM OR HE'LL KILL US ALL!
AH! JEEZ!
FWOOSH
SCRAPE

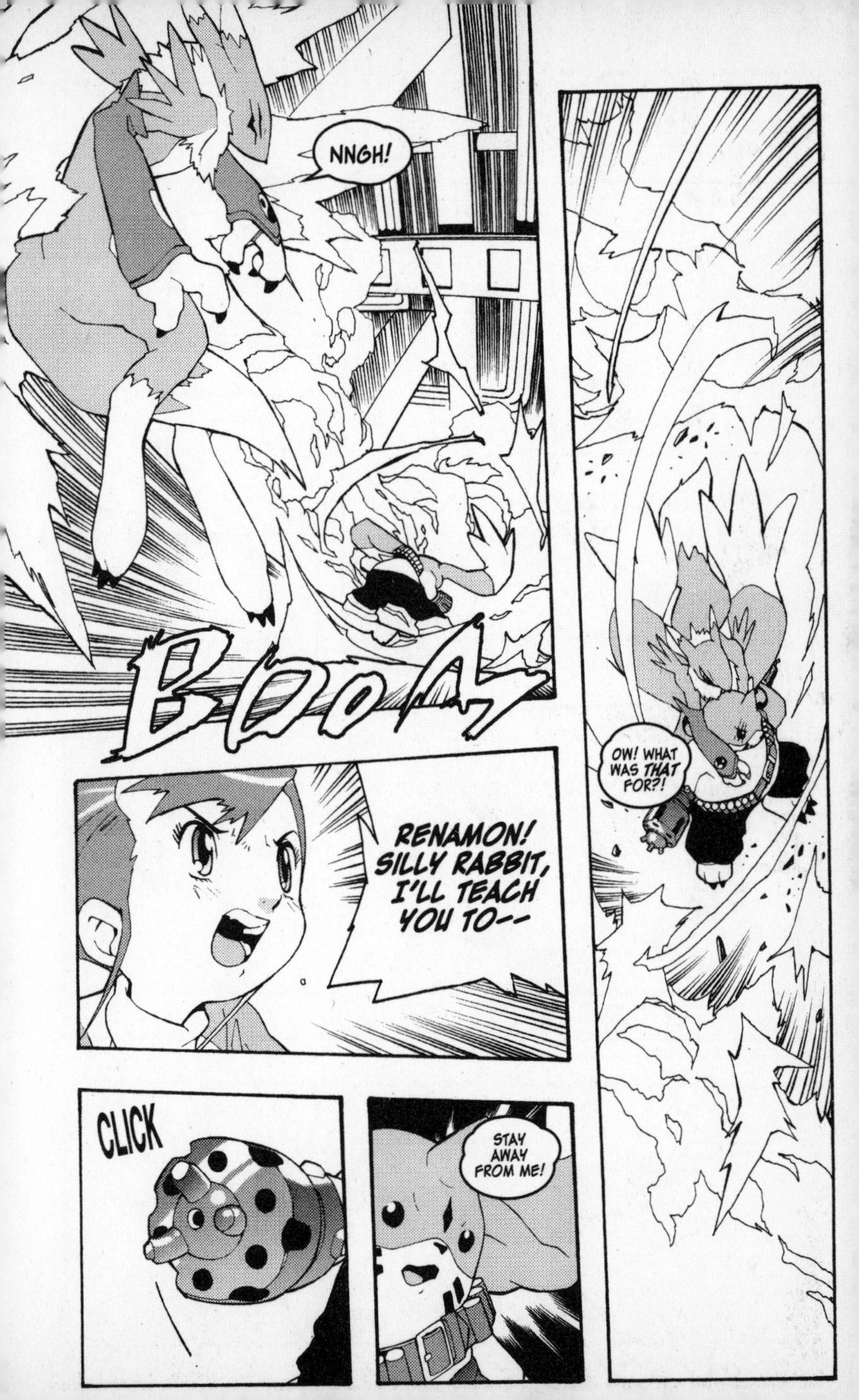
OW! WHAT WAS *THAT* FOR?!
NNGH!
BOOM
RENAMON! SILLY RABBIT, I'LL TEACH YOU TO--
STAY AWAY FROM ME!
CLICK

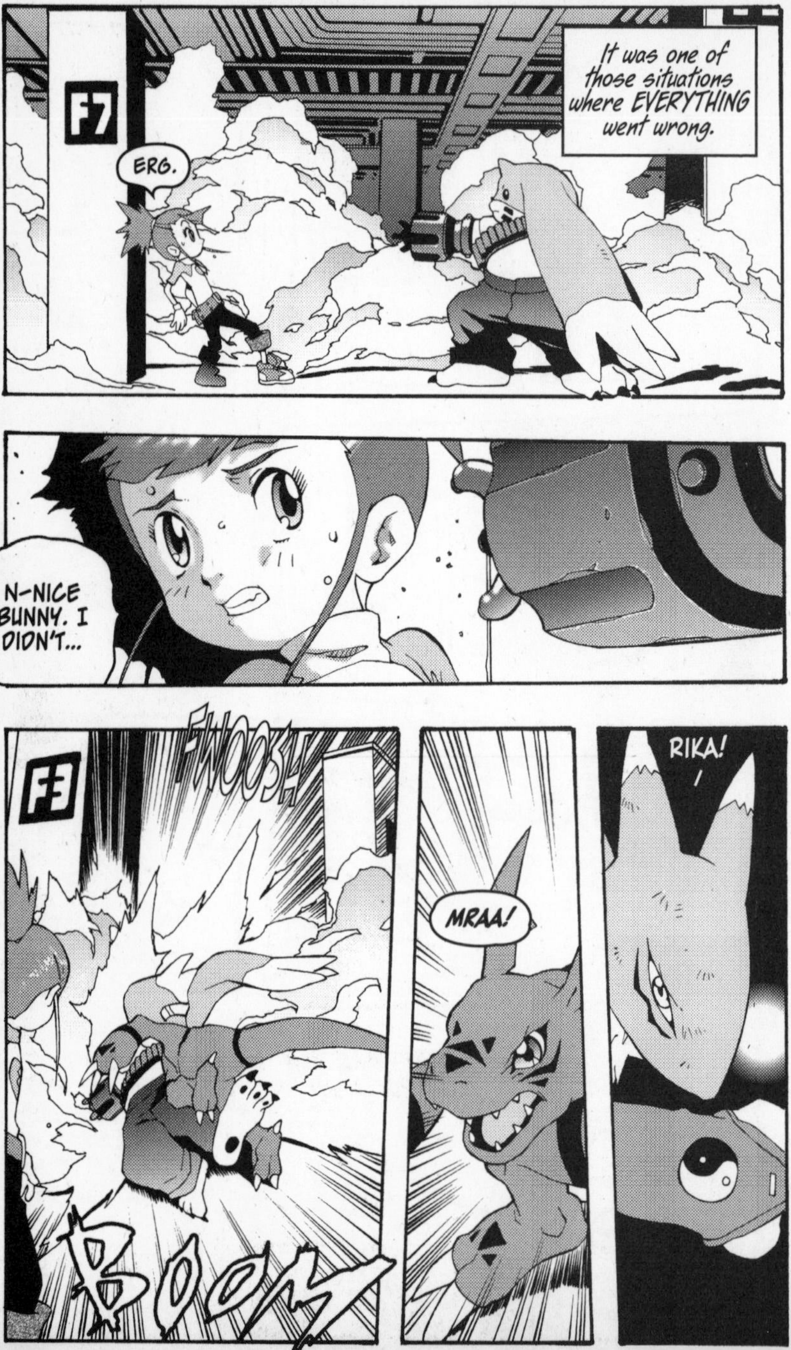
It was one of those situations where EVERYTHING went wrong.
F7
ERG.
N-NICE BUNNY. I DIDN'T...
RIKA!
MRAA!
F3
FWOOSH
BOOM

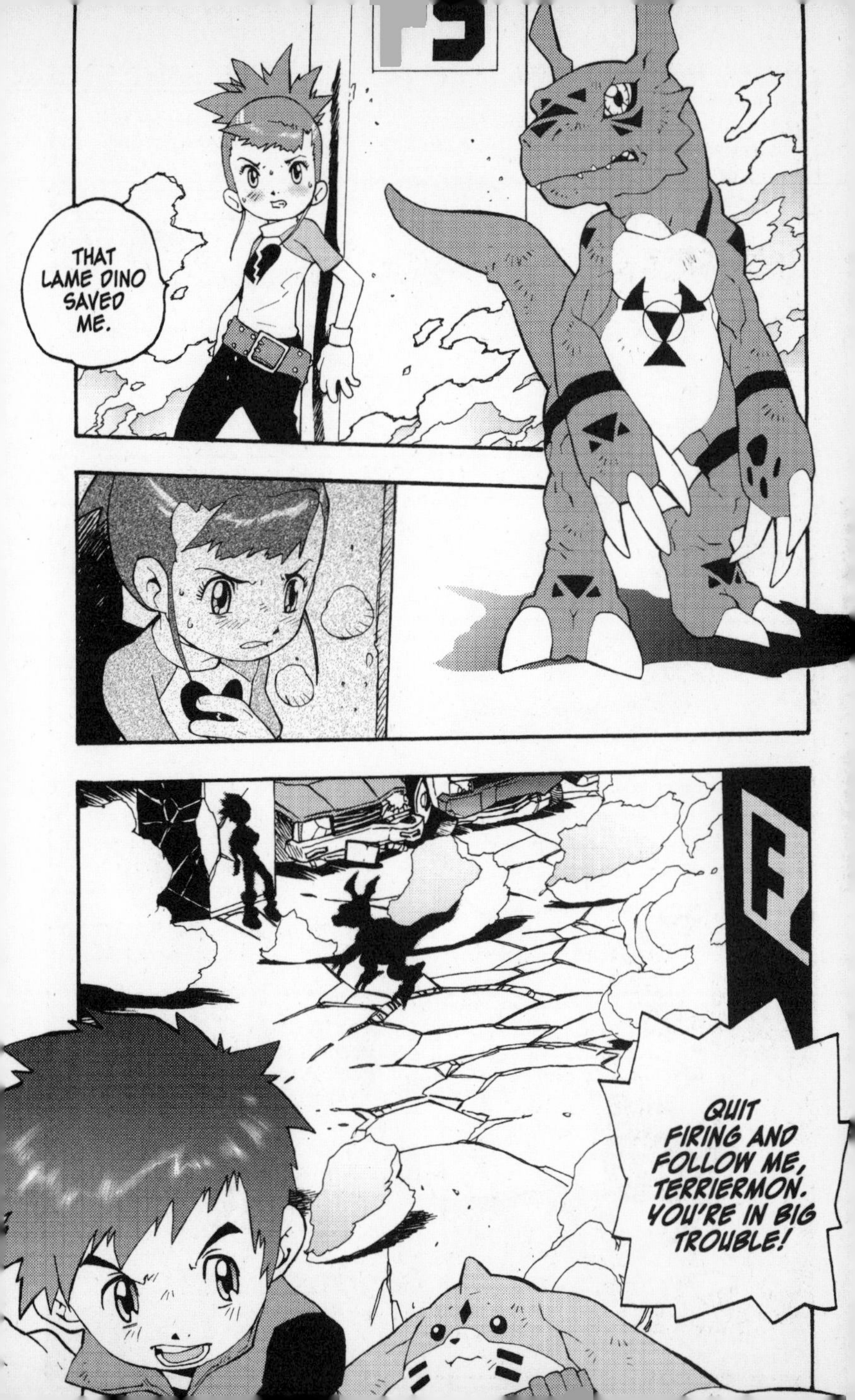
THAT LAME DINO SAVED ME.
QUIT FIRING AND FOLLOW ME, TERRIERMON. YOU'RE IN BIG TROUBLE!

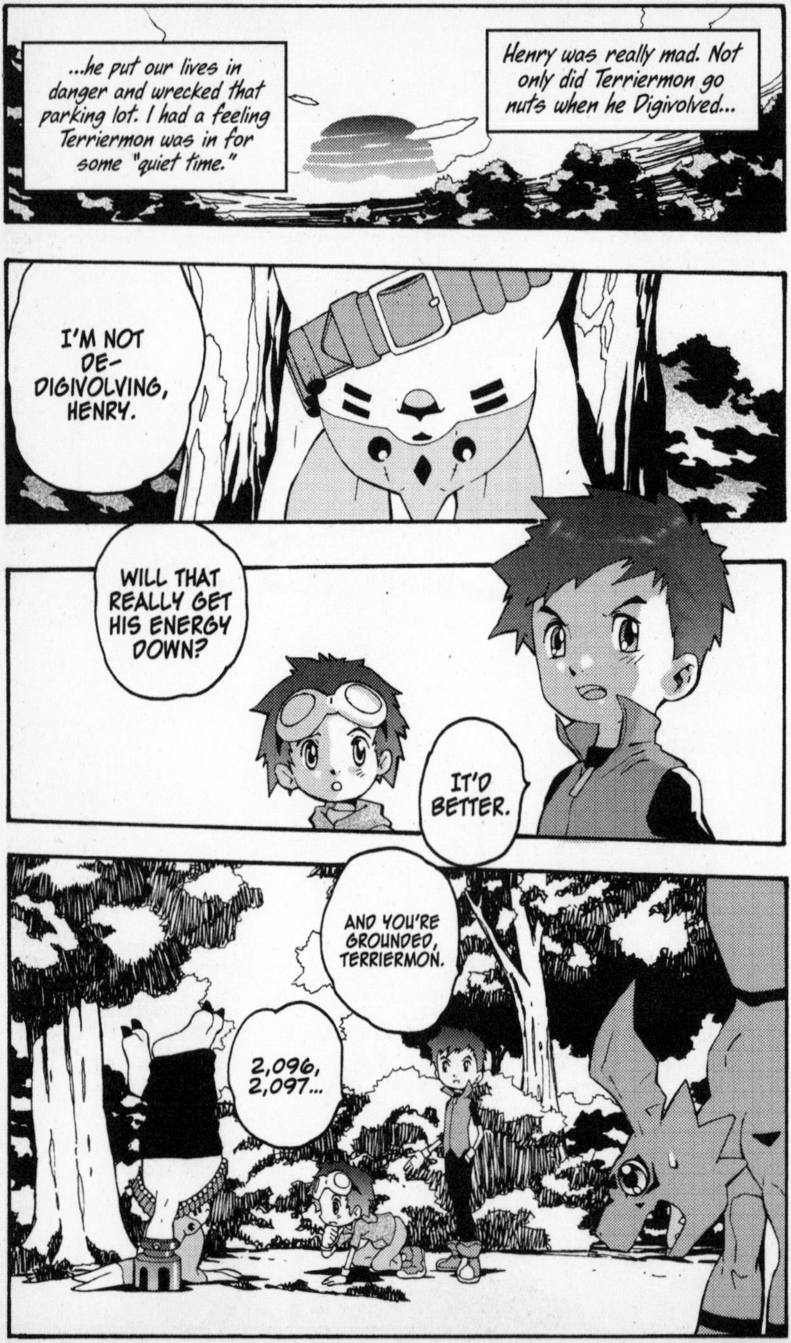
Henry was really mad. Not only did Terriermon go nuts when he Digivolved...
...he put our lives in danger and wrecked that parking lot. I had a feeling Terriermon was in for some "quiet time."
I'M NOT DE-DIGIVOLVING, HENRY.
WILL THAT REALLY GET HIS ENERGY DOWN?
IT'D BETTER.
AND YOU'RE GROUNDED, TERRIERMON.
2,096, 2,097...

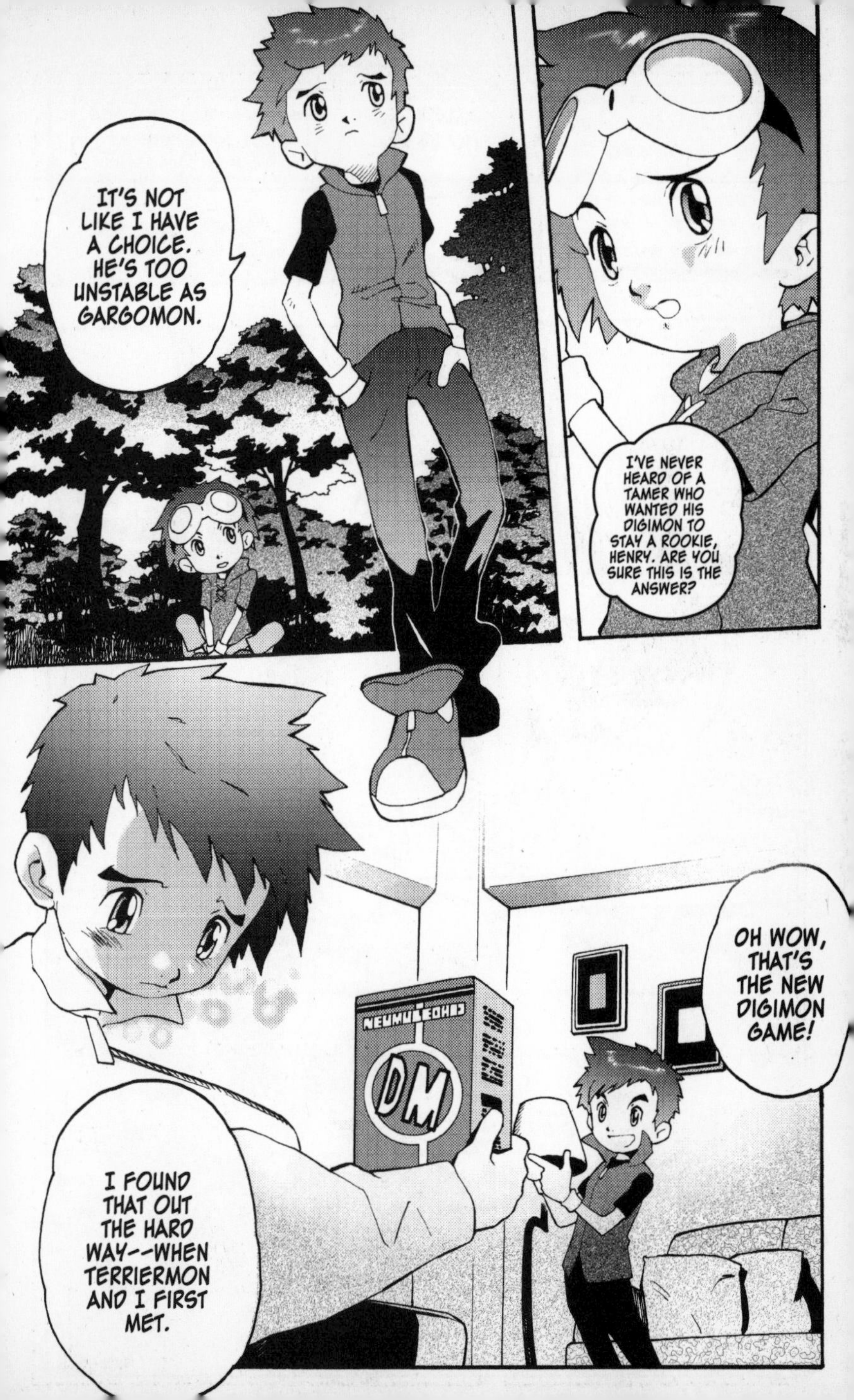
I'VE NEVER HEARD OF A TAMER WHO WANTED HIS DIGIMON TO STAY A ROOKIE, HENRY. ARE YOU SURE THIS IS THE ANSWER?
IT'S NOT LIKE I HAVE A CHOICE. HE'S TOO UNSTABLE AS GARGOMON.
OH WOW, THAT'S THE NEW DIGIMON GAME!
DM
I FOUND THAT OUT THE HARD WAY--WHEN TERRIERMON AND I FIRST MET.

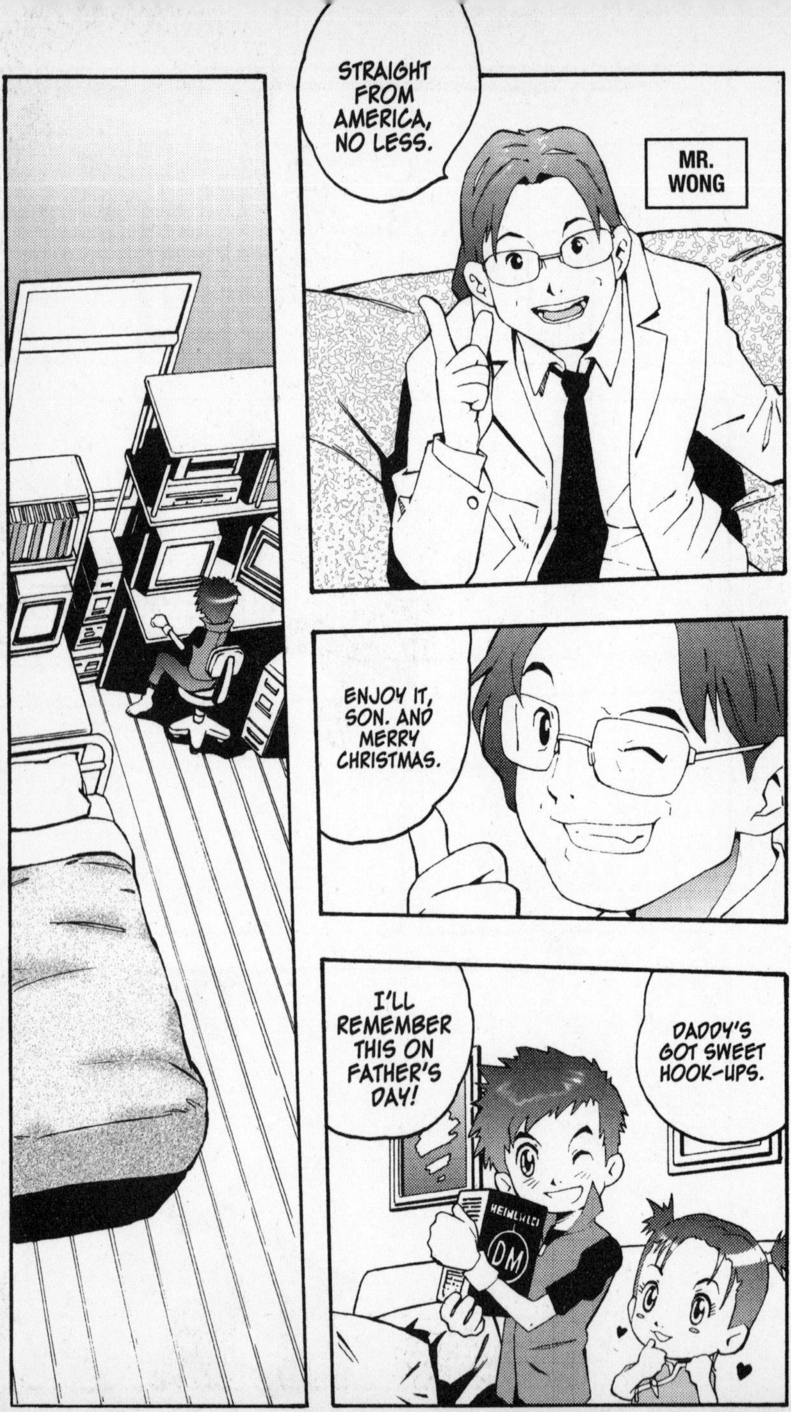
STRAIGHT FROM AMERICA, NO LESS.
MR. WONG
ENJOY IT, SON. AND MERRY CHRISTMAS.
DADDY'S GOT SWEET HOOK-UPS.
I'LL REMEMBER THIS ON FATHER'S DAY!

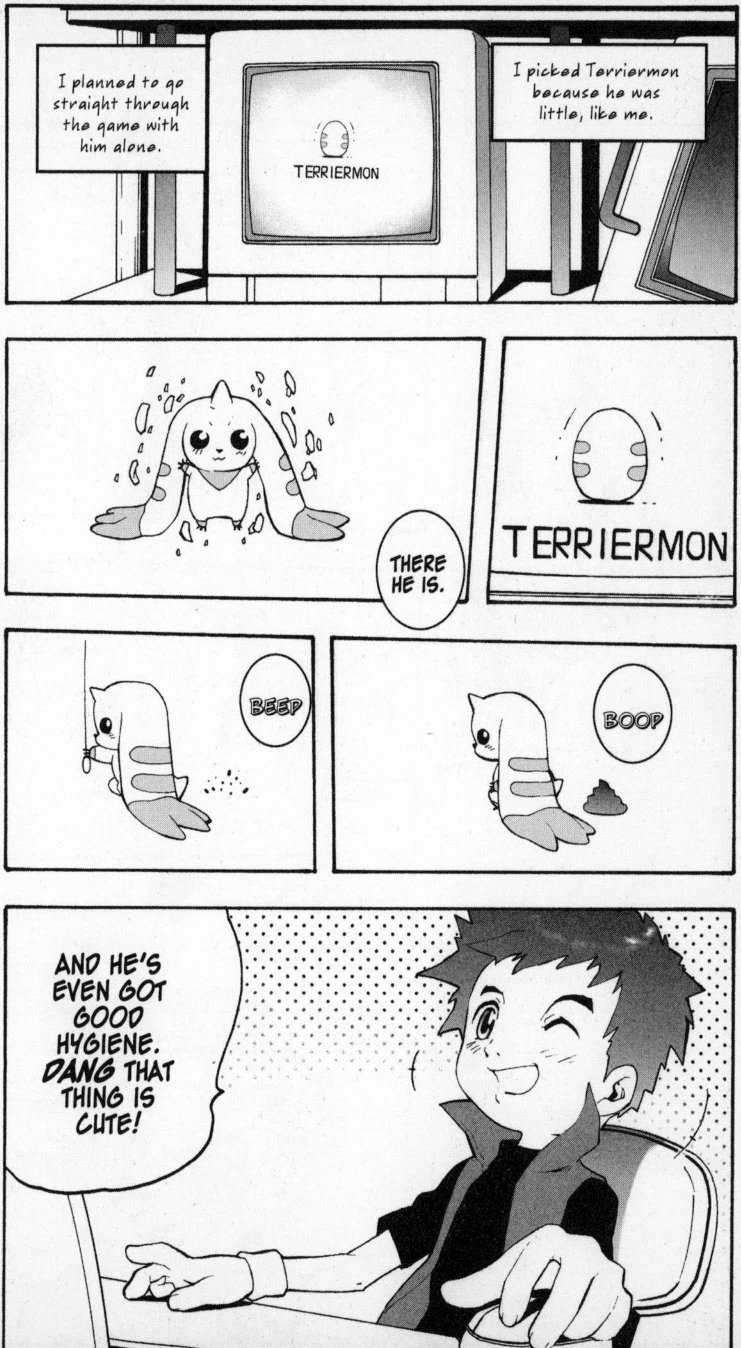
I picked Terriermon because he was little, like me.
I planned to go straight through the game with him alone.
TERRIERMON
TERRIERMON
THERE HE IS.
BOOP
BEEP
AND HE'S EVEN GOT GOOD HYGIENE. DANG THAT THING IS CUTE!

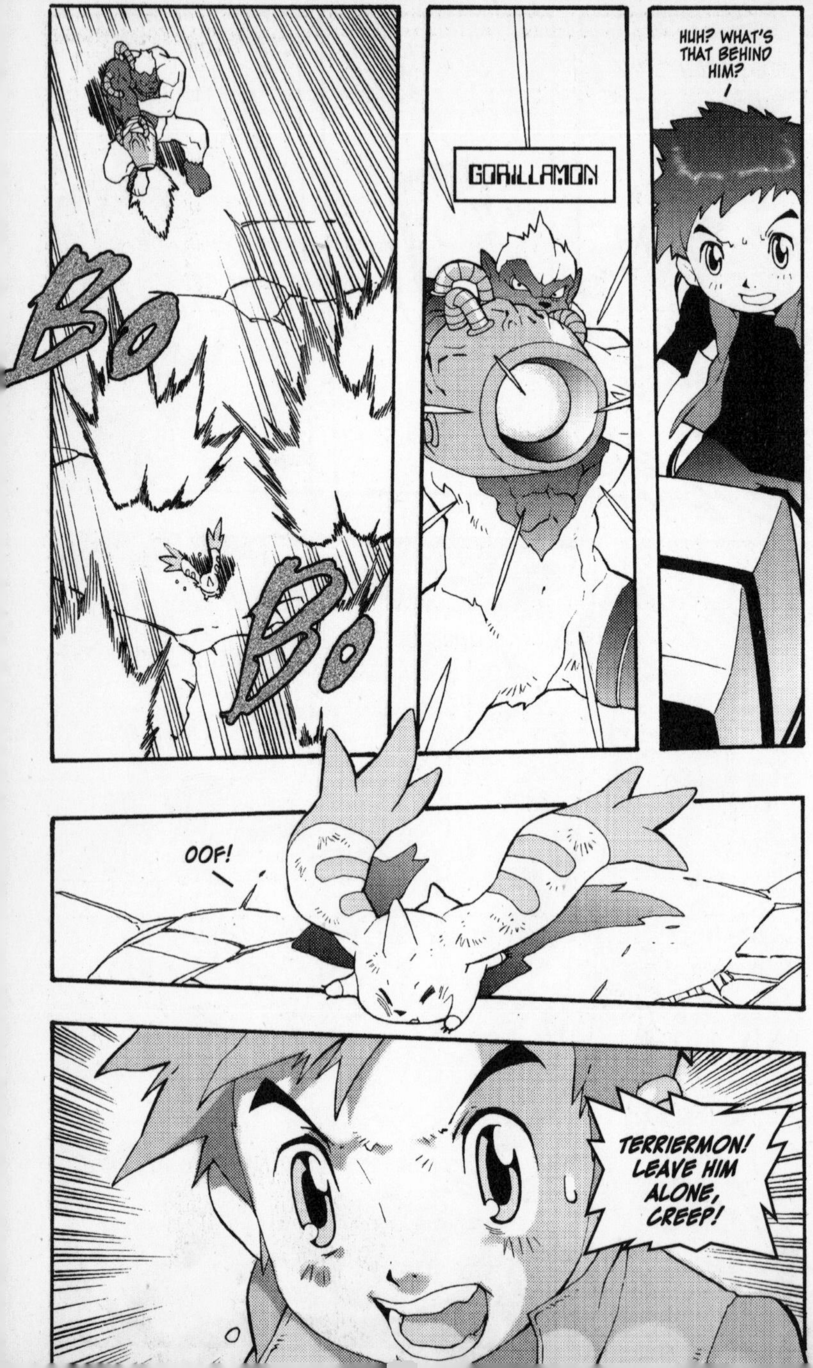
HUH? WHAT'S THAT BEHIND HIM?
GORILLAMON
BO
BO
OOF!
TERRIERMON! LEAVE HIM ALONE, CREEP!

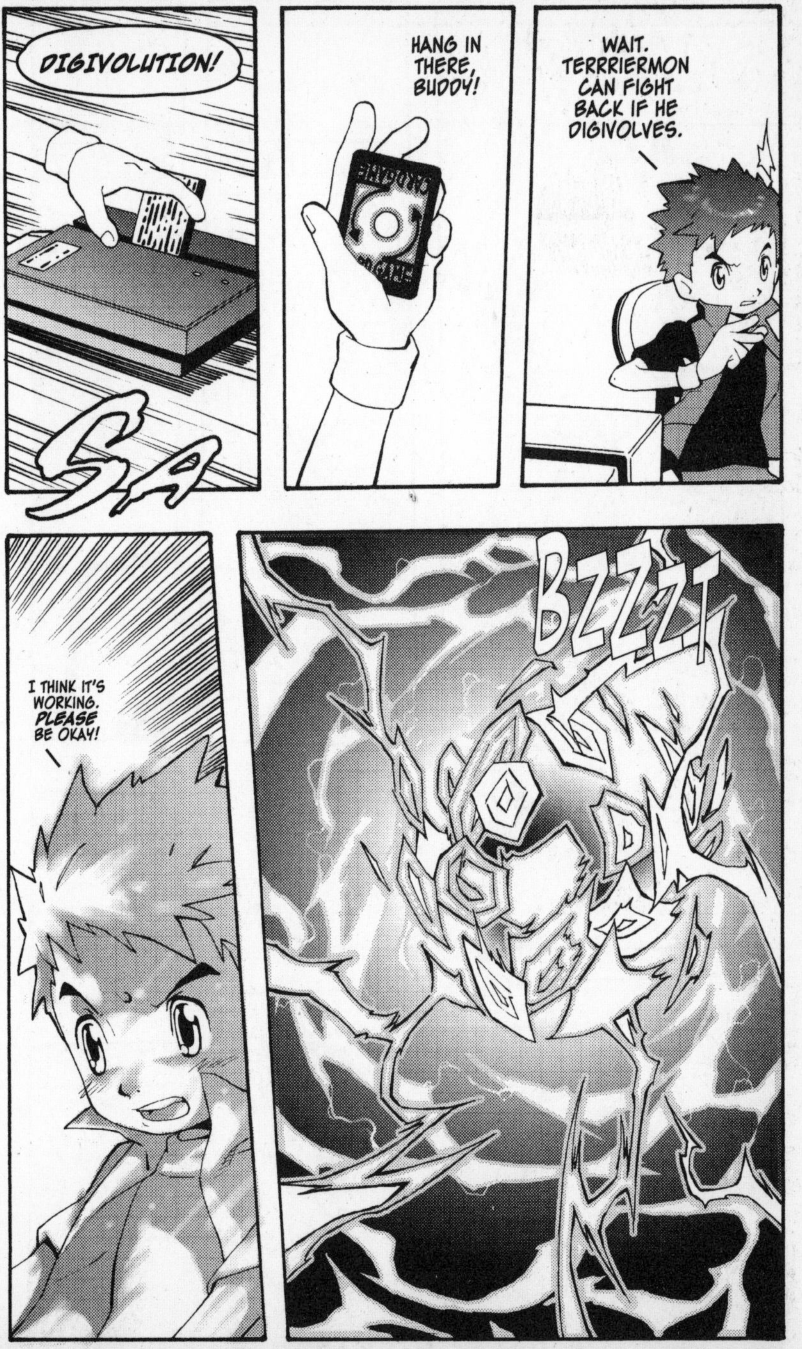
WAIT. TERRRIERMON CAN FIGHT BACK IF HE DIGIVOLVES.
HANG IN THERE, BUDDY!
DIGIVOLUTION!
SA
BZZZT
I THINK IT'S WORKING. PLEASE BE OKAY!

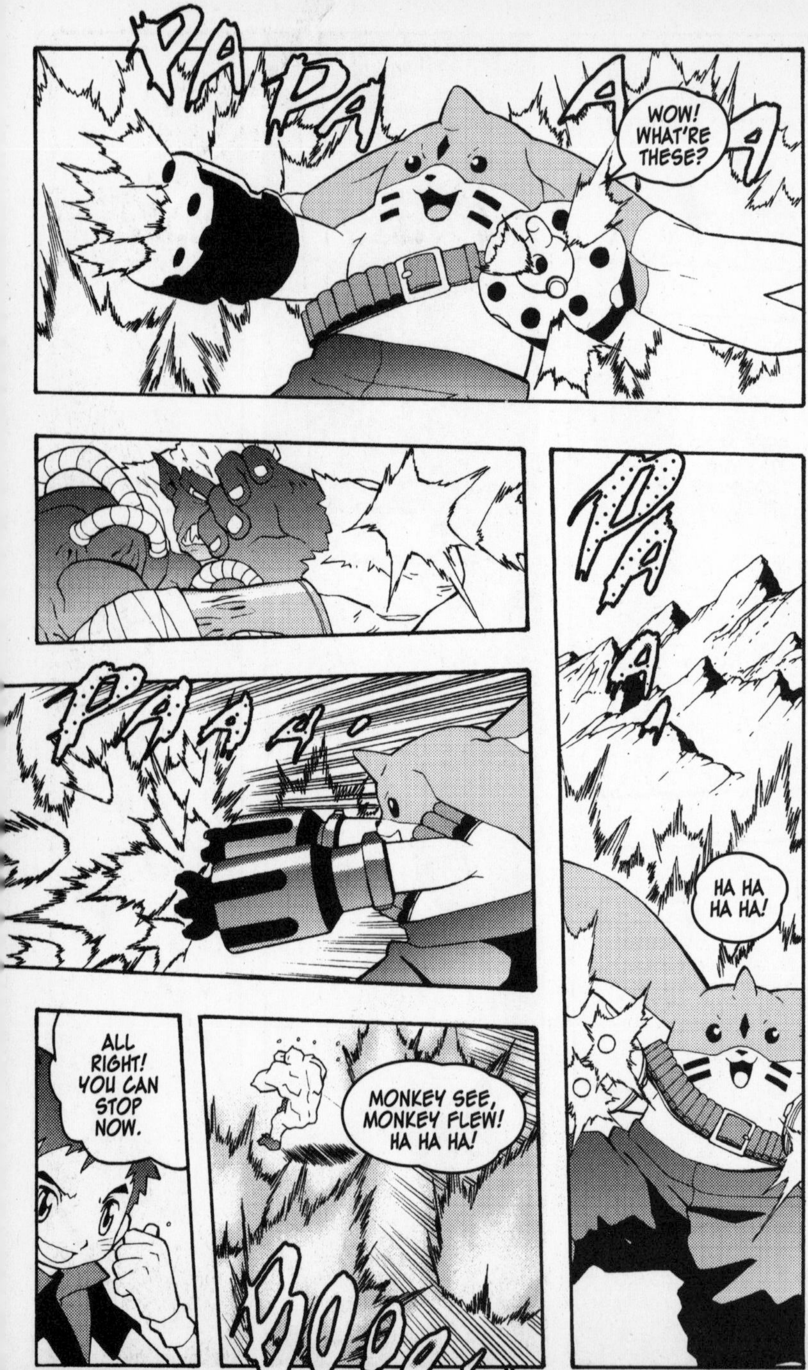
PAPA
AA
WOW! WHAT'RE THESE?
PA
PA
HA HA HA HA!
PAA
MONKEY SEE, MONKEY FLEW! HA HA HA!
BOOO..
ALL RIGHT! YOU CAN STOP NOW.

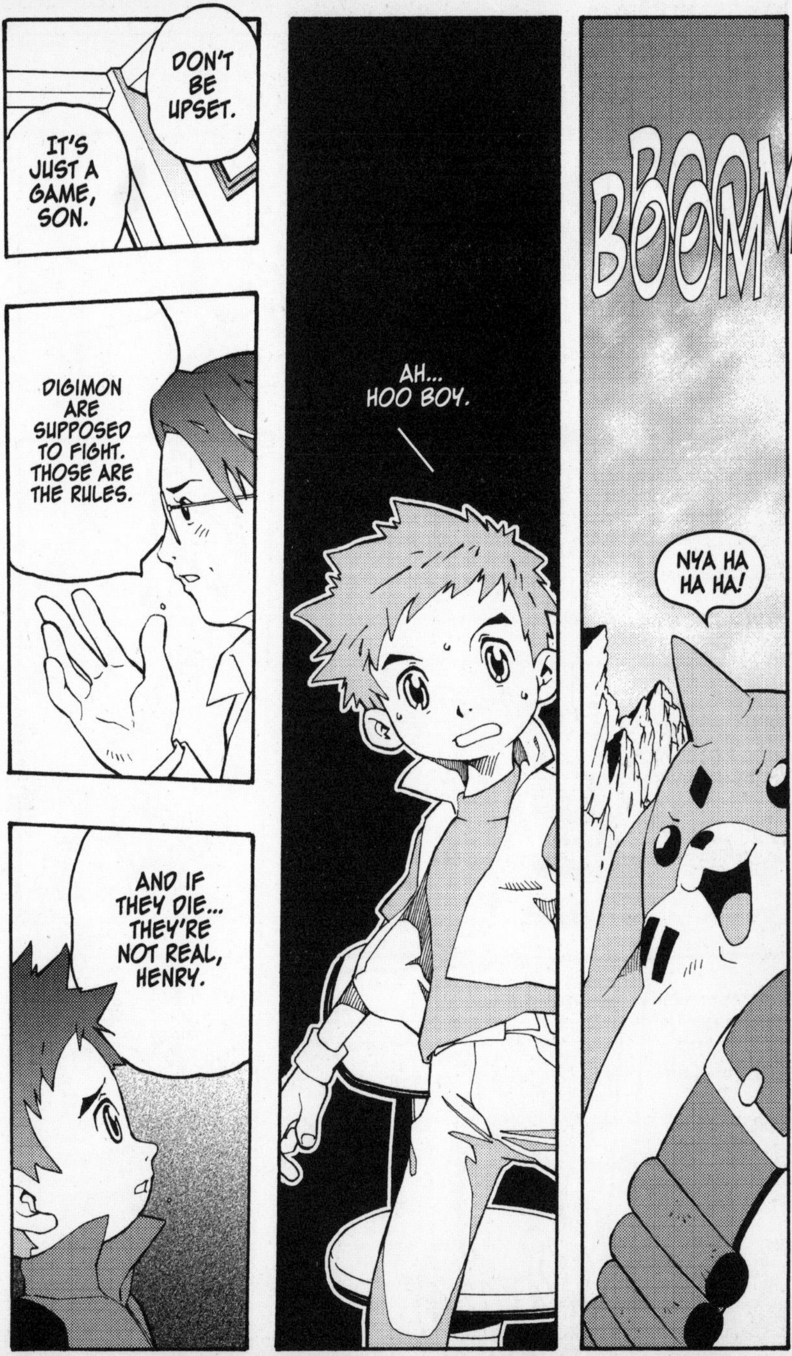
BOOM BOOM
NYA HA HA HA!
AH... HOO BOY.
DON'T BE UPSET.
IT'S JUST A GAME, SON.
DIGIMON ARE SUPPOSED TO FIGHT. THOSE ARE THE RULES.
AND IF THEY DIE... THEY'RE NOT REAL, HENRY.

SO, WHAT, I'M SUPPOSED TO JUST *NOT* CARE?!

NOT REAL?

BWEE

I WON'T LET YOU DIE, TERRIERMON.

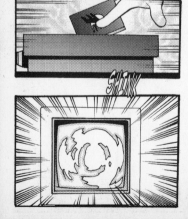

SHRINK

I WON'T!

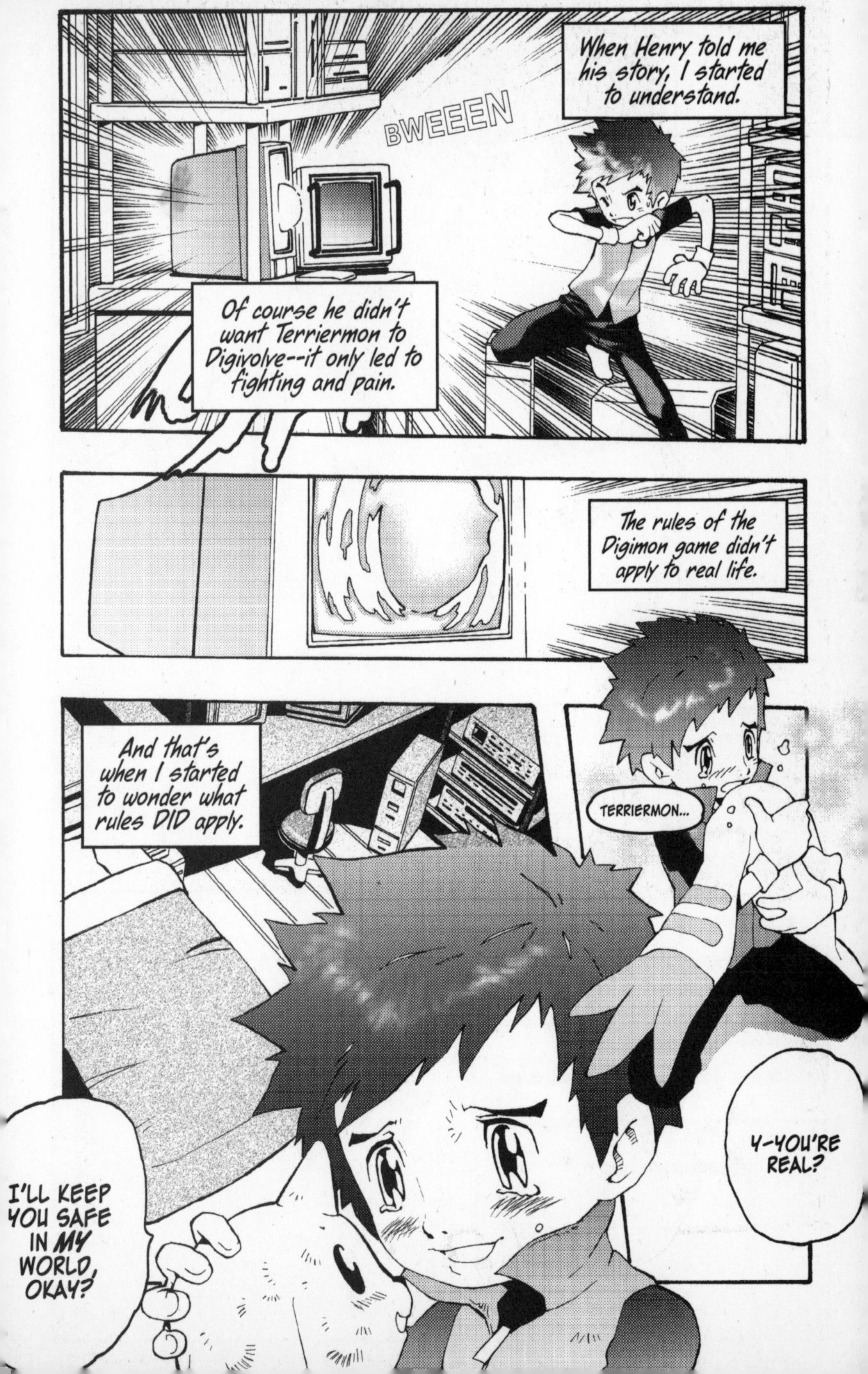
When Henry told me his story, I started to understand.
BWEEEN
Of course he didn't want Terriermon to Digivolve--it only led to fighting and pain.
The rules of the Digimon game didn't apply to real life.
TERRIERMON...
And that's when I started to wonder what rules DID apply.
Y-YOU'RE REAL?
I'LL KEEP YOU SAFE IN MY WORLD, OKAY?

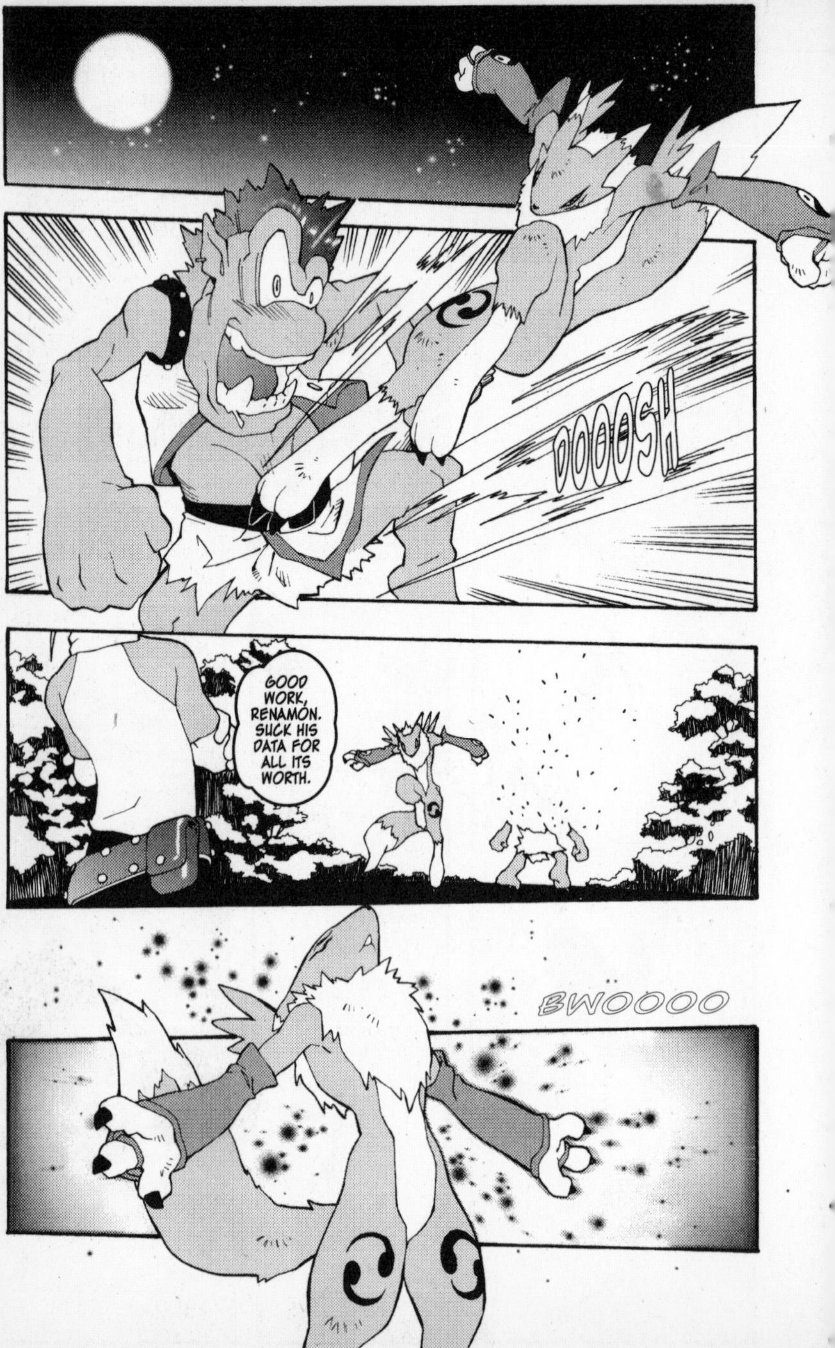
DOOOSH
GOOD WORK, RENAMON. SUCK HIS DATA FOR ALL ITS WORTH.
BWOOOO

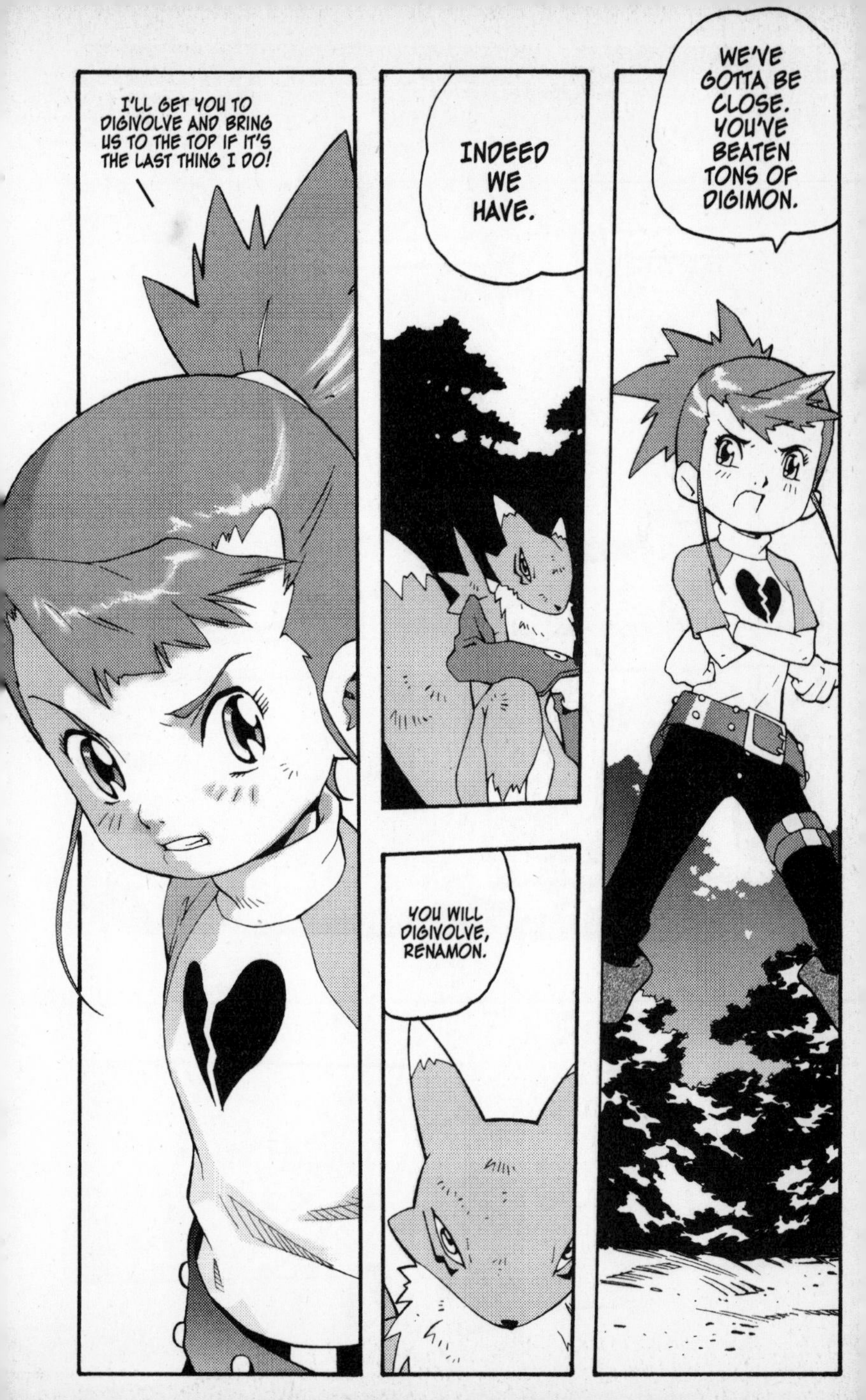
WE'VE GOTTA BE CLOSE. YOU'VE BEATEN TONS OF DIGIMON.
INDEED WE HAVE.
YOU WILL DIGIVOLVE, RENAMON.
I'LL GET YOU TO DIGIVOLVE AND BRING US TO THE TOP IF IT'S THE LAST THING I DO!

CHAPTER 4: SECRETS AND ANGER MANAGEMENT

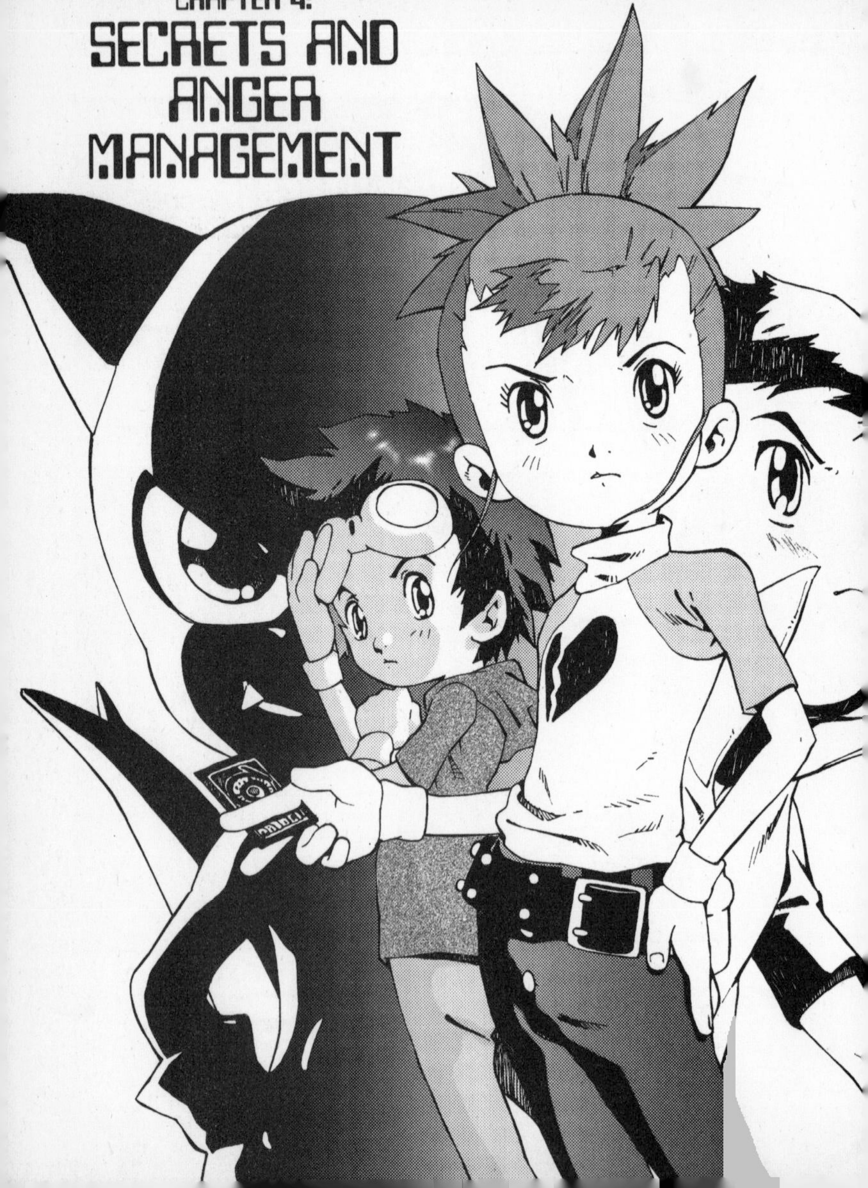

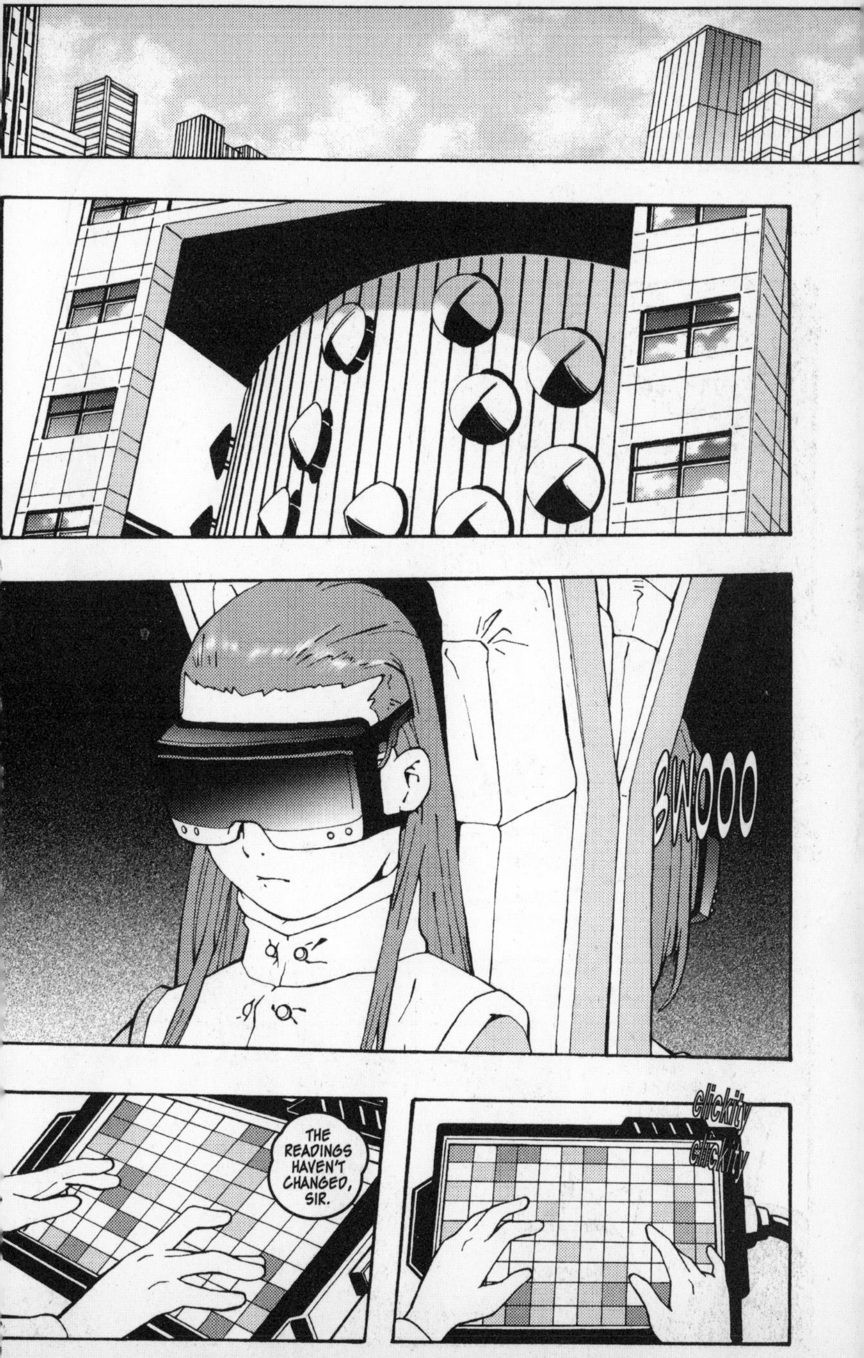
BWOOO
clickity
clickity
THE READINGS HAVEN'T CHANGED, SIR.

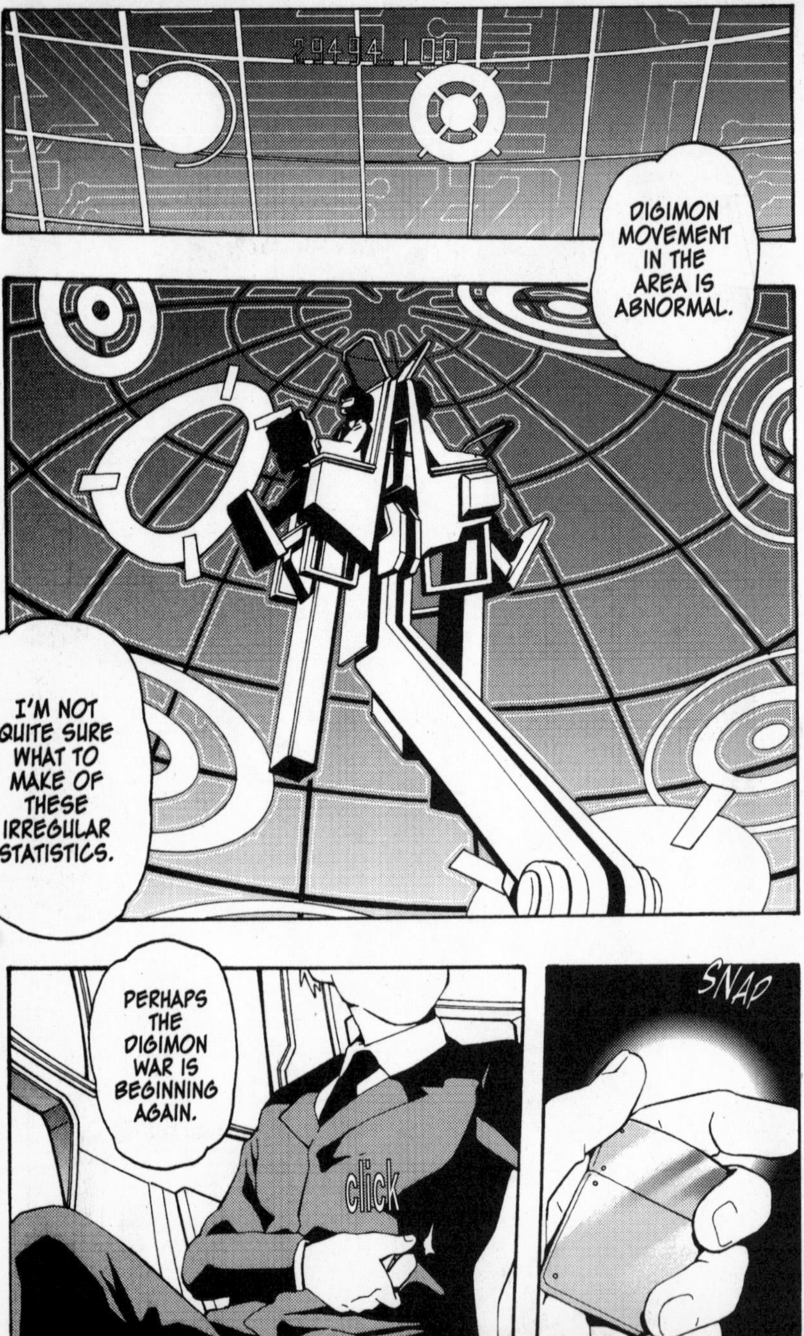
DIGIMON MOVEMENT IN THE AREA IS ABNORMAL.
I'M NOT QUITE SURE WHAT TO MAKE OF THESE IRREGULAR STATISTICS.
SNAP
PERHAPS THE DIGIMON WAR IS BEGINNING AGAIN.
click

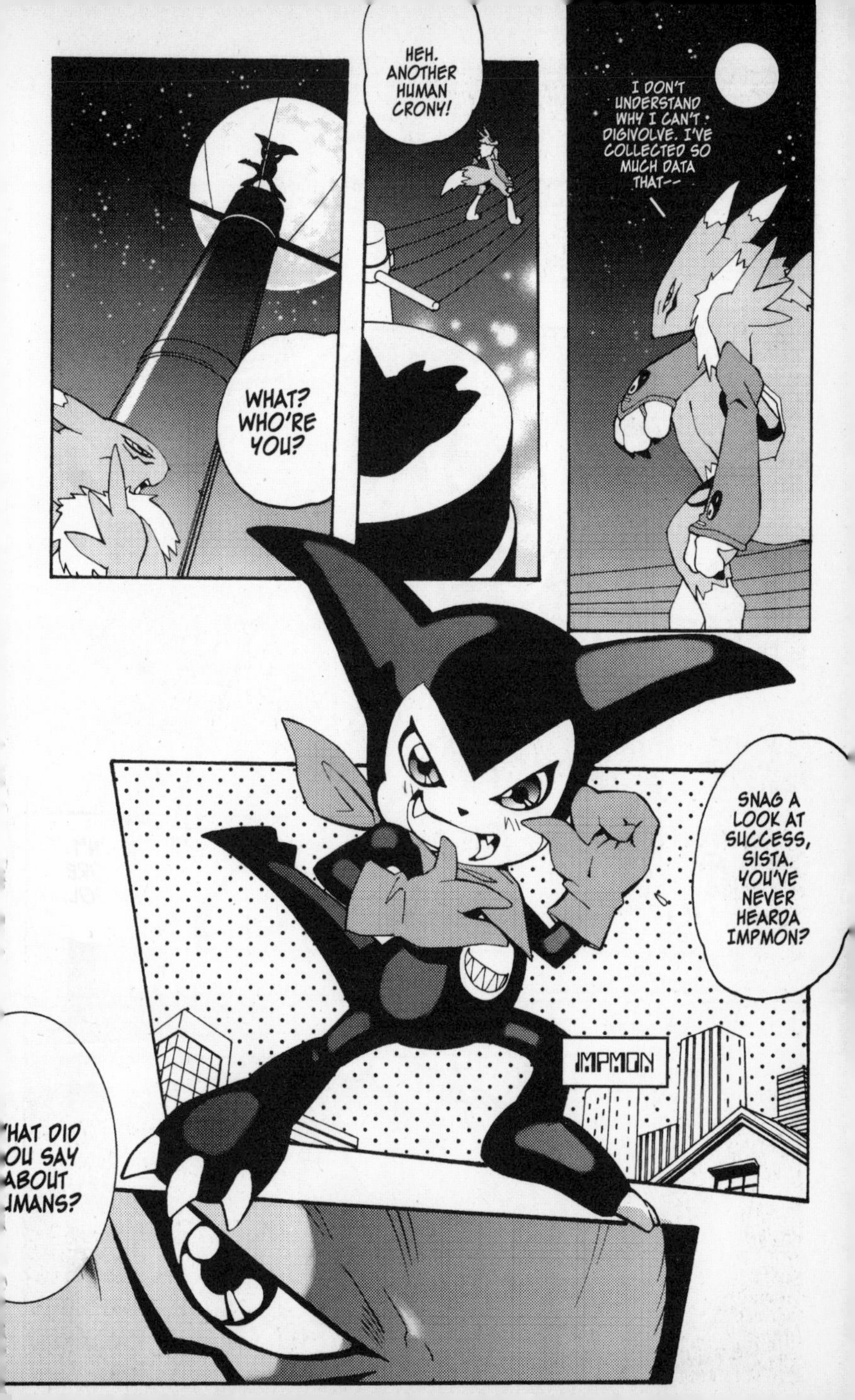
I DON'T UNDERSTAND WHY I CAN'T DIGIVOLVE. I'VE COLLECTED SO MUCH DATA THAT--
HEH. ANOTHER HUMAN CRONY!
WHAT? WHO'RE YOU?
SNAG A LOOK AT SUCCESS, SISTA. YOU'VE NEVER HEARDA IMPMON?
IMPMON
HAT DID OU SAY ABOUT IMANS?

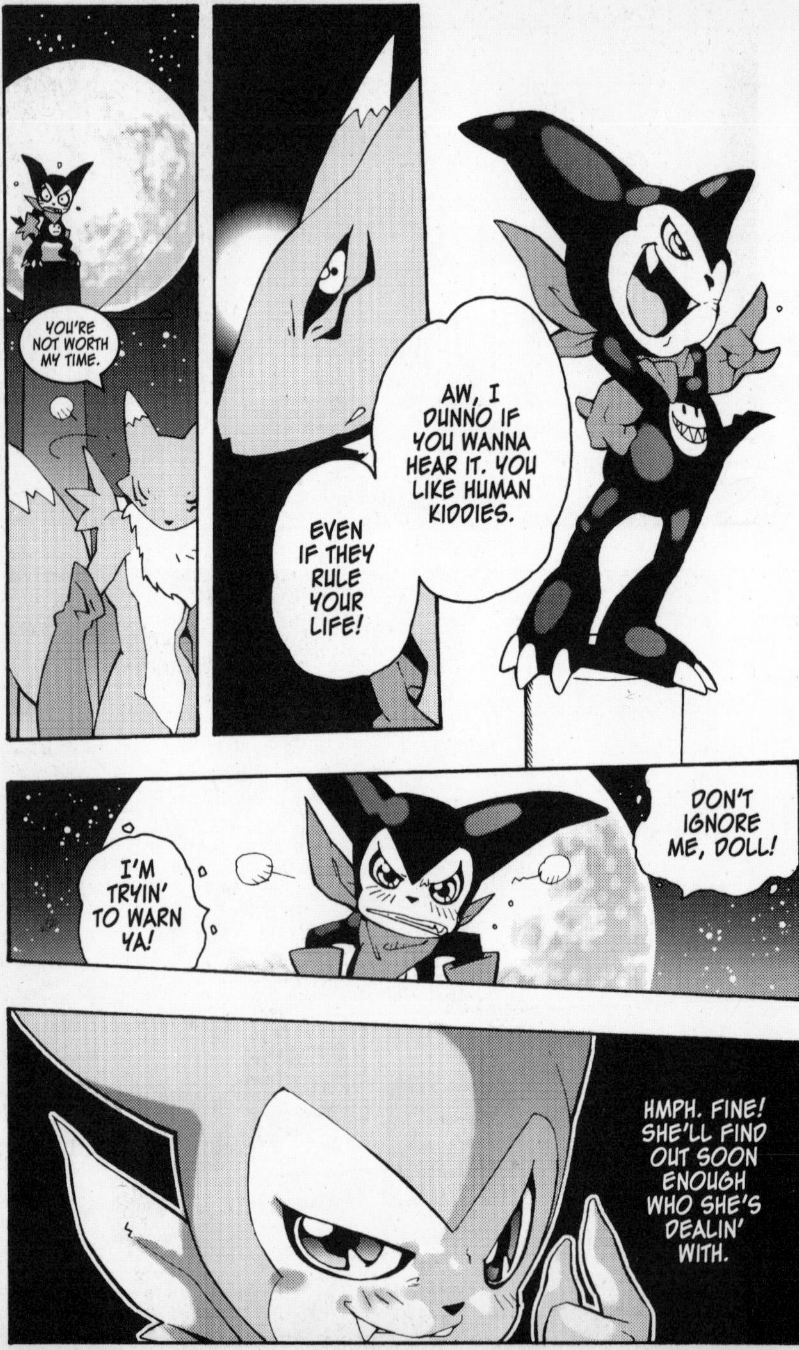
AW, I DUNNO IF YOU WANNA HEAR IT. YOU LIKE HUMAN KIDDIES.
EVEN IF THEY RULE YOUR LIFE!
YOU'RE NOT WORTH MY TIME.
DON'T IGNORE ME, DOLL!
I'M TRYIN' TO WARN YA!
HMPH. FINE! SHE'LL FIND OUT SOON ENOUGH WHO SHE'S DEALIN' WITH.

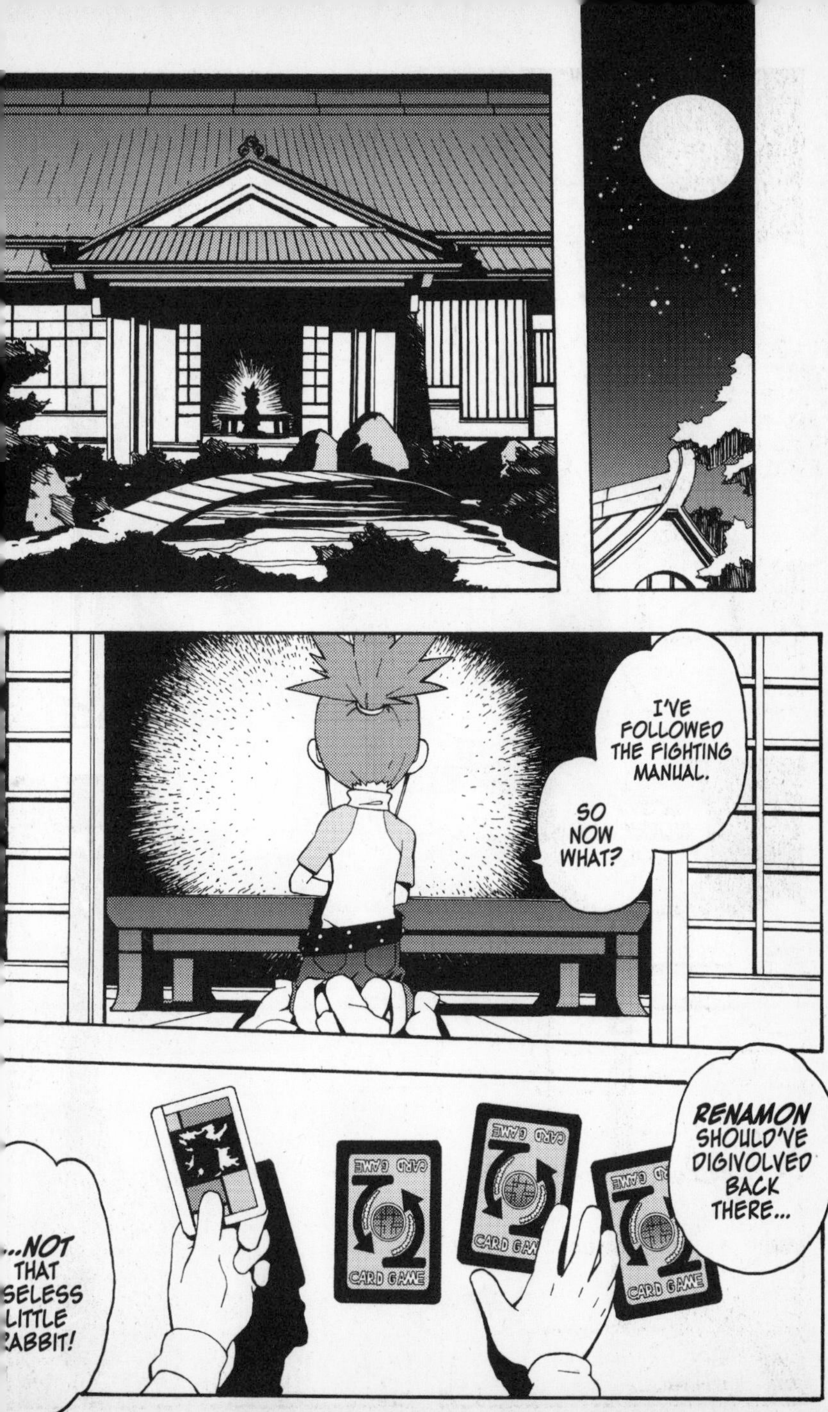
I'VE FOLLOWED THE FIGHTING MANUAL.
SO NOW WHAT?
RENAMON SHOULD'VE DIGIVOLVED BACK THERE...
...NOT THAT SELESS LITTLE ABBIT!

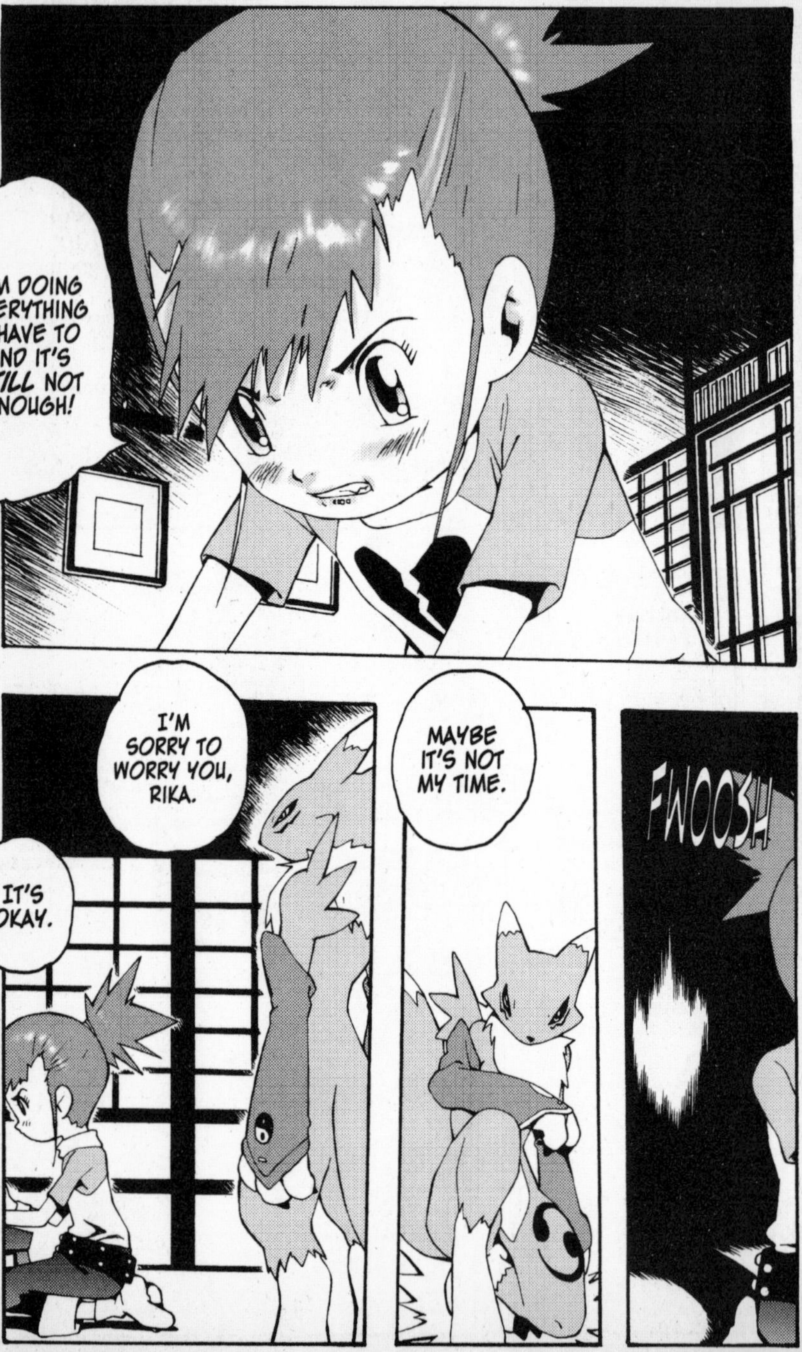
I'M DOING EVERYTHING I HAVE TO AND IT'S *STILL* NOT ENOUGH!
FWOOSH
MAYBE IT'S NOT MY TIME.
I'M SORRY TO WORRY YOU, RIKA.
IT'S OKAY.

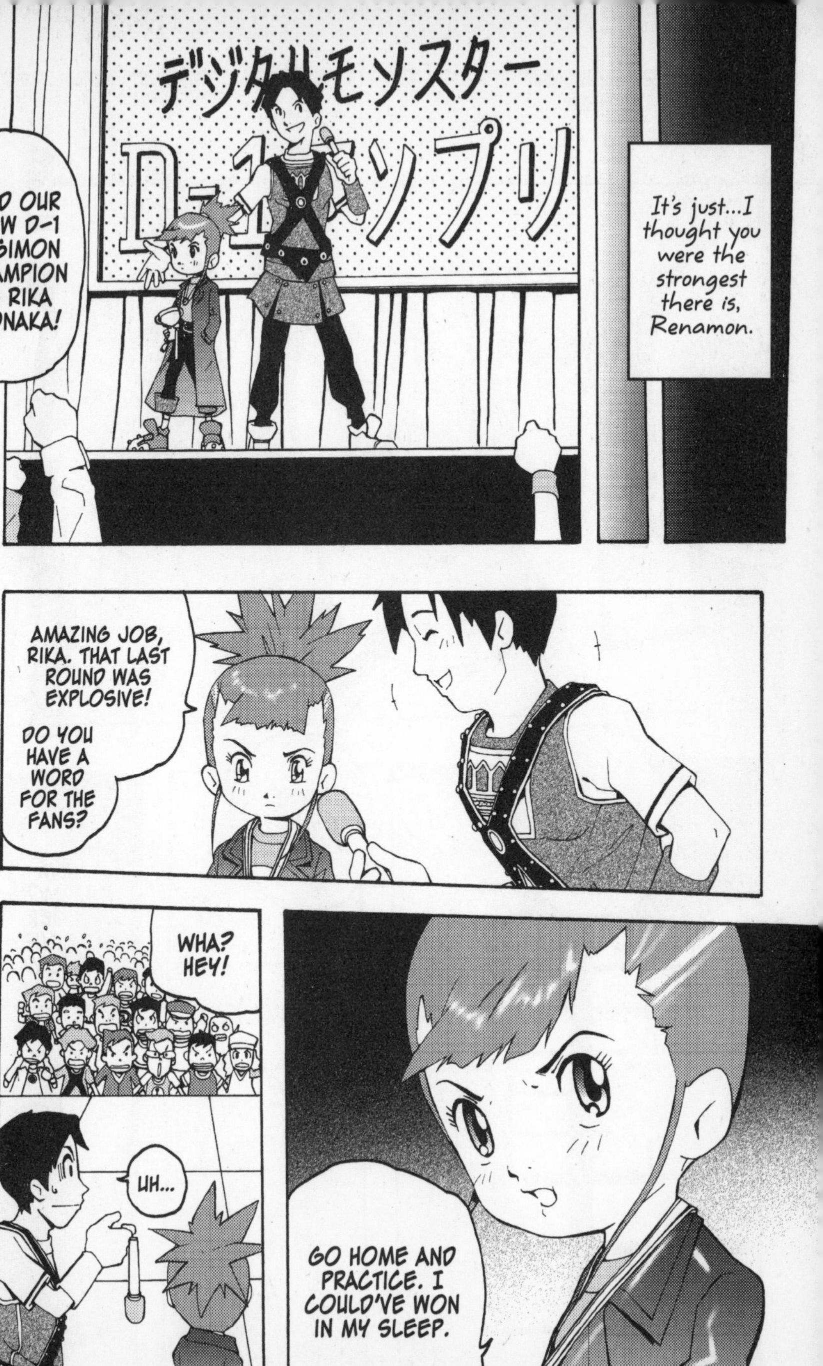
デジタルモンスター
It's just...I thought you were the strongest there is, Renamon.
AND OUR NEW D-1 DIGIMON CHAMPION IS RIKA NONAKA!
AMAZING JOB, RIKA. THAT LAST ROUND WAS EXPLOSIVE!
DO YOU HAVE A WORD FOR THE FANS?
GO HOME AND PRACTICE. I COULD'VE WON IN MY SLEEP.
WHA? HEY!
UH...

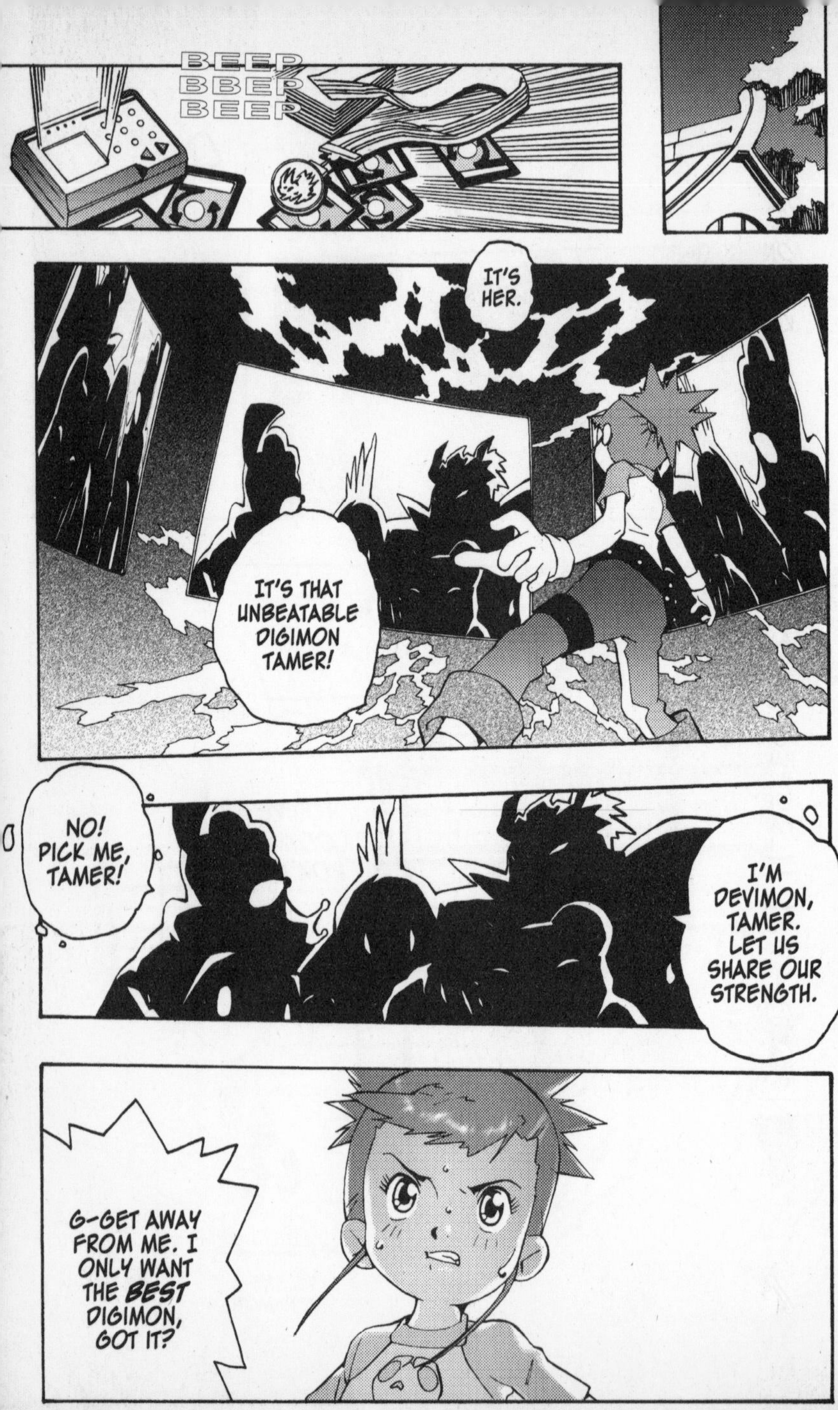
BEEP
BBEP
BEEP
IT'S HER.
IT'S THAT UNBEATABLE DIGIMON TAMER!
I'M DEVIMON, TAMER. LET US SHARE OUR STRENGTH.
NO! PICK ME, TAMER!
G-GET AWAY FROM ME. I ONLY WANT THE *BEST* DIGIMON, GOT IT?

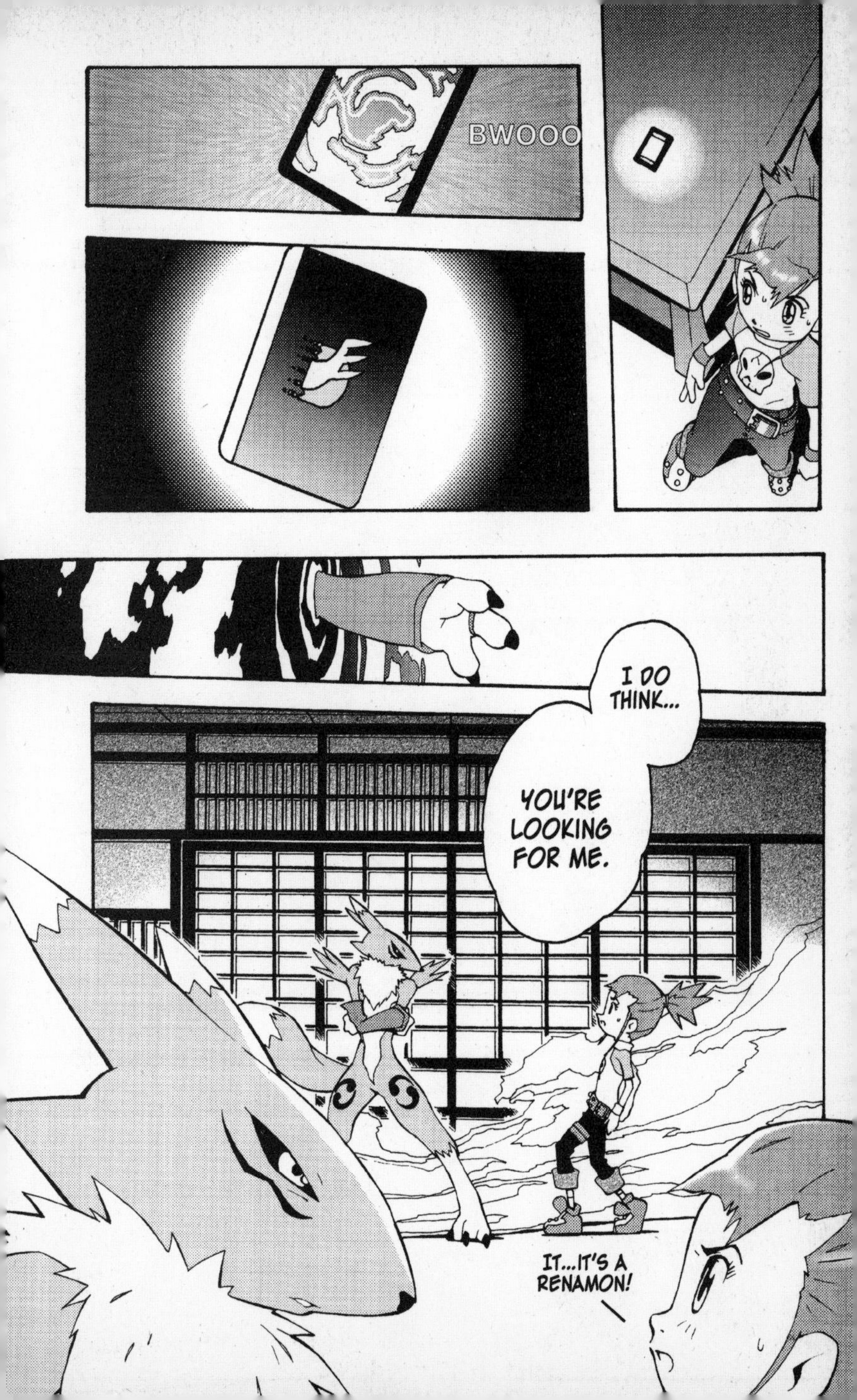
BWOOO
I DO THINK...
YOU'RE LOOKING FOR ME.
IT...IT'S A RENAMON!

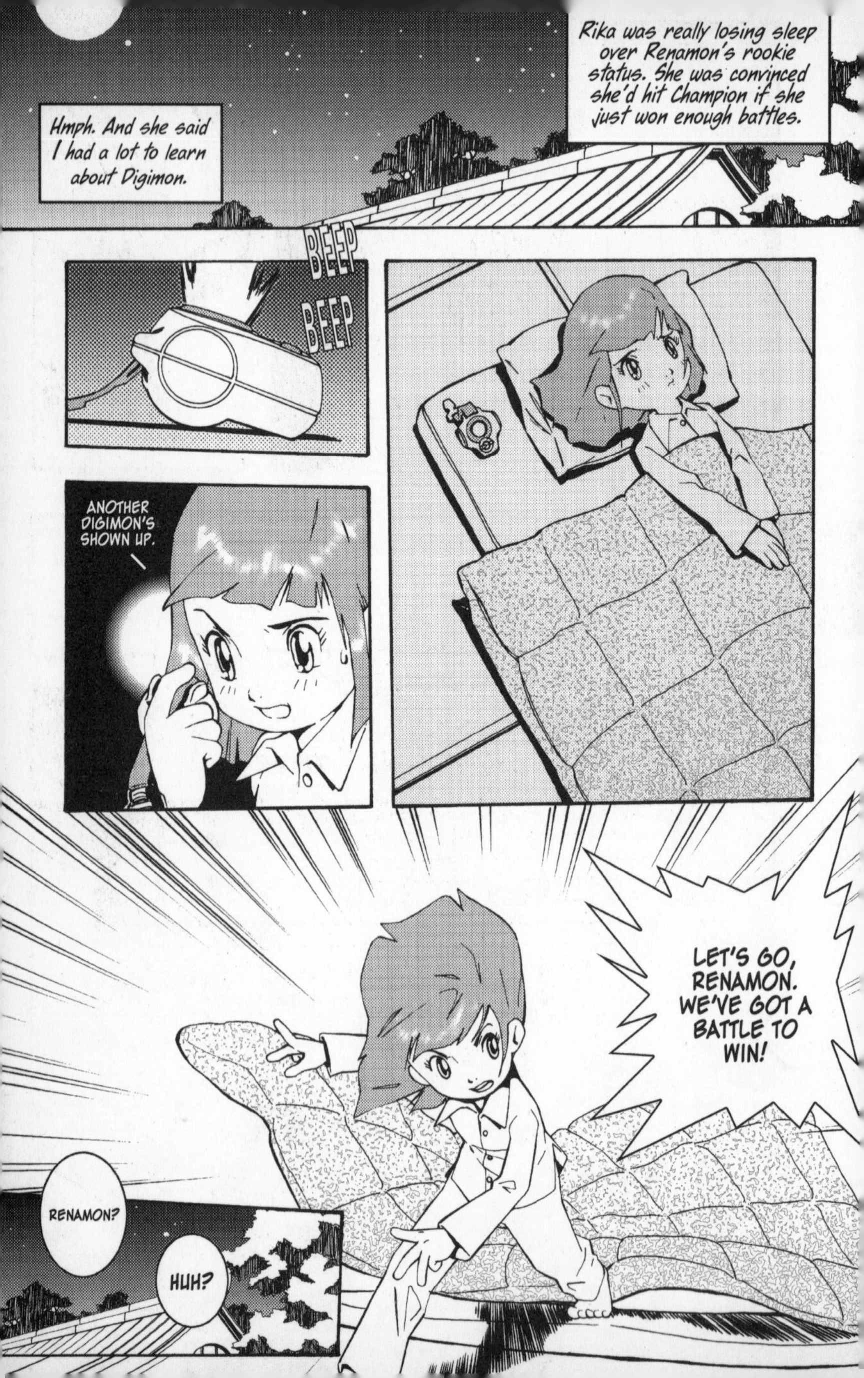
Rika was really losing sleep over Renamon's rookie status. She was convinced she'd hit Champion if she just won enough battles.
Hmph. And she said I had a lot to learn about Digimon.
BEEP BEEP
ANOTHER DIGIMON'S SHOWN UP.
LET'S GO, RENAMON. WE'VE GOT A BATTLE TO WIN!
RENAMON?
HUH?

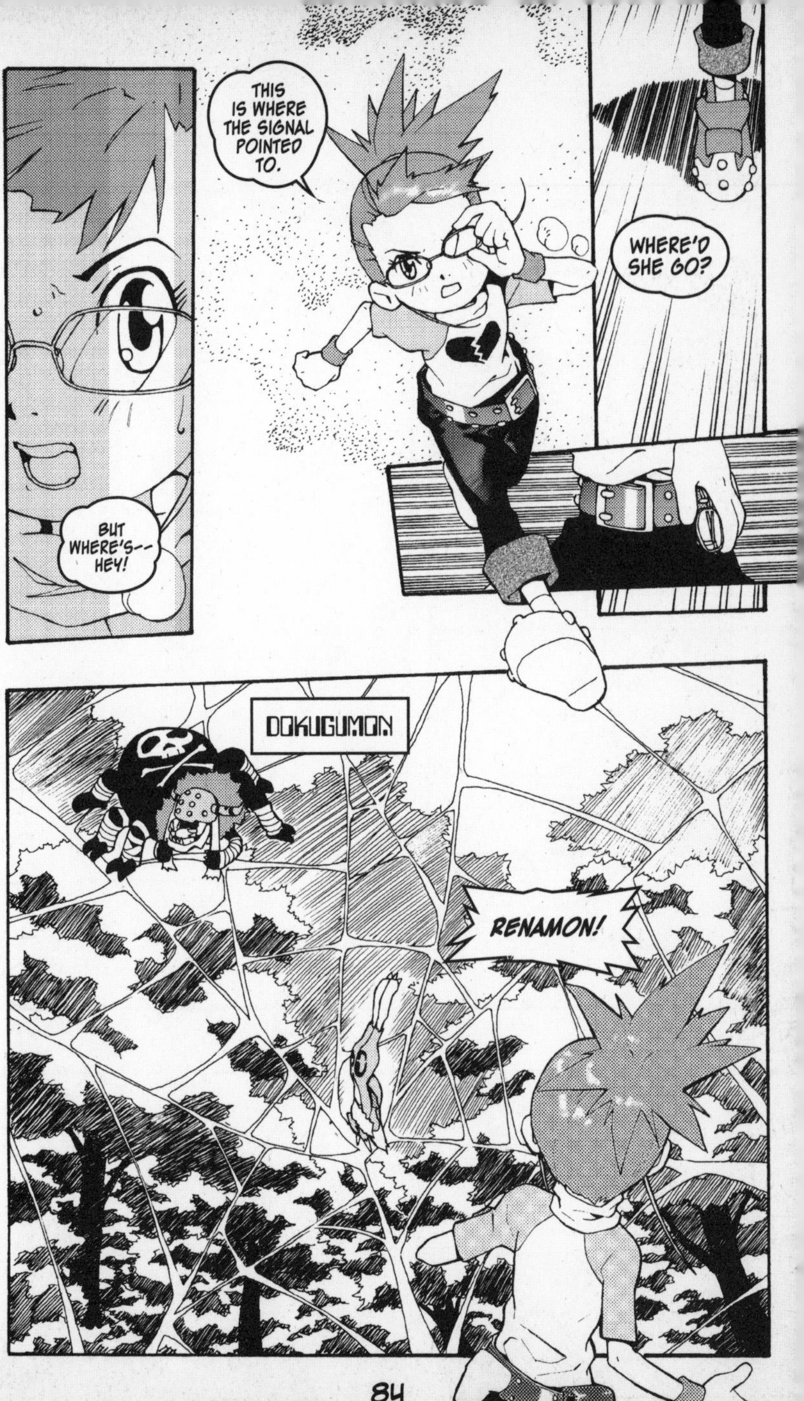
WHERE'D SHE GO?
THIS IS WHERE THE SIGNAL POINTED TO.
BUT WHERE'S-- HEY!
DOKUGUMON
RENAMON!

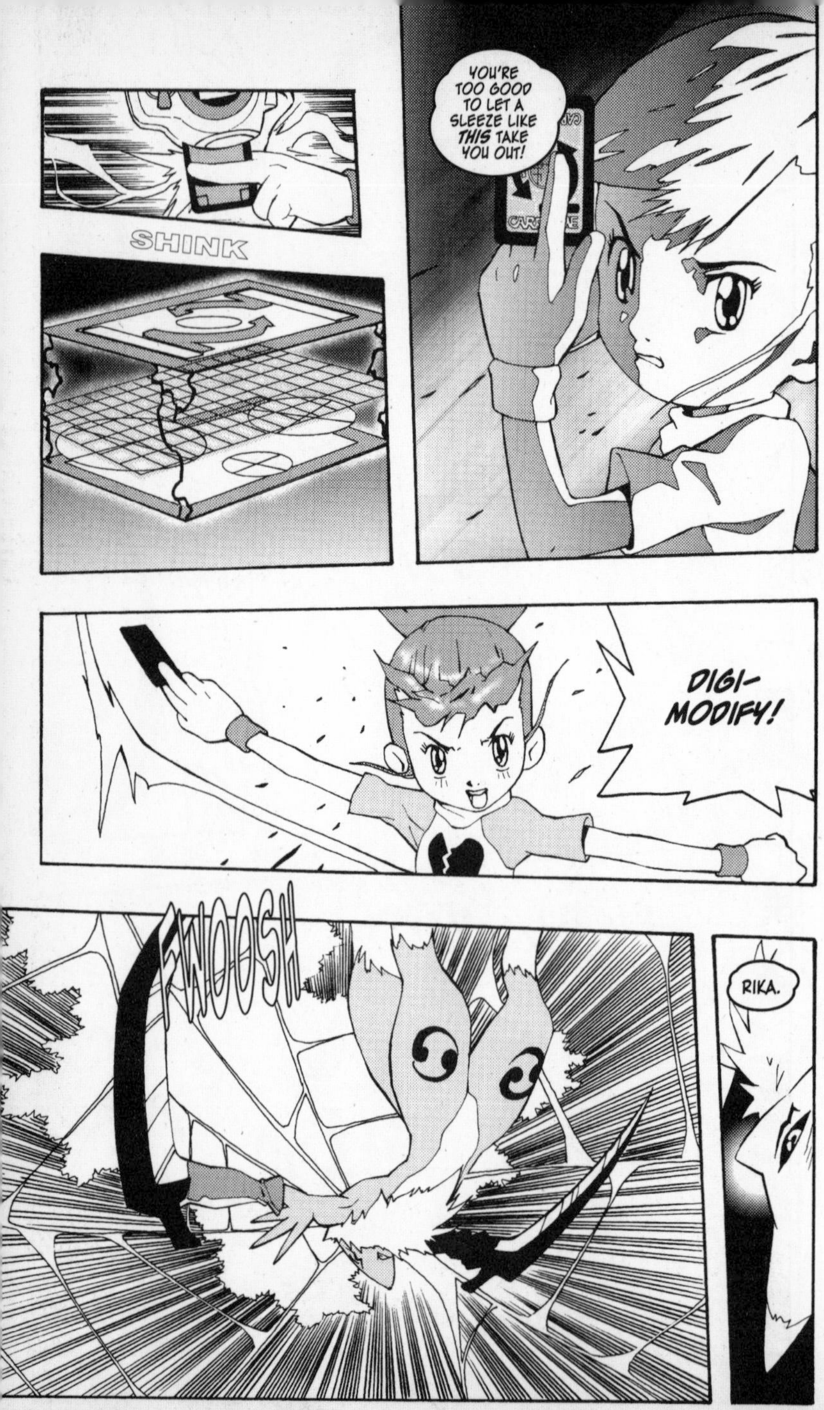
YOU'RE TOO GOOD TO LET A SLEEZE LIKE THIS TAKE YOU OUT!
SHINK
DIGI-MODIFY!
RIKA.
FWOOSH

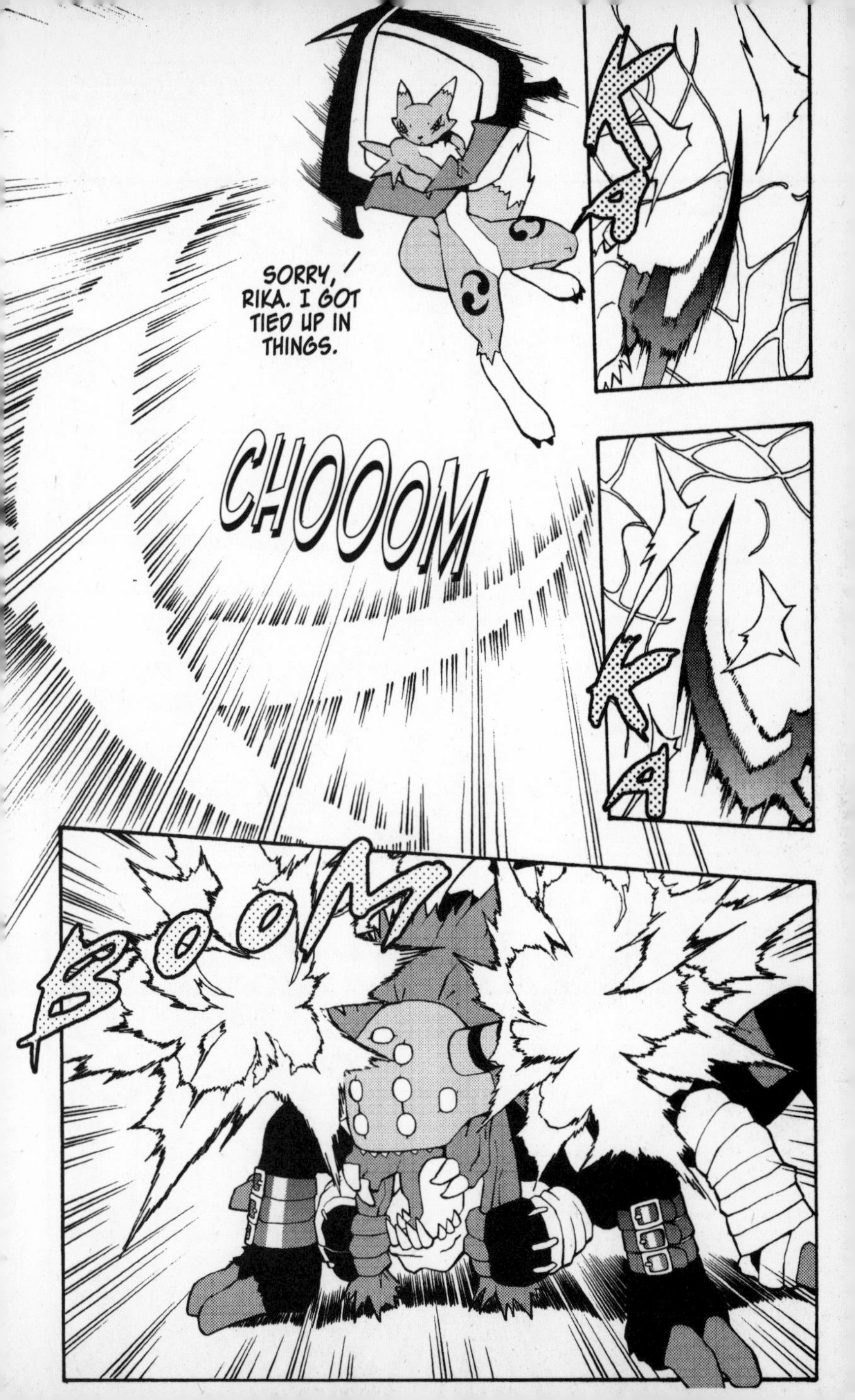
SORRY, RIKA. I GOT TIED UP IN THINGS.
CHOOOM
BOOM

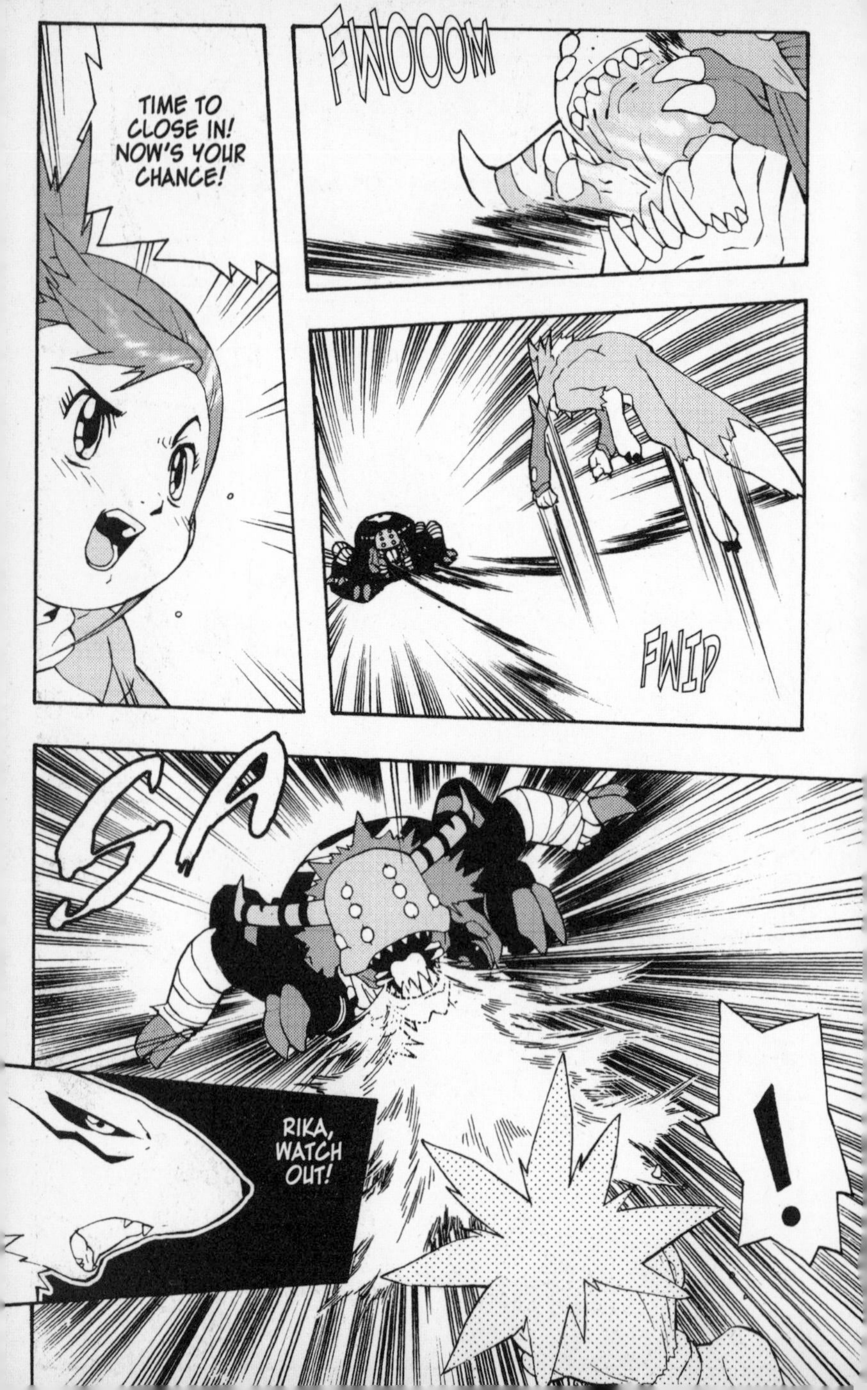
FWOOOM
FWIP
TIME TO CLOSE IN! NOW'S YOUR CHANCE!
SA
!
RIKA, WATCH OUT!

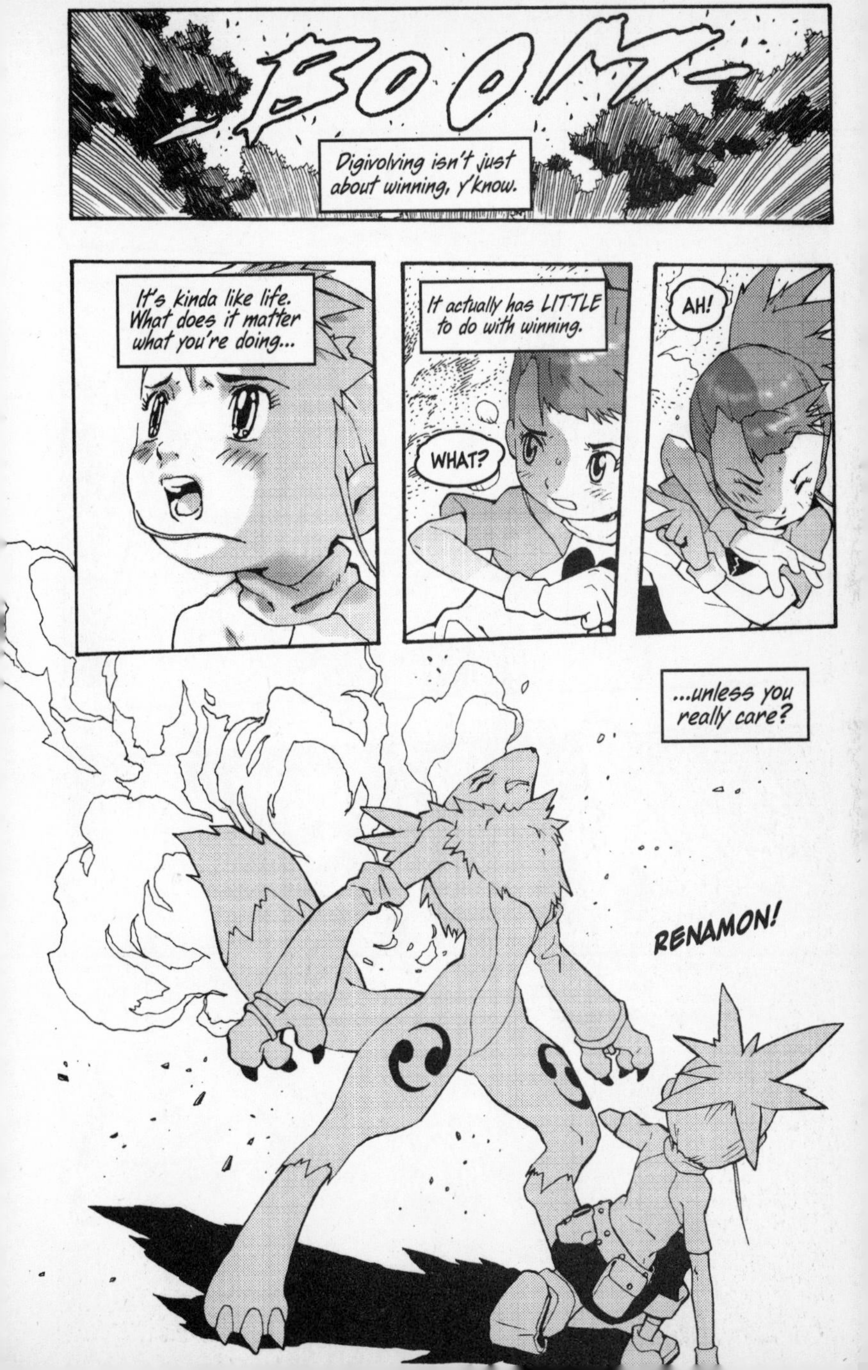
BOOM
Digivolving isn't just about winning, y'know.
AH!
It actually has LITTLE to do with winning.
WHAT?
It's kinda like life. What does it matter what you're doing...
...unless you really care?
RENAMON!

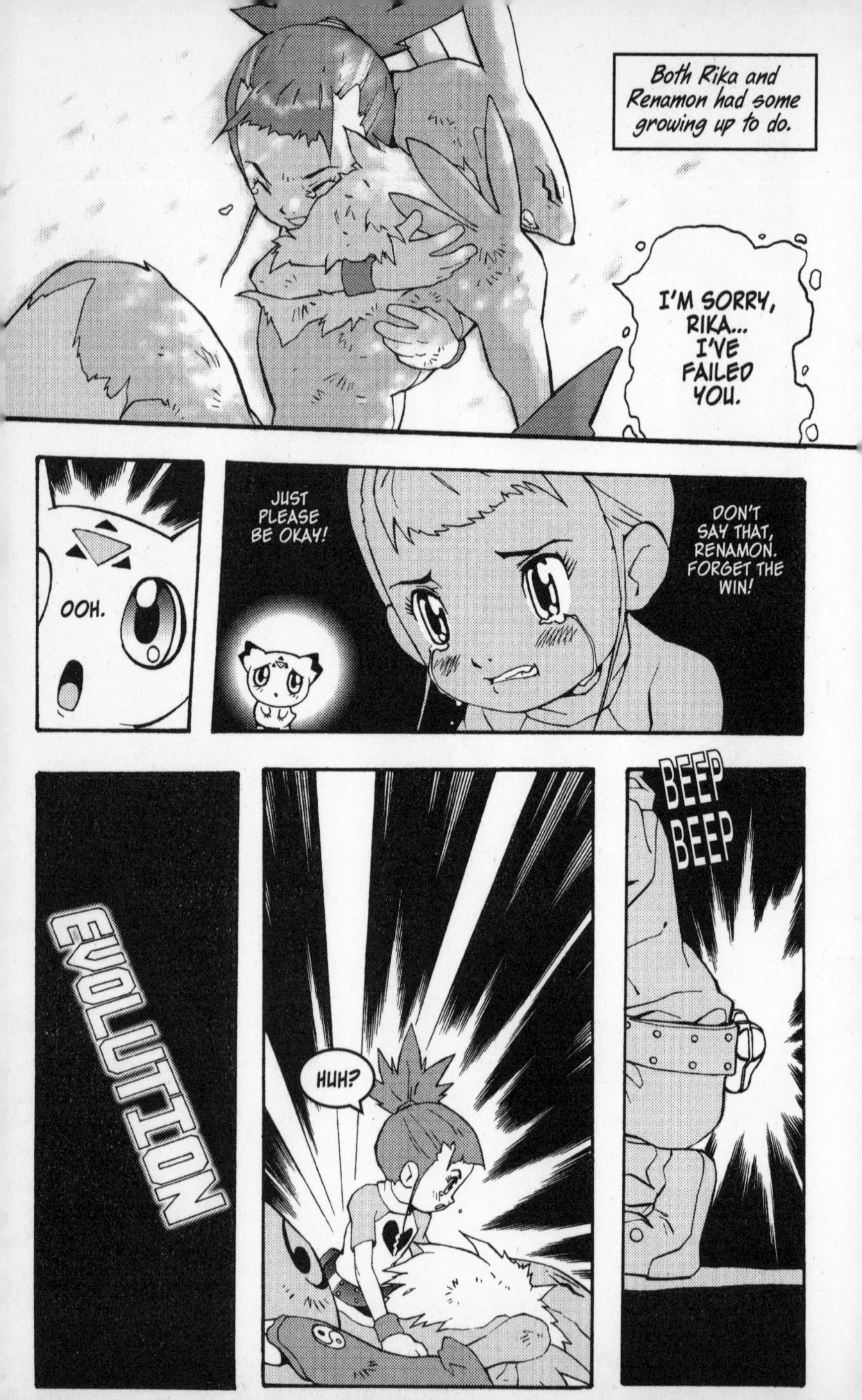
Both Rika and Renamon had some growing up to do.
I'M SORRY, RIKA... I'VE FAILED YOU.
DON'T SAY THAT, RENAMON. FORGET THE WIN!
JUST PLEASE BE OKAY!
OOH.
BEEP BEEP
HUH?
EVOLUTION

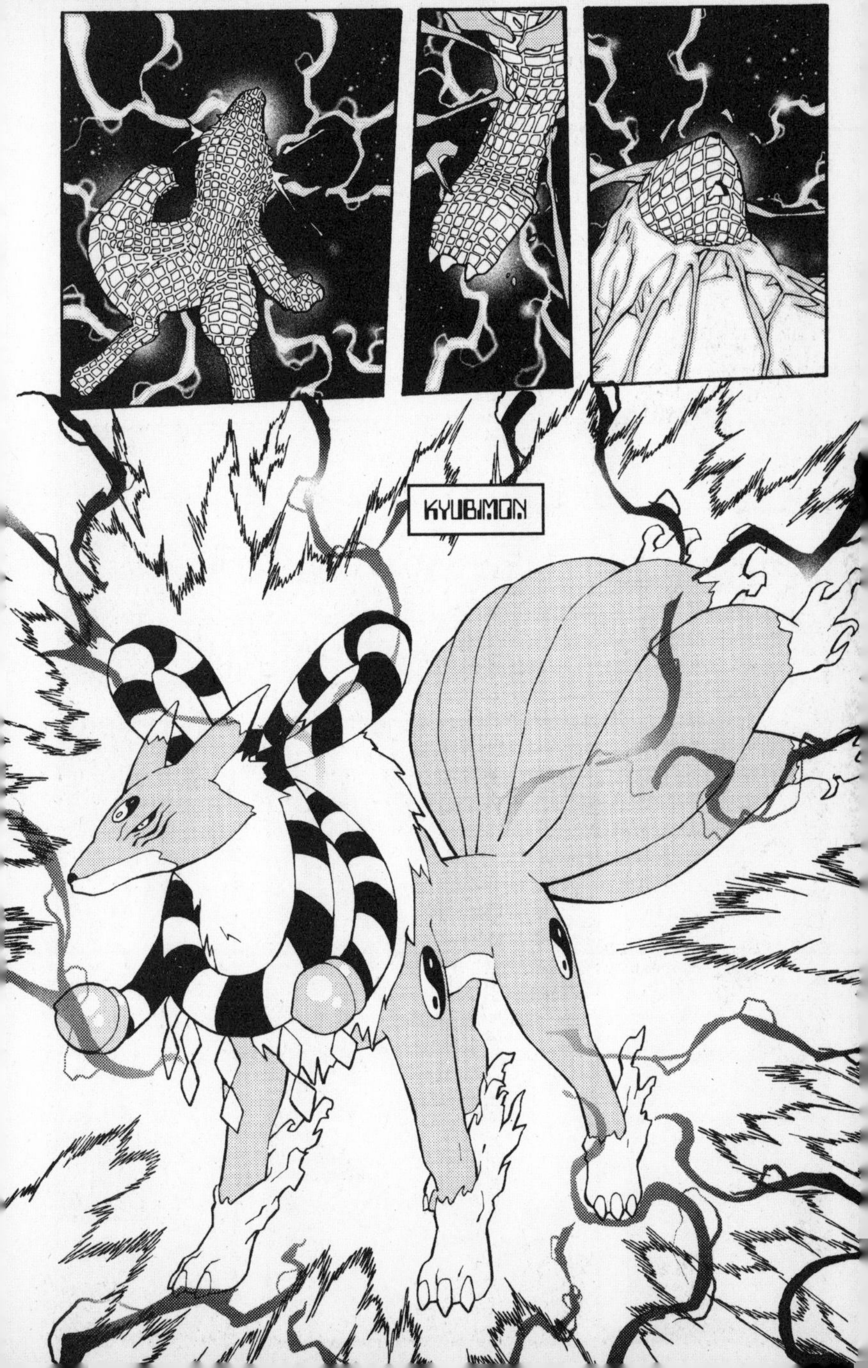
KYUBIMON

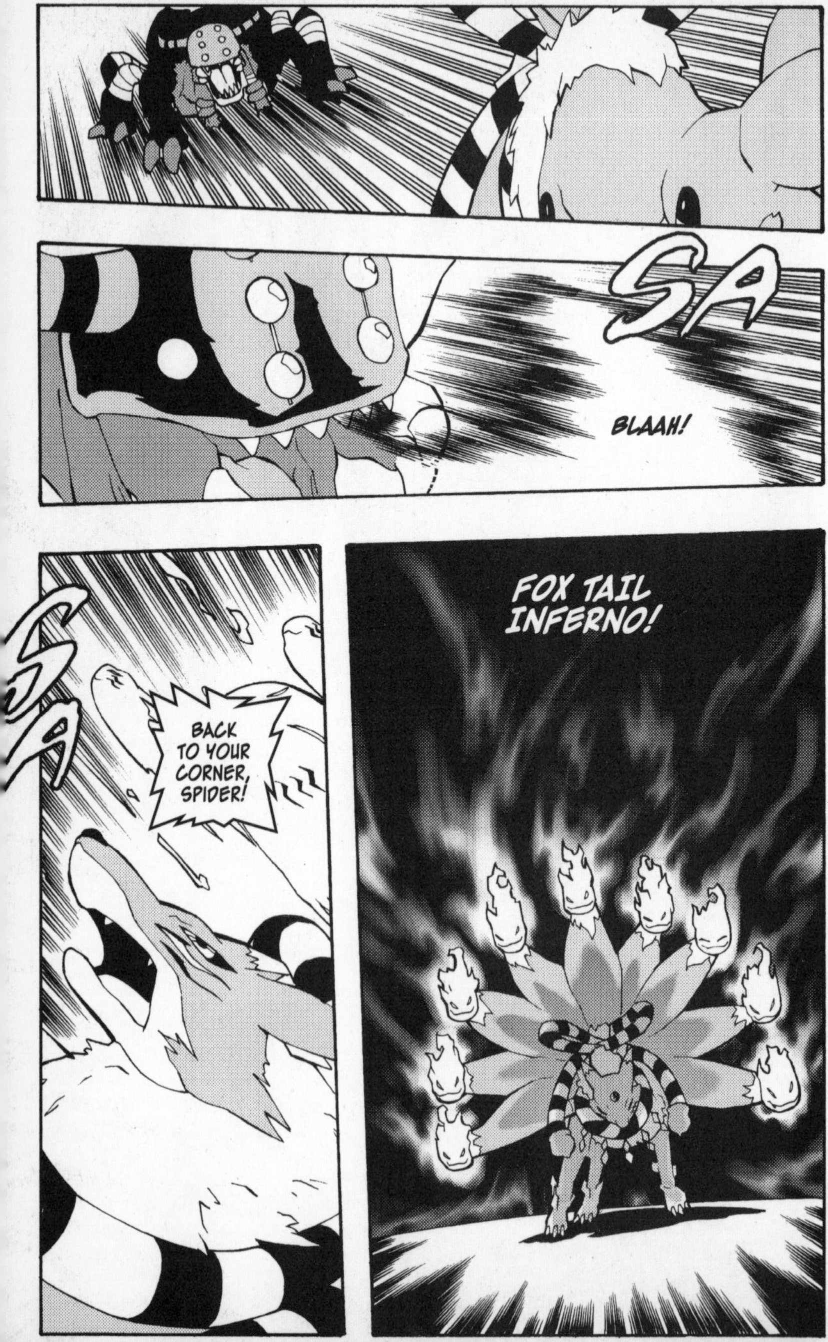

SA
BLAAH!
FOX TAIL INFERNO!
SA
BACK TO YOUR CORNER, SPIDER!

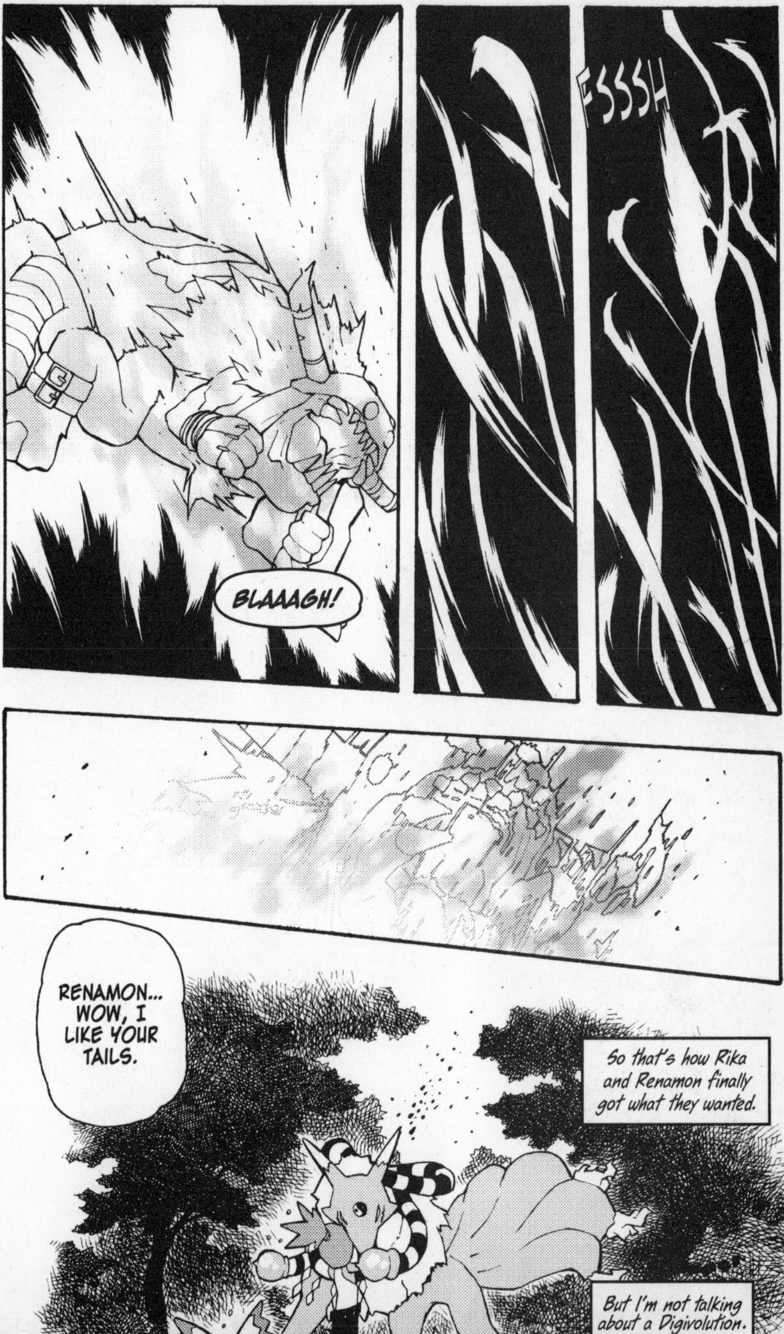
FSSSH
BLAAAGH!
RENAMON... WOW, I LIKE YOUR TAILS.
So that's how Rika and Renamon finally got what they wanted.
But I'm not talking about a Digivolution.

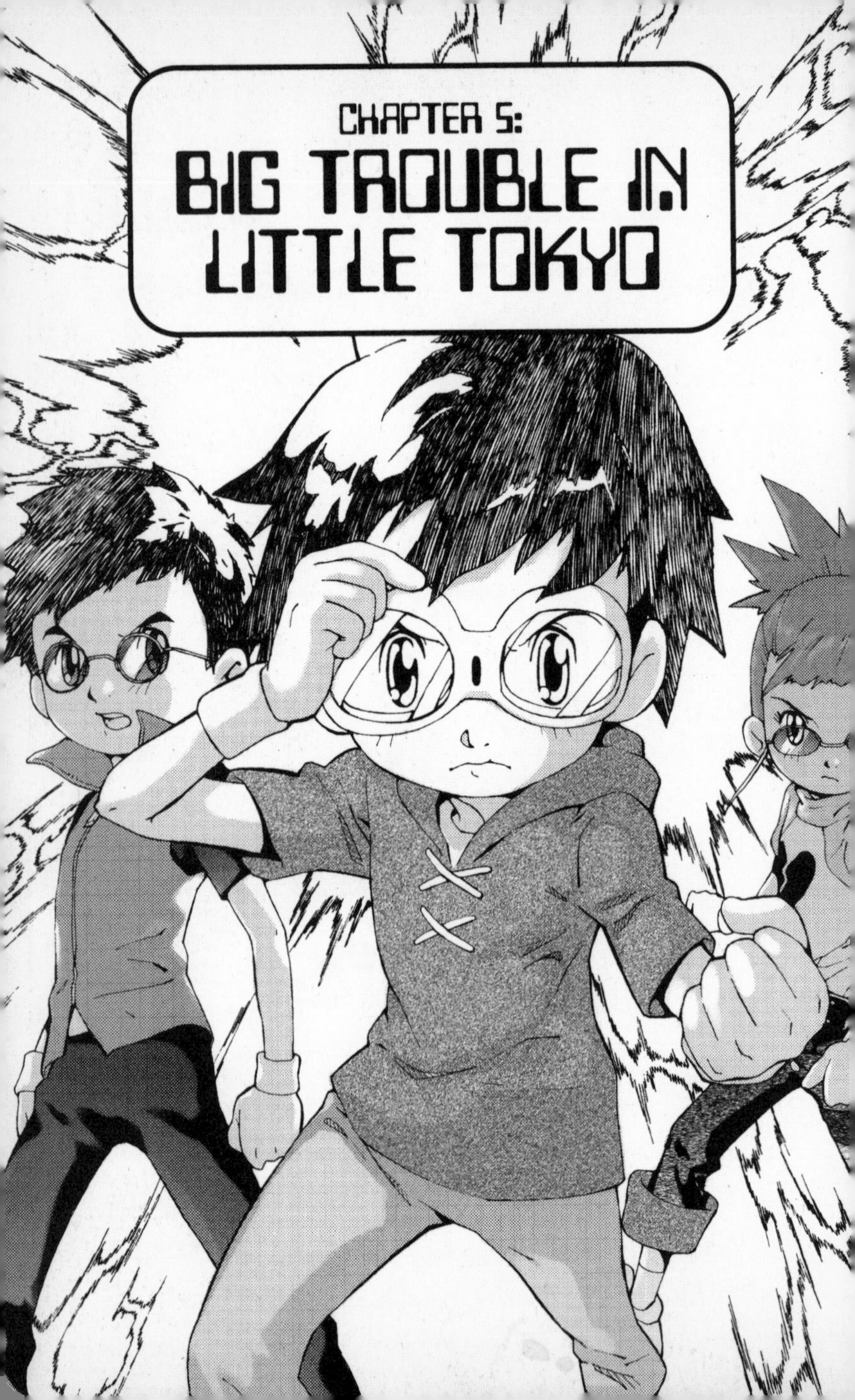
CHAPTER 5:
BIG TROUBLE IN LITTLE TOKYO

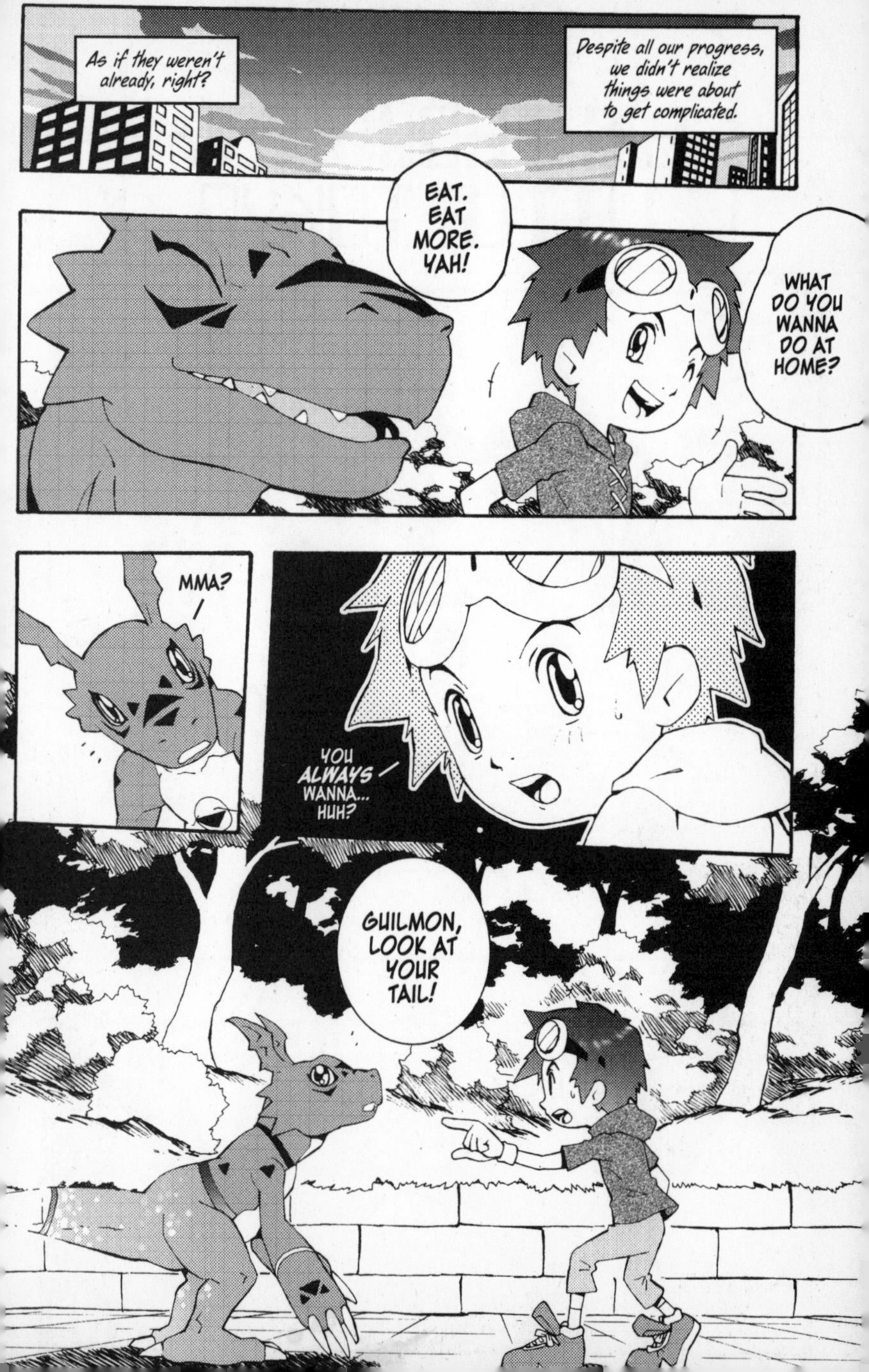
Despite all our progress, we didn't realize things were about to get complicated.
As if they weren't already, right?
WHAT DO YOU WANNA DO AT HOME?
EAT. EAT MORE. YAH!
YOU ALWAYS WANNA... HUH?
MMA?
...
GUILMON, LOOK AT YOUR TAIL!

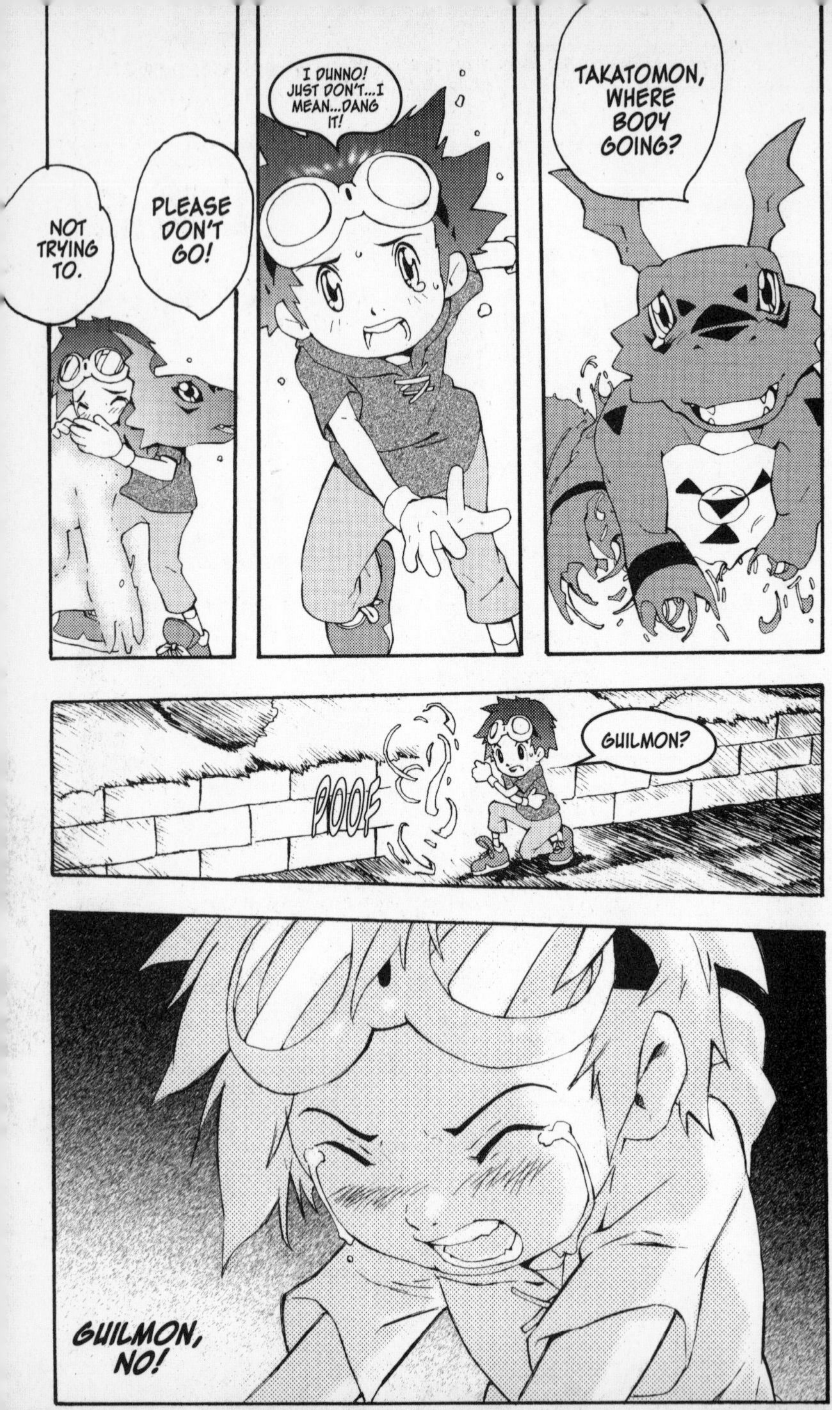
TAKATOMON, WHERE BODY GOING?
I DUNNO! JUST DON'T...I MEAN...DANG IT!
PLEASE DON'T GO!
NOT TRYING TO.
GUILMON?
POOF
GUILMON, NO!

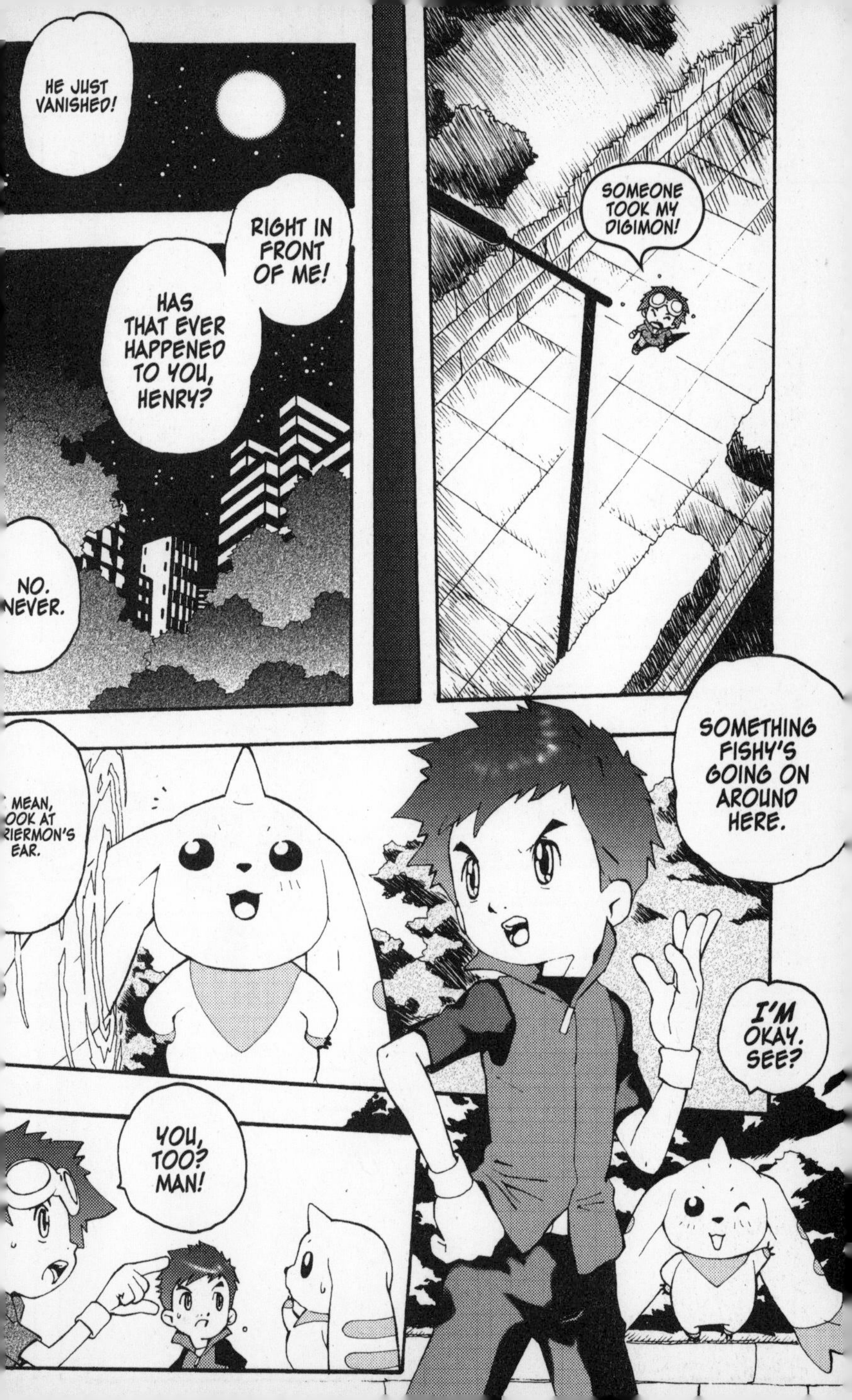
SOMEONE TOOK MY DIGIMON!
HE JUST VANISHED!
RIGHT IN FRONT OF ME!
HAS THAT EVER HAPPENED TO YOU, HENRY?
NO. NEVER.
SOMETHING FISHY'S GOING ON AROUND HERE.
I'M OKAY. SEE?
MEAN, OOK AT RIERMON'S EAR.
YOU, TOO? MAN!

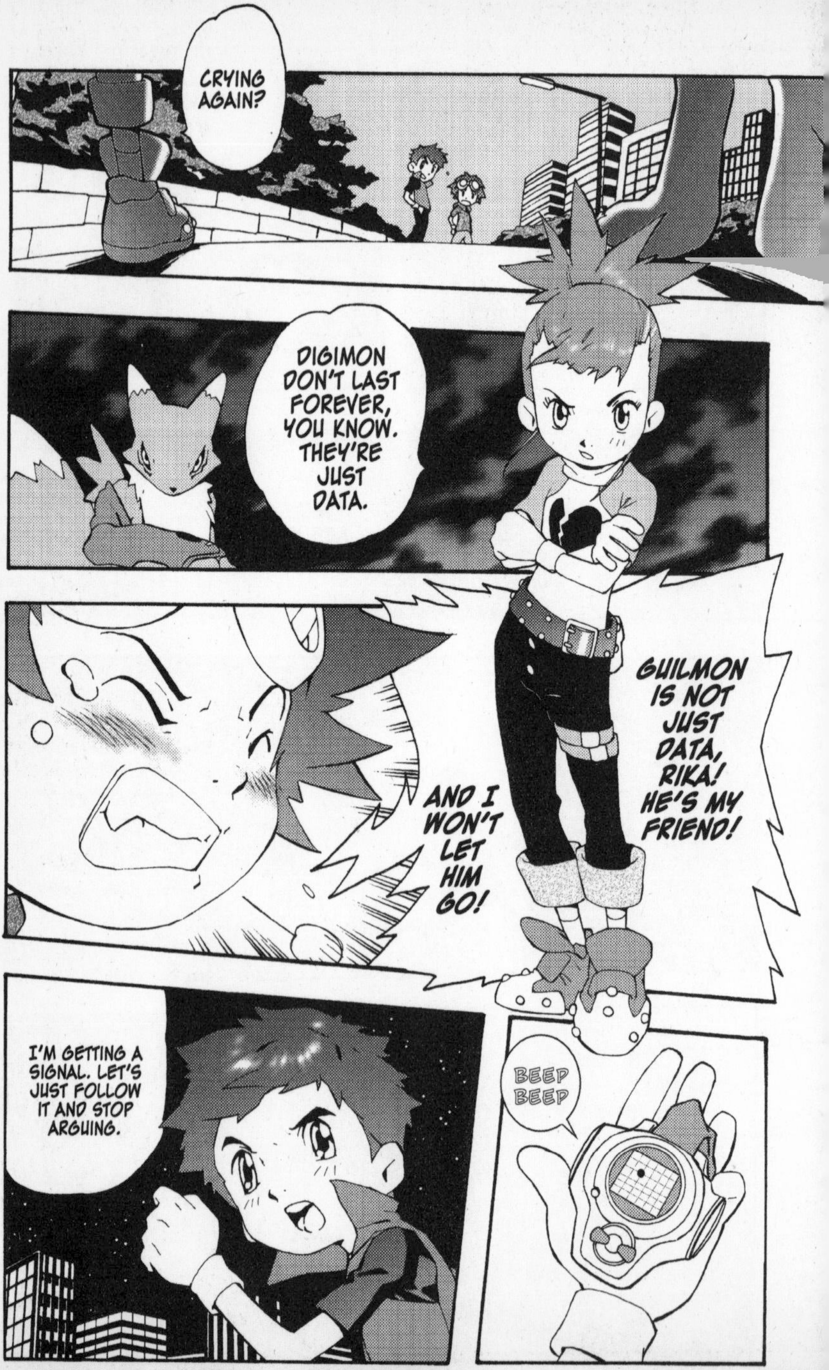
CRYING AGAIN?
DIGIMON DON'T LAST FOREVER, YOU KNOW. THEY'RE JUST DATA.
GUILMON IS NOT JUST DATA, RIKA! HE'S MY FRIEND!
AND I WON'T LET HIM GO!
BEEP BEEP
I'M GETTING A SIGNAL. LET'S JUST FOLLOW IT AND STOP ARGUING.

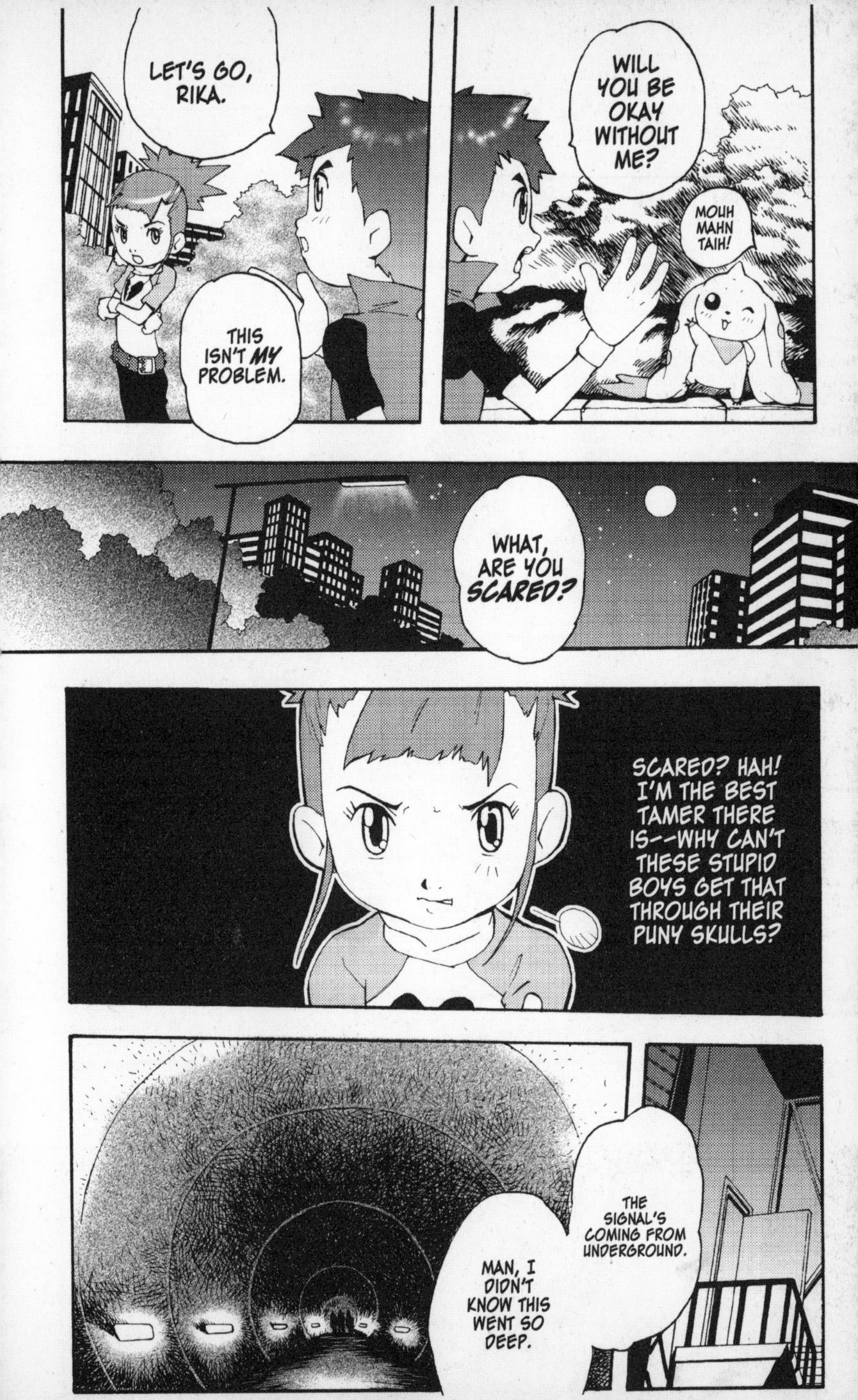
WILL YOU BE OKAY WITHOUT ME?
MOUH MAHN TAIH!
LET'S GO, RIKA.
THIS ISN'T *MY* PROBLEM.
WHAT, ARE YOU *SCARED?*
SCARED? HAH! I'M THE BEST TAMER THERE IS--WHY CAN'T THESE STUPID BOYS GET THAT THROUGH THEIR PUNY SKULLS?
THE SIGNAL'S COMING FROM UNDERGROUND.
MAN, I DIDN'T KNOW THIS WENT SO DEEP.

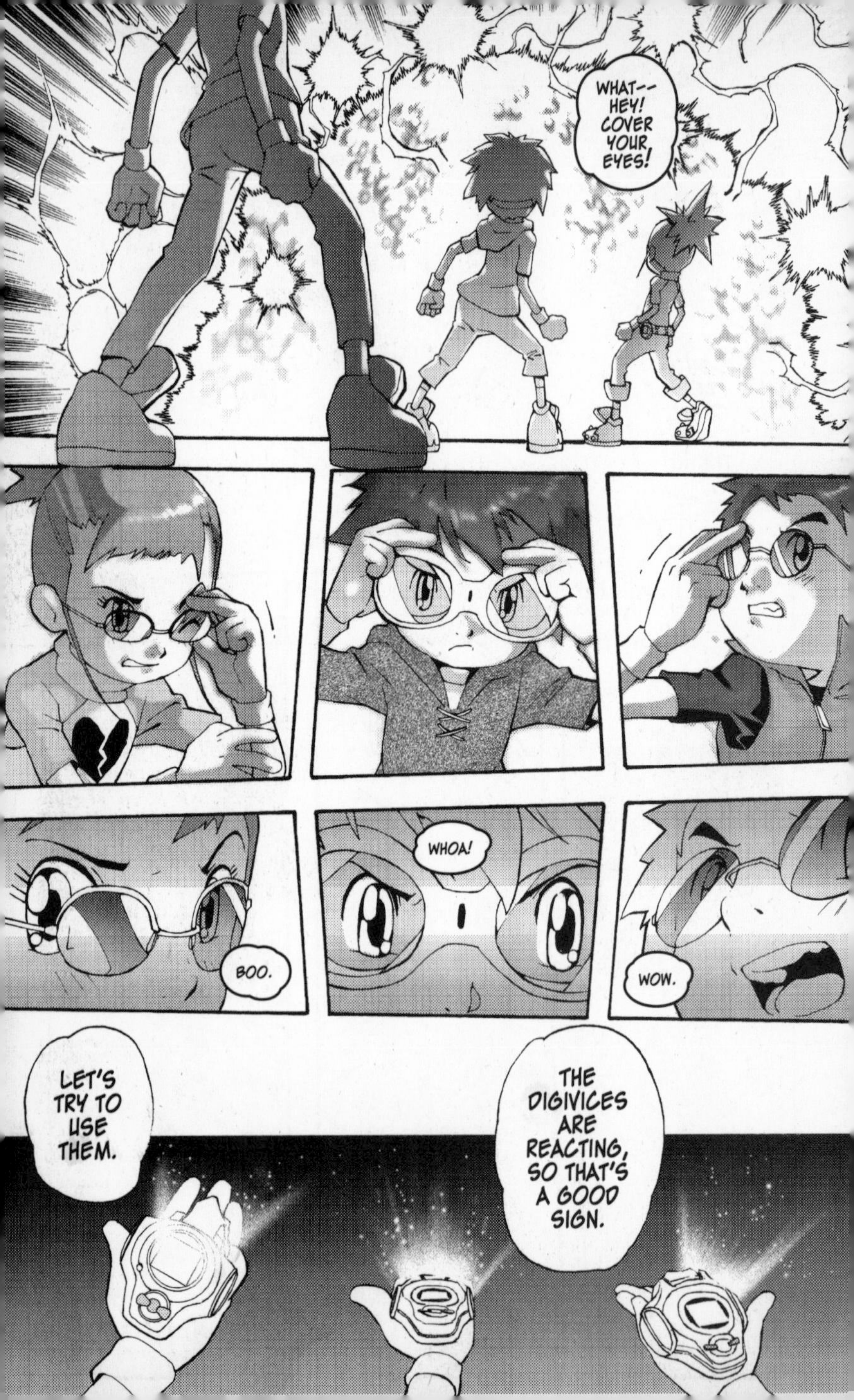
WHAT-- HEY! COVER YOUR EYES!
WOW.
WHOA!
BOO.
THE DIGIVICES ARE REACTING, SO THAT'S A GOOD SIGN.
LET'S TRY TO USE THEM.

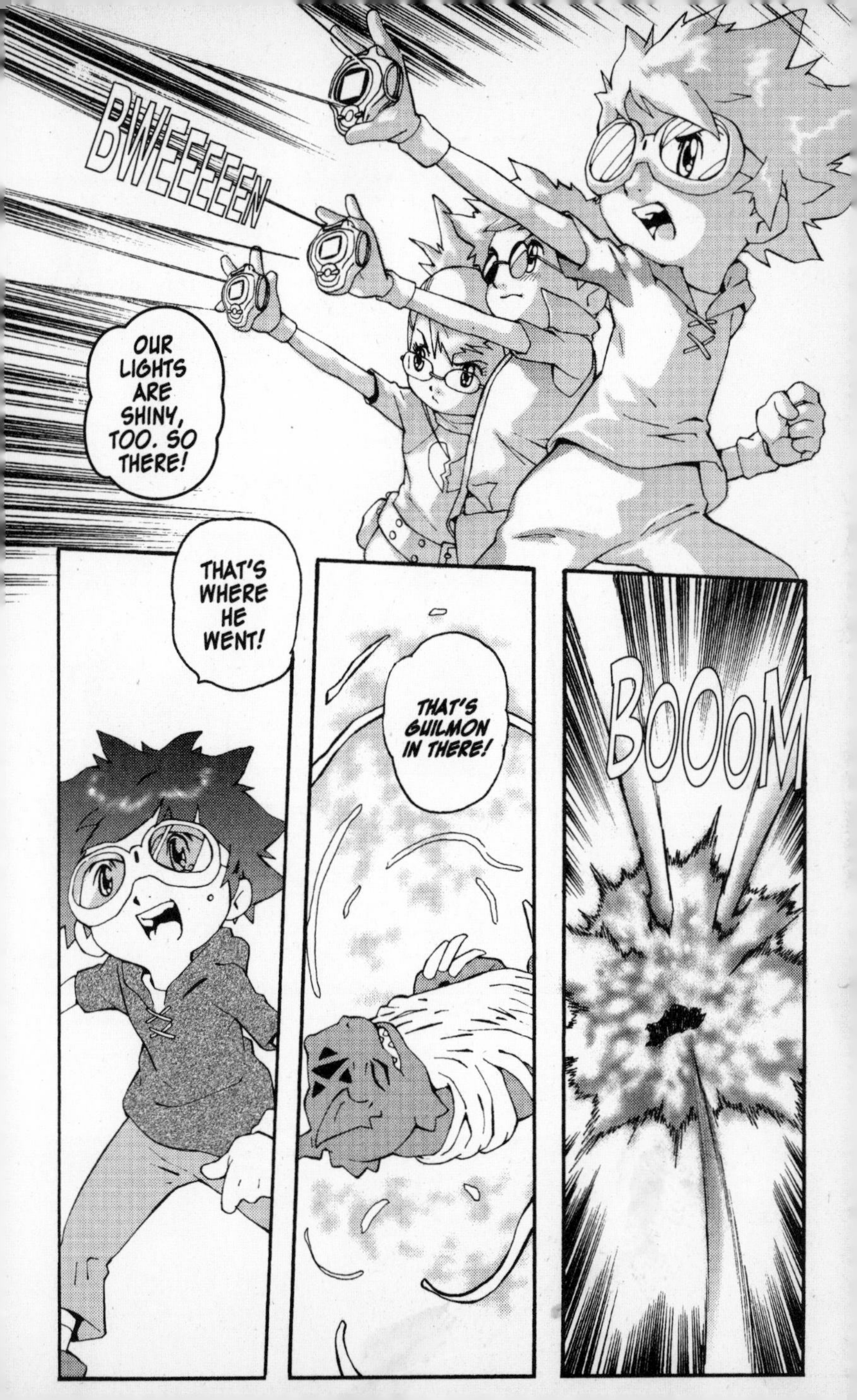
BWEEEEEEN
OUR LIGHTS ARE SHINY, TOO. SO THERE!
BOOOM
THAT'S GUILMON IN THERE!
THAT'S WHERE HE WENT!

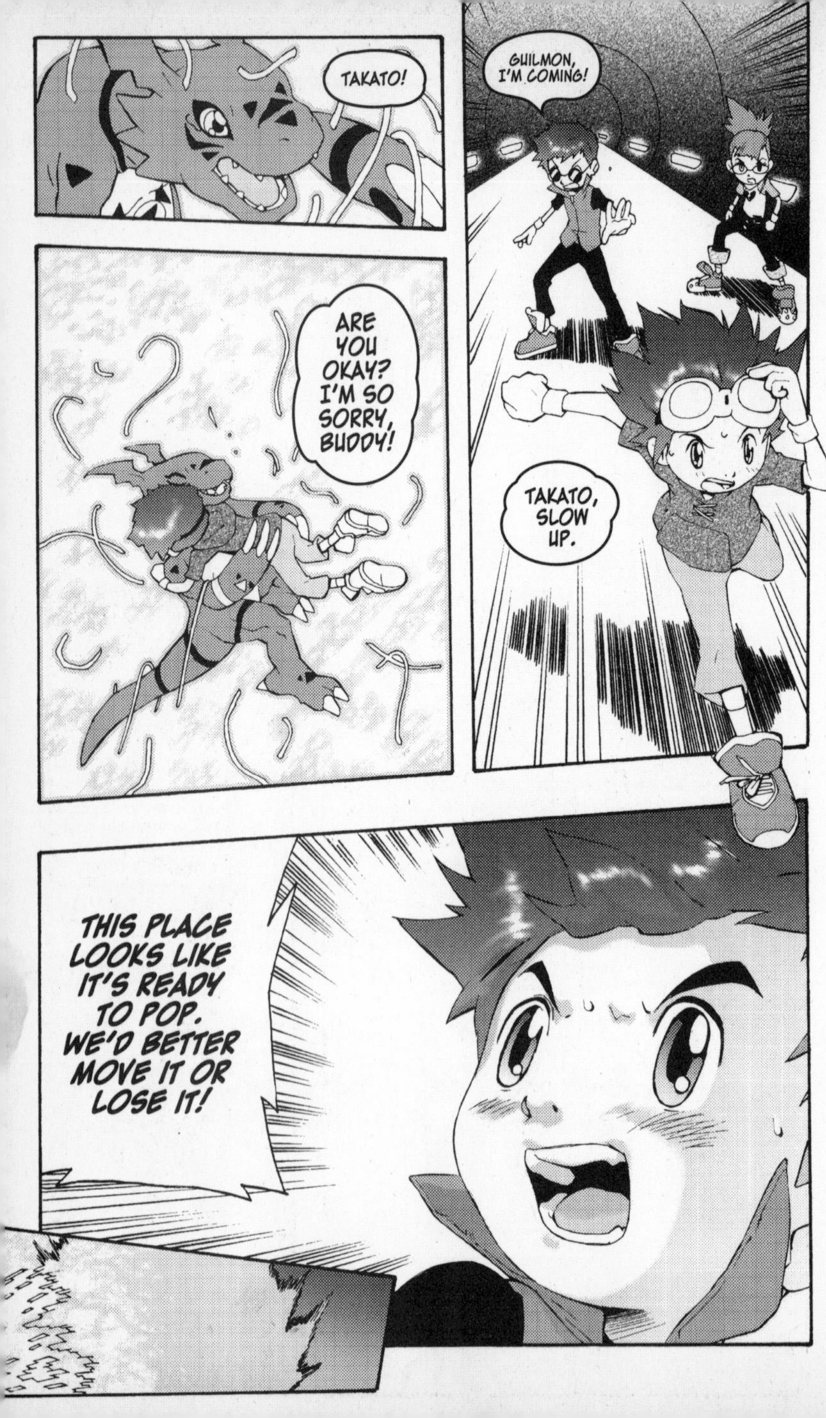
GUILMON, I'M COMING!
TAKATO, SLOW UP.
TAKATO!
ARE YOU OKAY? I'M SO SORRY, BUDDY!
THIS PLACE LOOKS LIKE IT'S READY TO POP. WE'D BETTER MOVE IT OR LOSE IT!

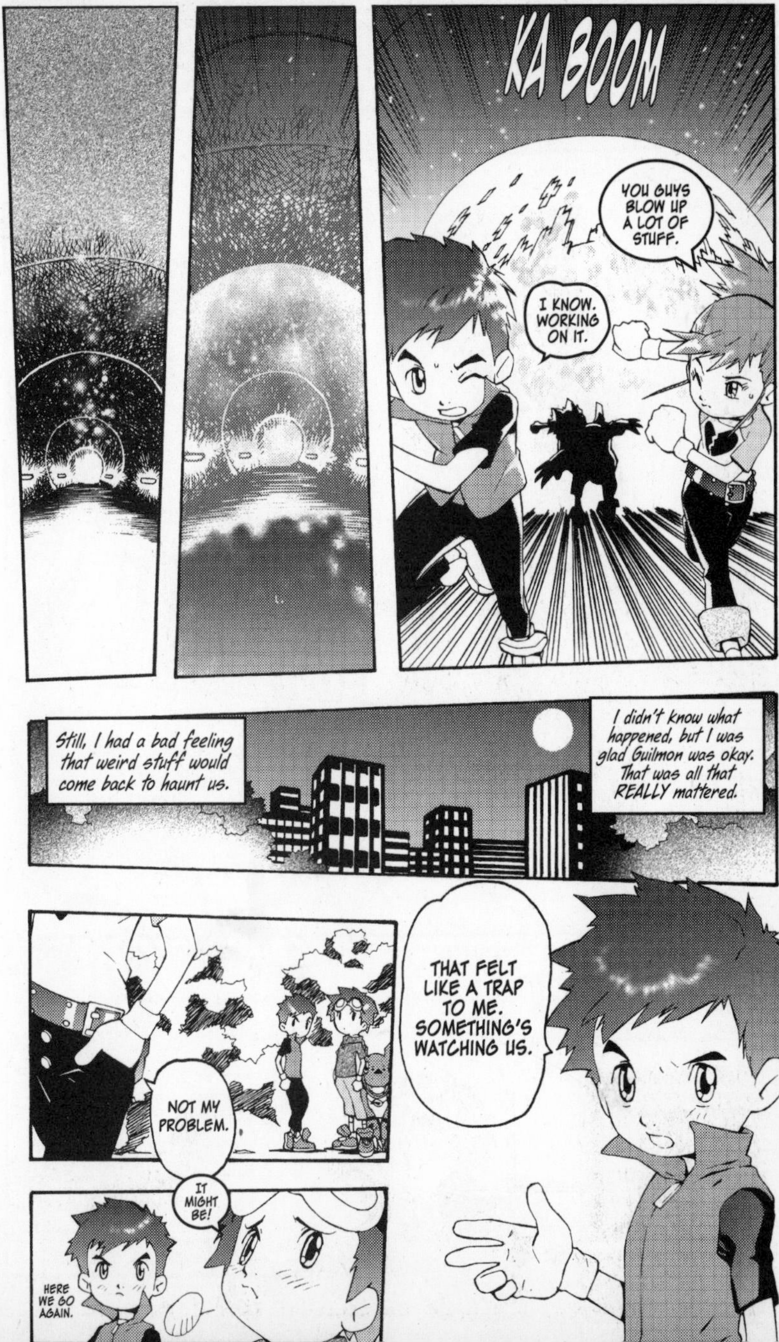
KA BOOM
YOU GUYS BLOW UP A LOT OF STUFF.
I KNOW. WORKING ON IT.
I didn't know what happened, but I was glad Guilmon was okay. That was all that REALLY mattered.
Still, I had a bad feeling that weird stuff would come back to haunt us.
THAT FELT LIKE A TRAP TO ME. SOMETHING'S WATCHING US.
NOT MY PROBLEM.
IT MIGHT BE!
HERE WE GO AGAIN.

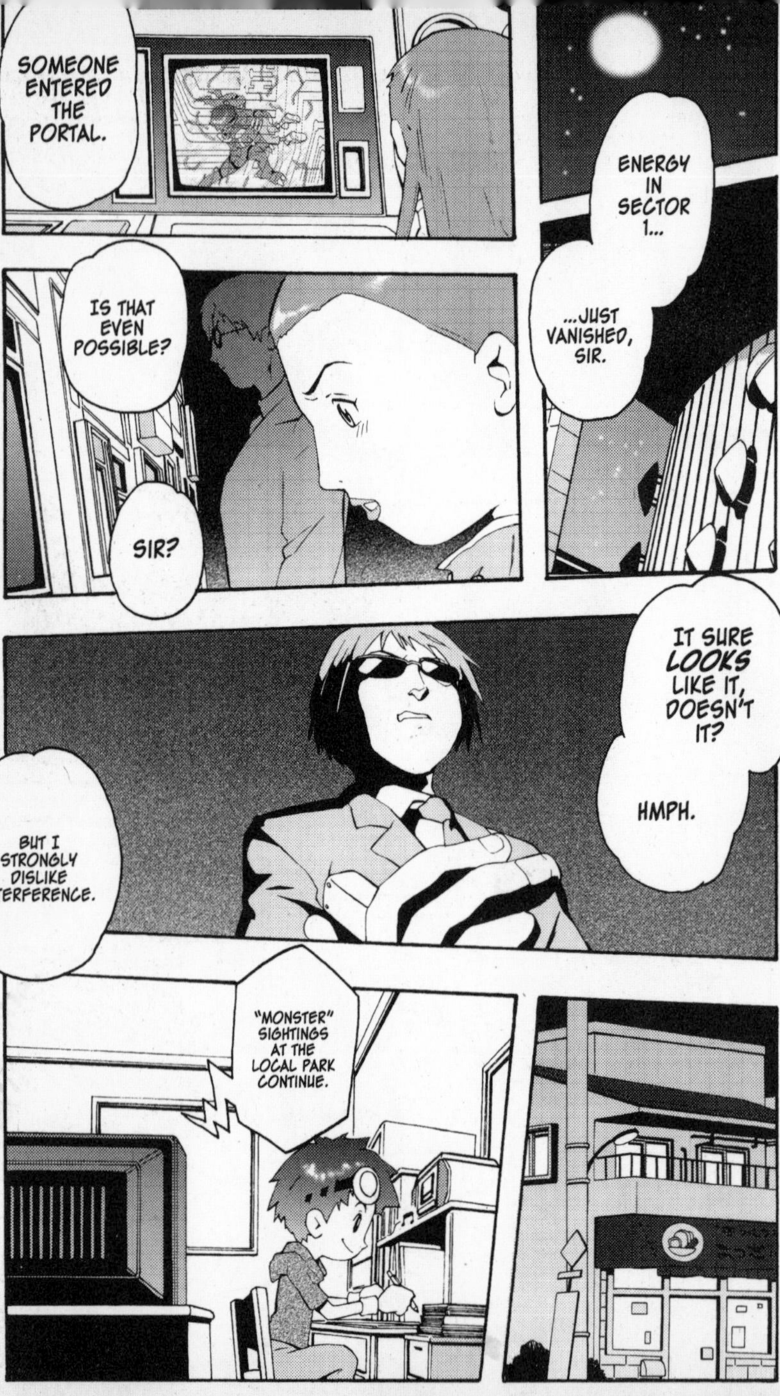
ENERGY IN SECTOR 1...
...JUST VANISHED, SIR.
SOMEONE ENTERED THE PORTAL.
IS THAT EVEN POSSIBLE?
SIR?
IT SURE *LOOKS* LIKE IT, DOESN'T IT?
HMPH.
BUT I STRONGLY DISLIKE INTERFERENCE.
"MONSTER" SIGHTINGS AT THE LOCAL PARK CONTINUE.

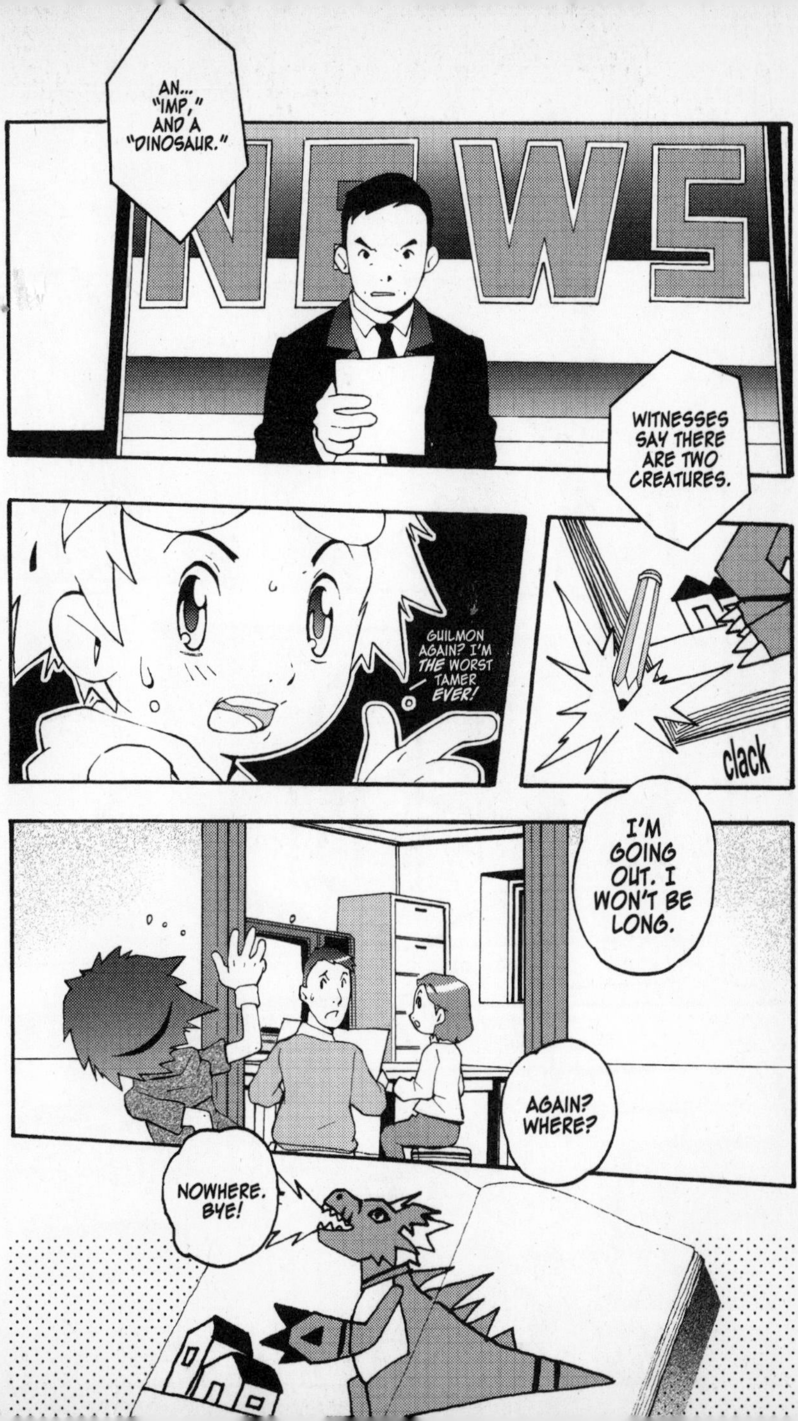
WITNESSES SAY THERE ARE TWO CREATURES.
AN... "IMP," AND A "DINOSAUR."
clack
GUILMON AGAIN? I'M *THE* WORST TAMER *EVER!*
I'M GOING OUT. I WON'T BE LONG.
AGAIN? WHERE?
NOWHERE. BYE!

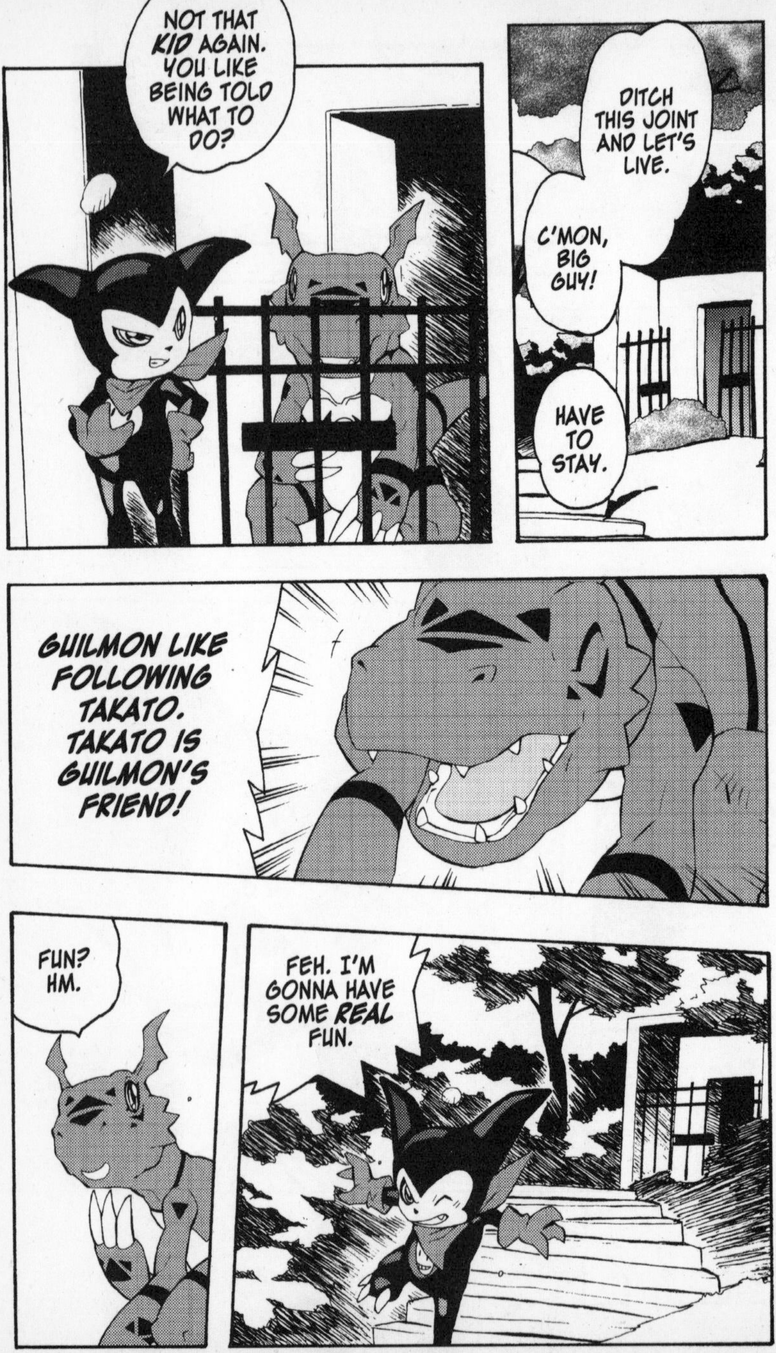
DITCH THIS JOINT AND LET'S LIVE.
C'MON, BIG GUY!
HAVE TO STAY.
NOT THAT *KID* AGAIN. YOU LIKE BEING TOLD WHAT TO DO?
GUILMON LIKE FOLLOWING TAKATO. TAKATO IS GUILMON'S FRIEND!
FEH. I'M GONNA HAVE SOME *REAL* FUN.
FUN? HM.

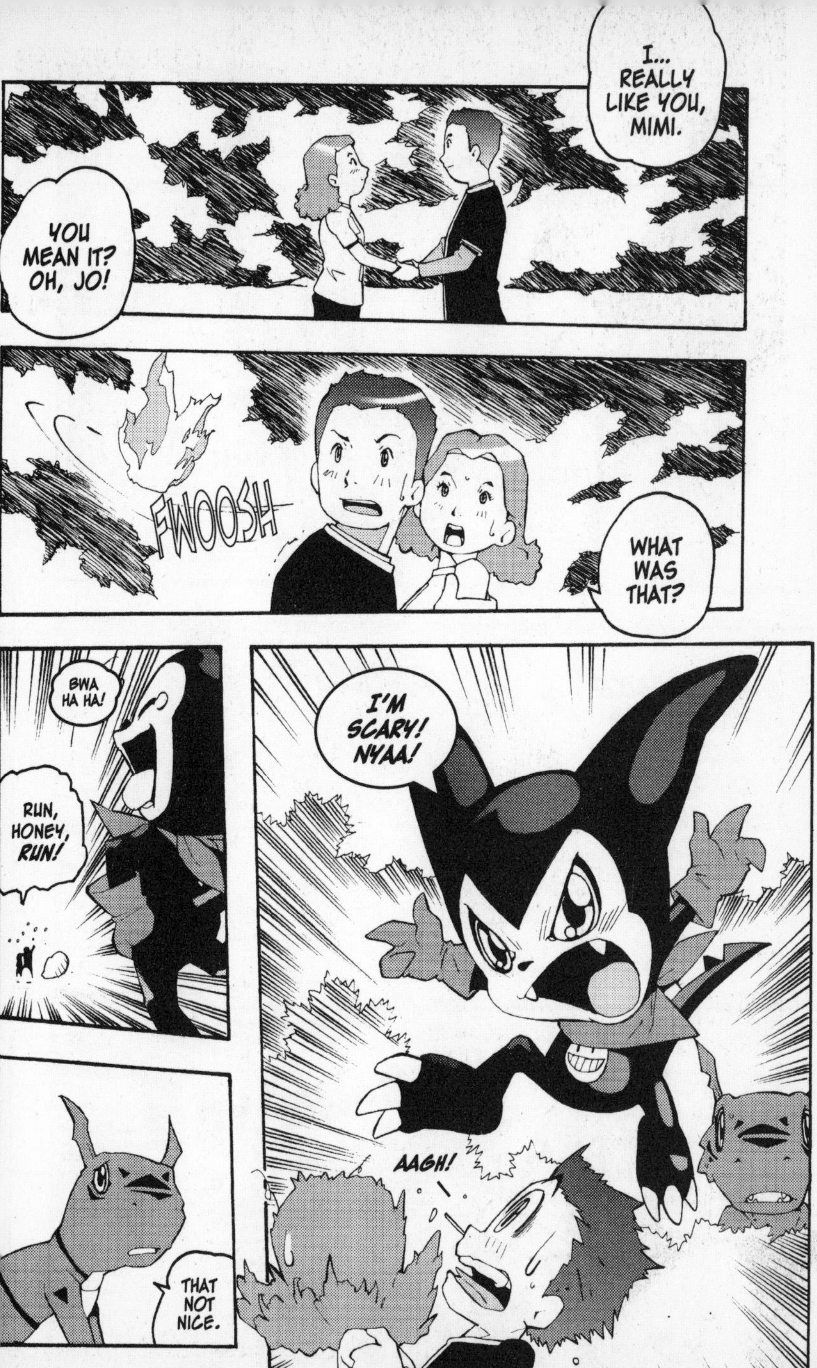
I... REALLY LIKE YOU, MIMI.
YOU MEAN IT? OH, JO!
FWOOSH
WHAT WAS THAT?
I'M SCARY! NYAA!
AAGH!
BWA HA HA!
RUN, HONEY, RUN!
THAT NOT NICE.

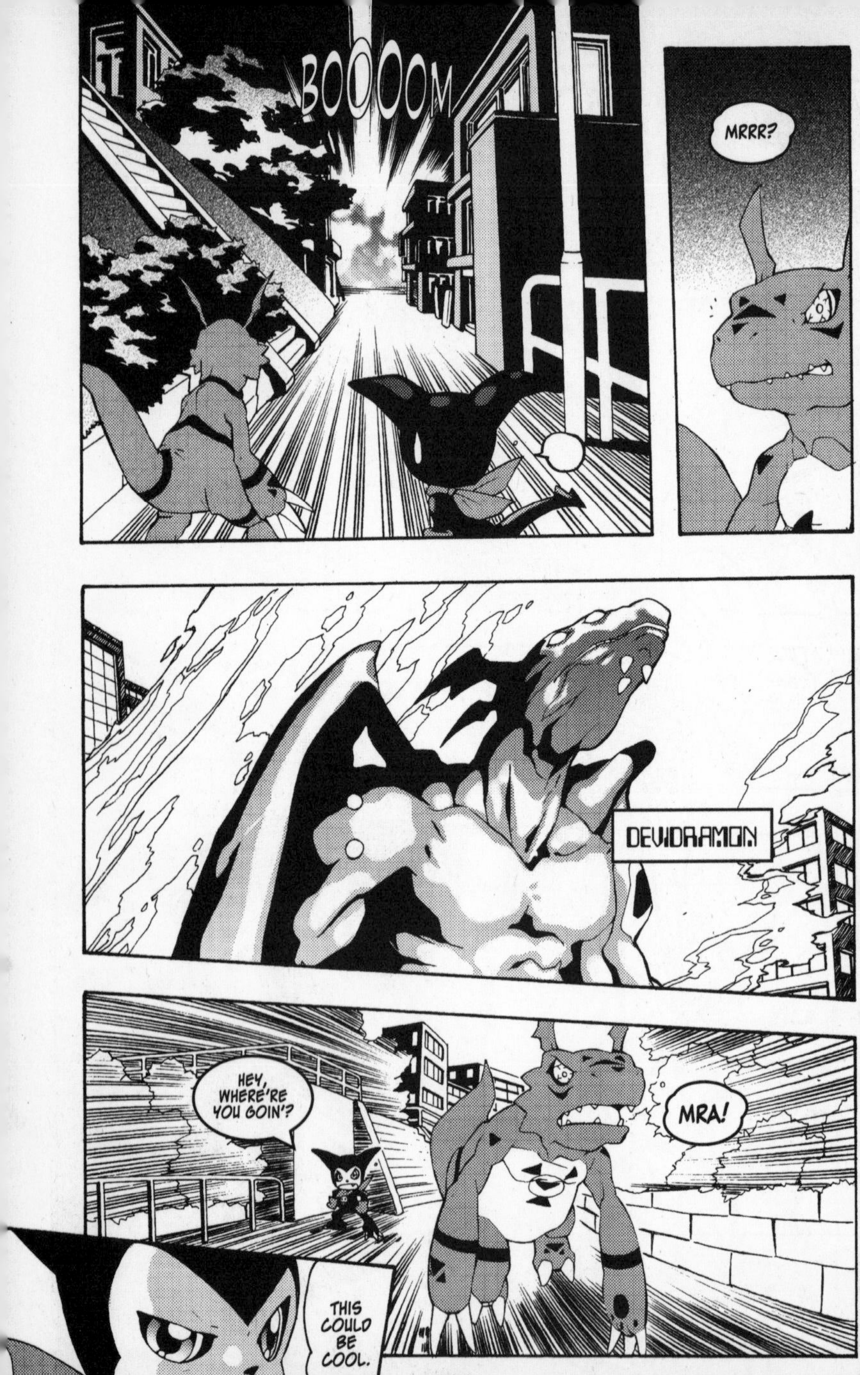
MRRR?
BOOOOM
DEVIDRAMON
MRA!
HEY, WHERE'RE YOU GOIN'?
THIS COULD BE COOL.

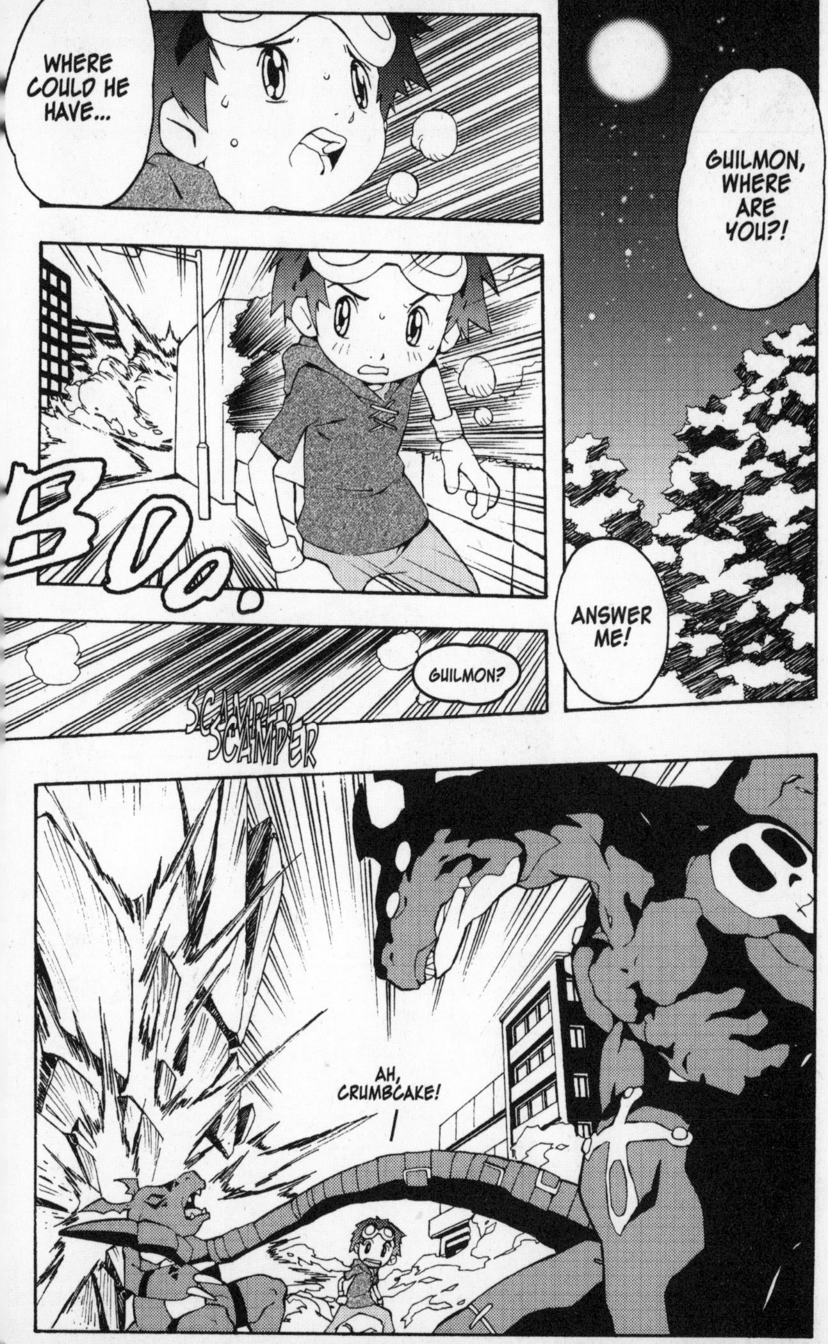
GUILMON, WHERE ARE YOU?!
ANSWER ME!
WHERE COULD HE HAVE...
BOO.
GUILMON?
SCAMPER SCAMPER
AH, CRUMBCAKE!

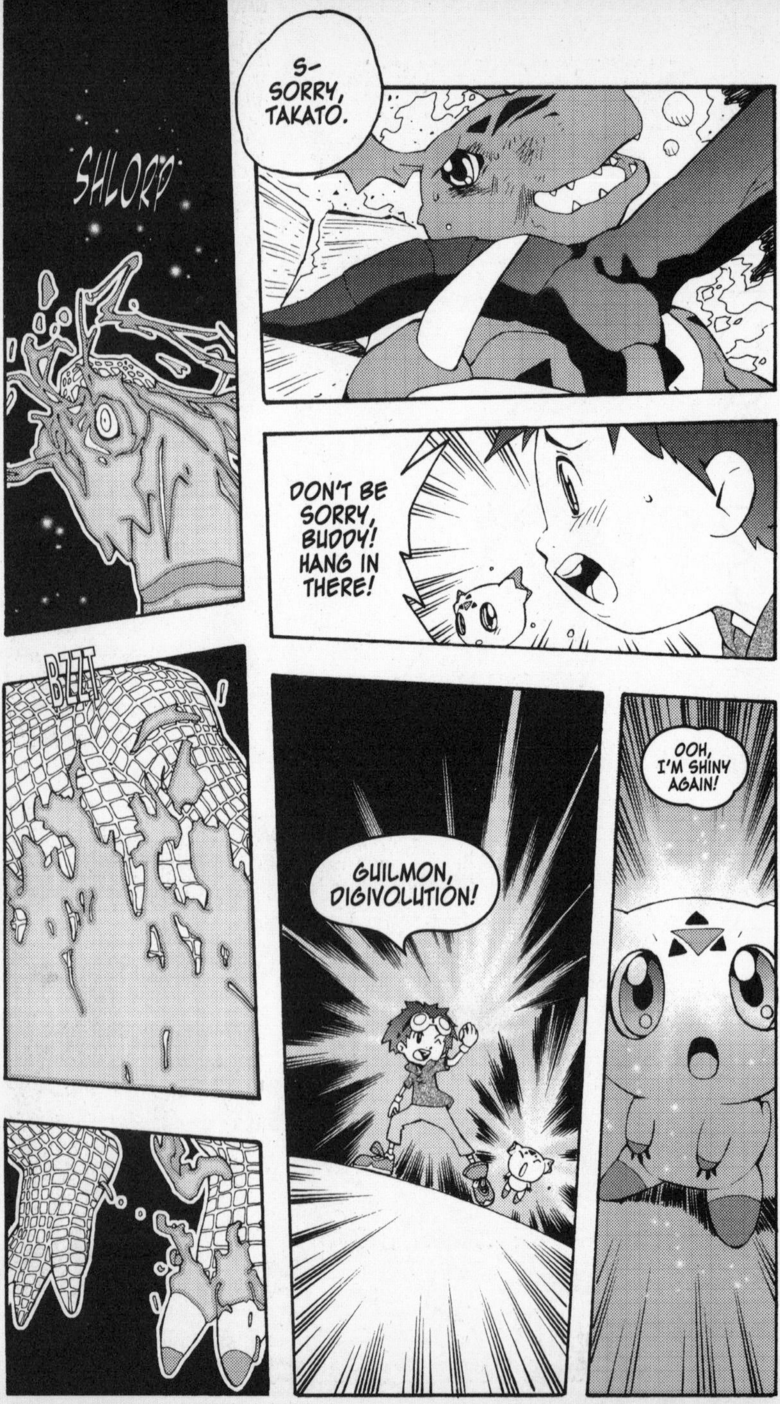
S-SORRY, TAKATO.
DON'T BE SORRY, BUDDY! HANG IN THERE!
SHLORP
OOH, I'M SHINY AGAIN!
GUILMON, DIGIVOLUTION!
BZZT

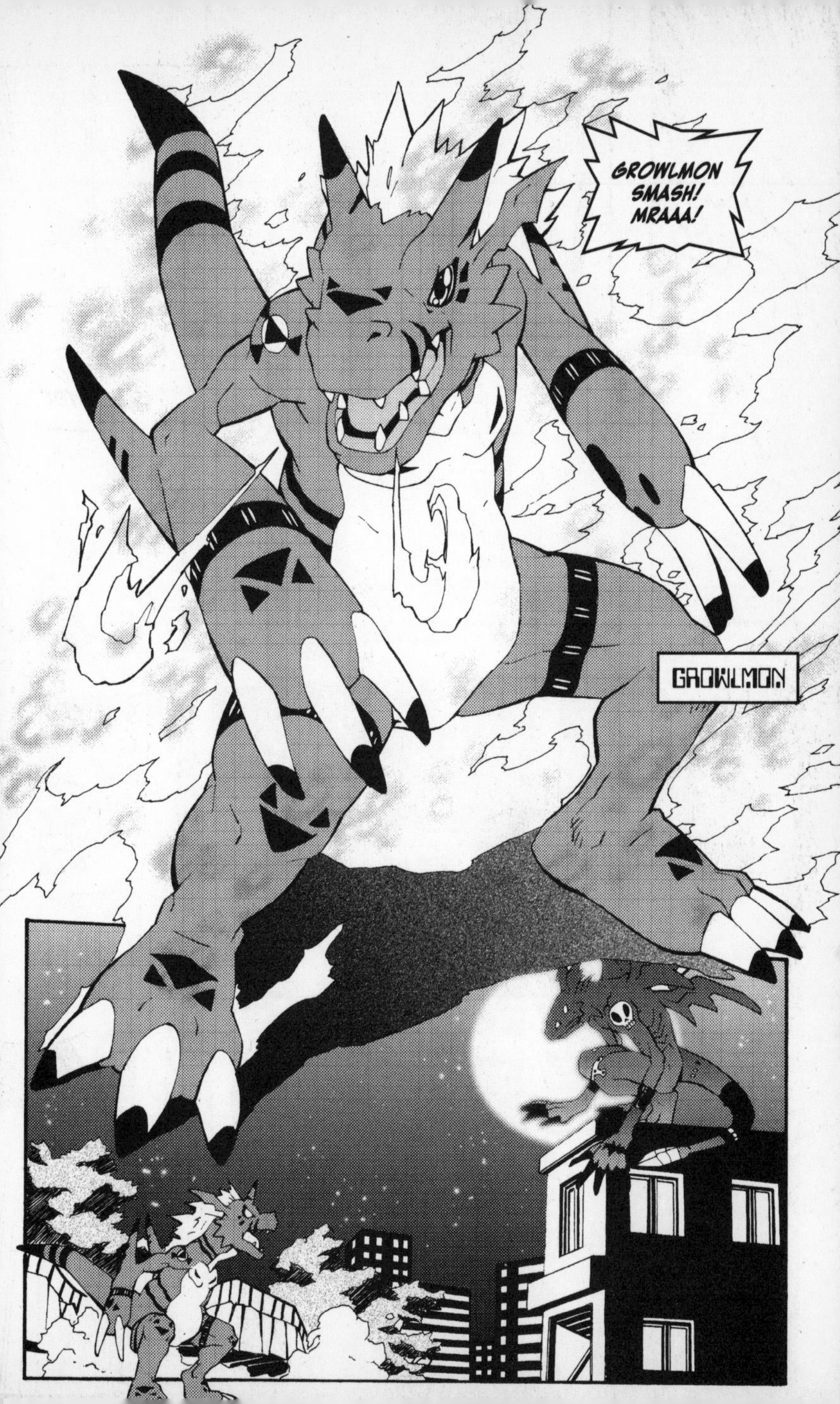
GROWLMON SMASH! MRAAA!
GROWLMON

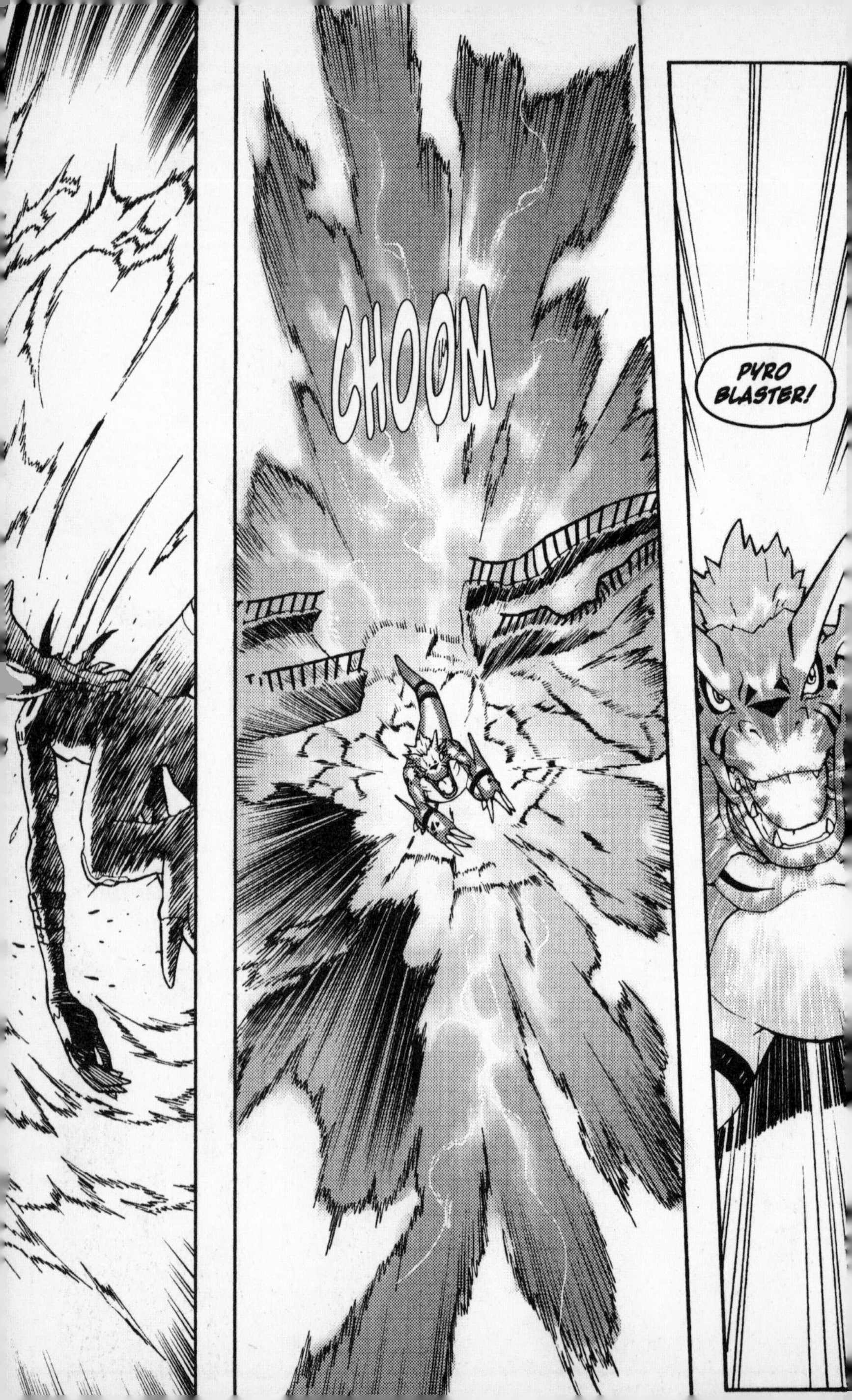
PYRO BLASTER!
CHOOM

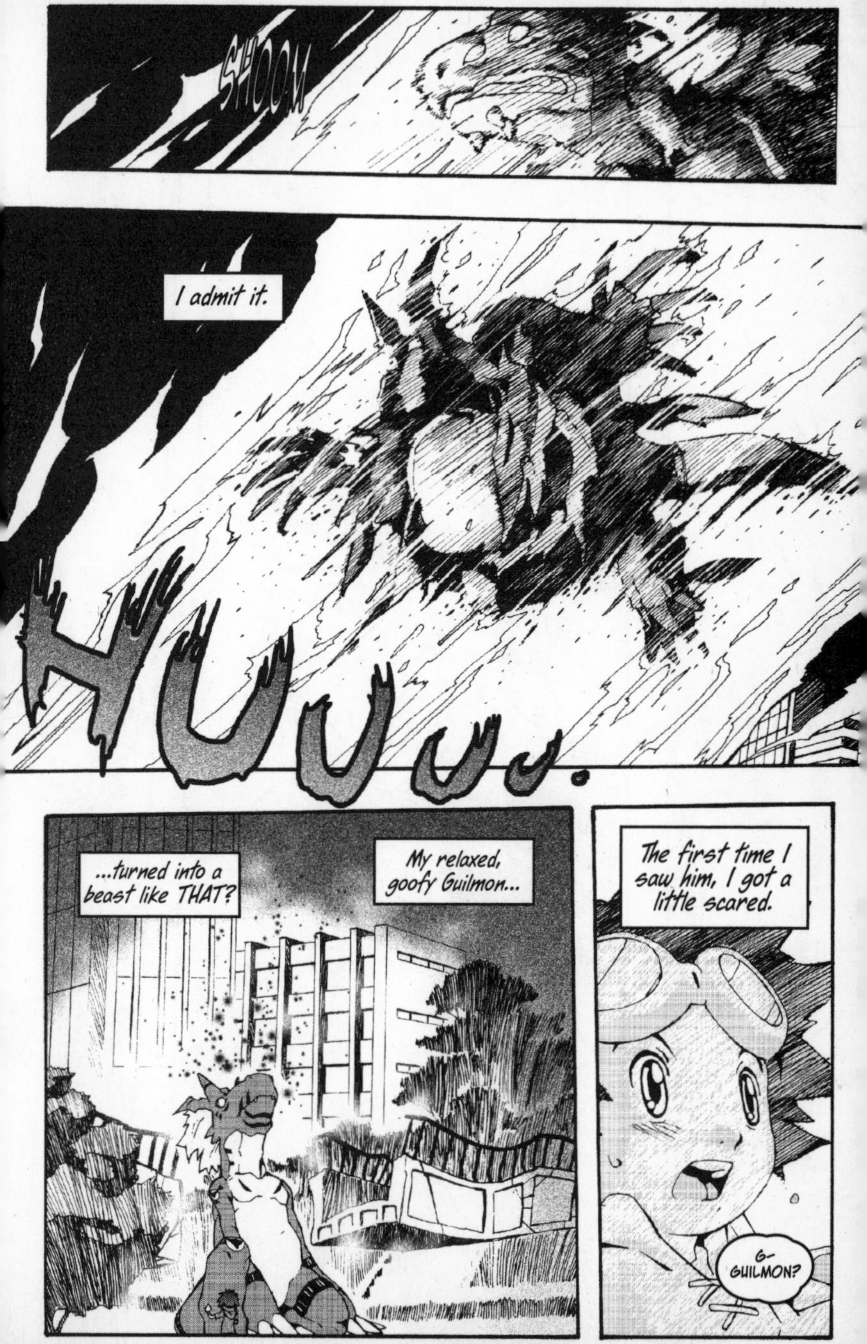
SHOOM
I admit it.
HUUUU.
The first time I saw him, I got a little scared.
G-GUILMON?
My relaxed, goofy Guilmon...
...turned into a beast like THAT?

CHAPTER 6: DAZED AND CONFUSED

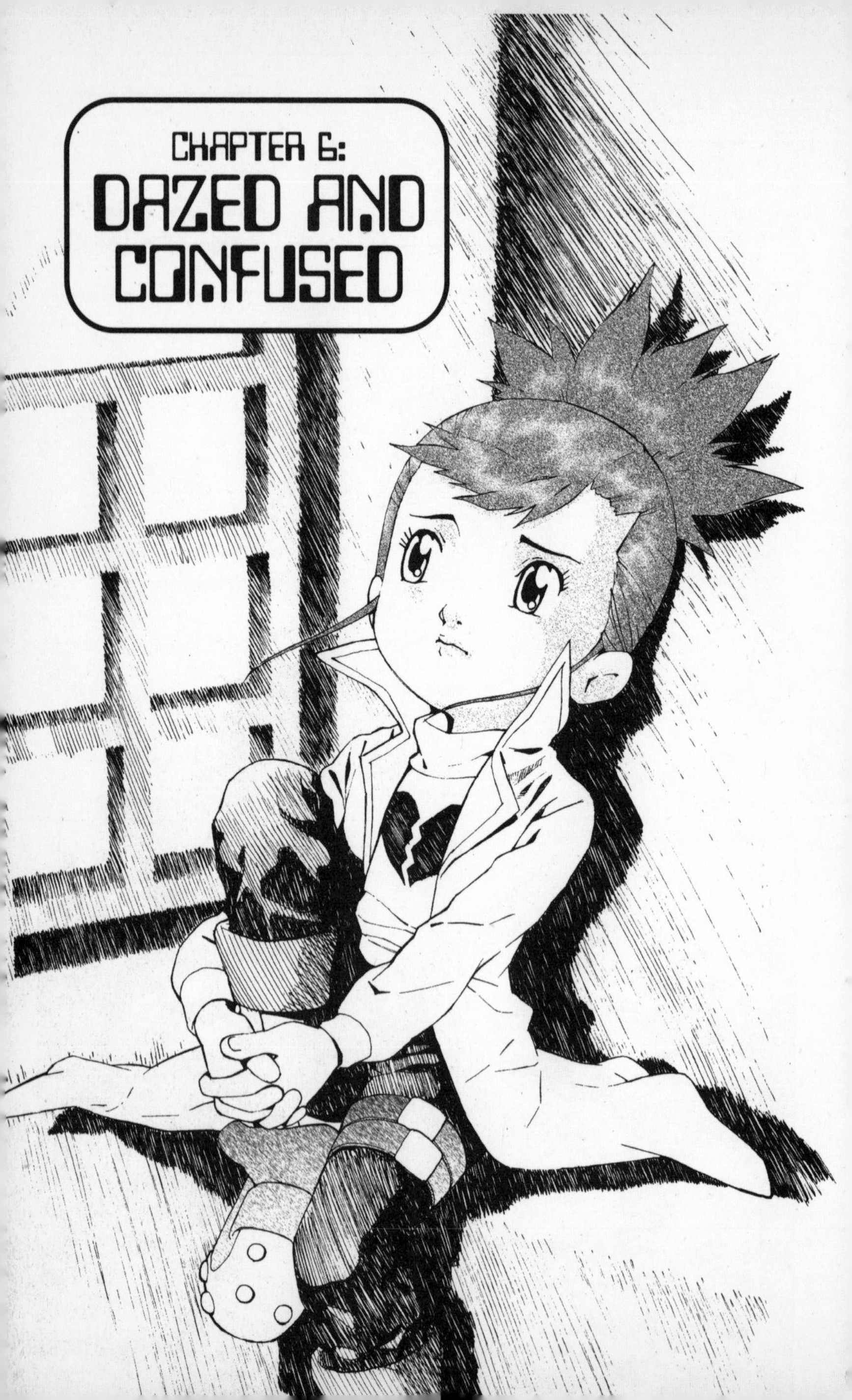

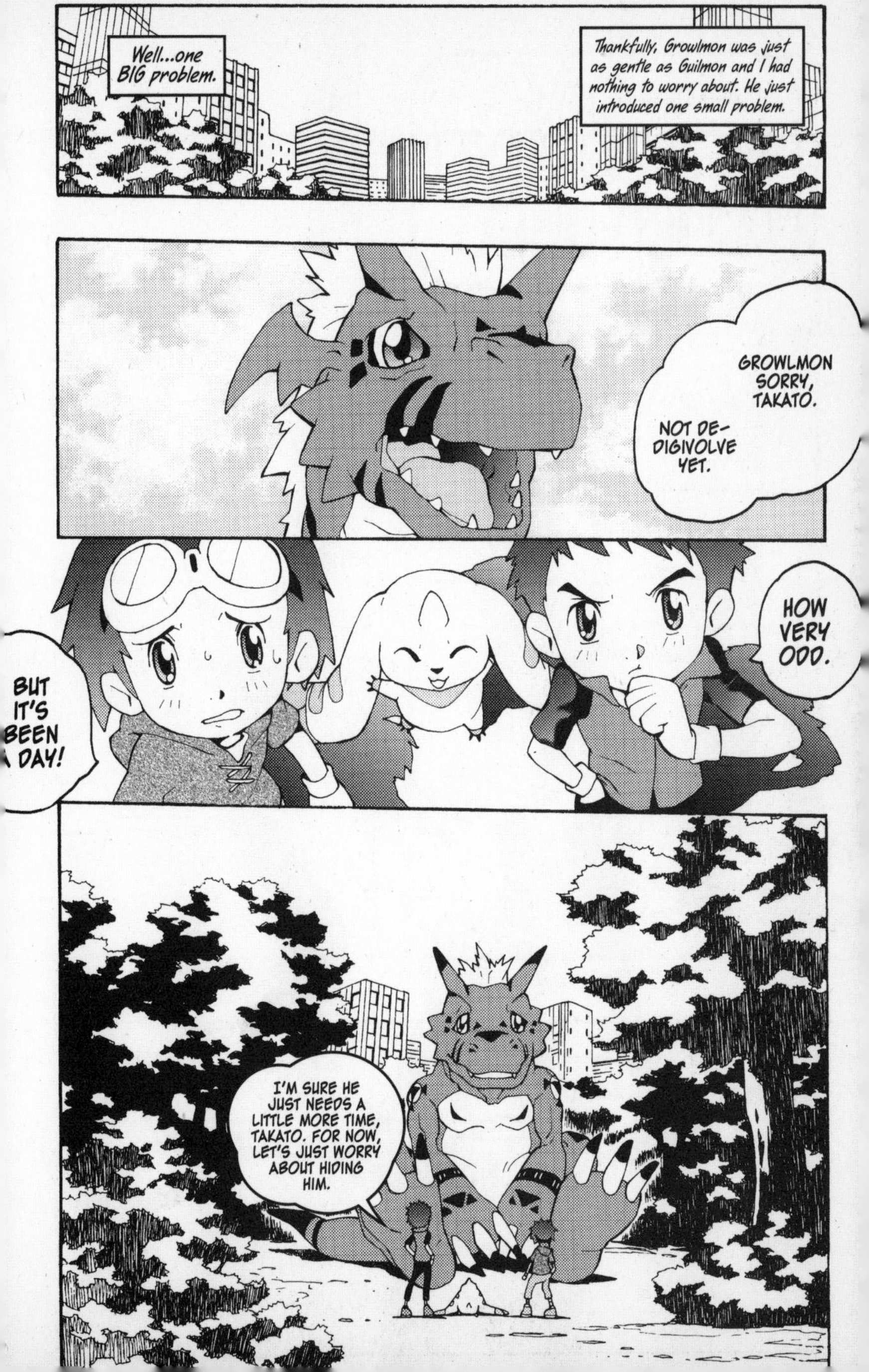
Thankfully, Growlmon was just as gentle as Guilmon and I had nothing to worry about. He just introduced one small problem.
Well...one BIG problem.
GROWLMON SORRY, TAKATO.
NOT DE-DIGIVOLVE YET.
HOW VERY ODD.
BUT IT'S BEEN DAY!
I'M SURE HE JUST NEEDS A LITTLE MORE TIME, TAKATO. FOR NOW, LET'S JUST WORRY ABOUT HIDING HIM.

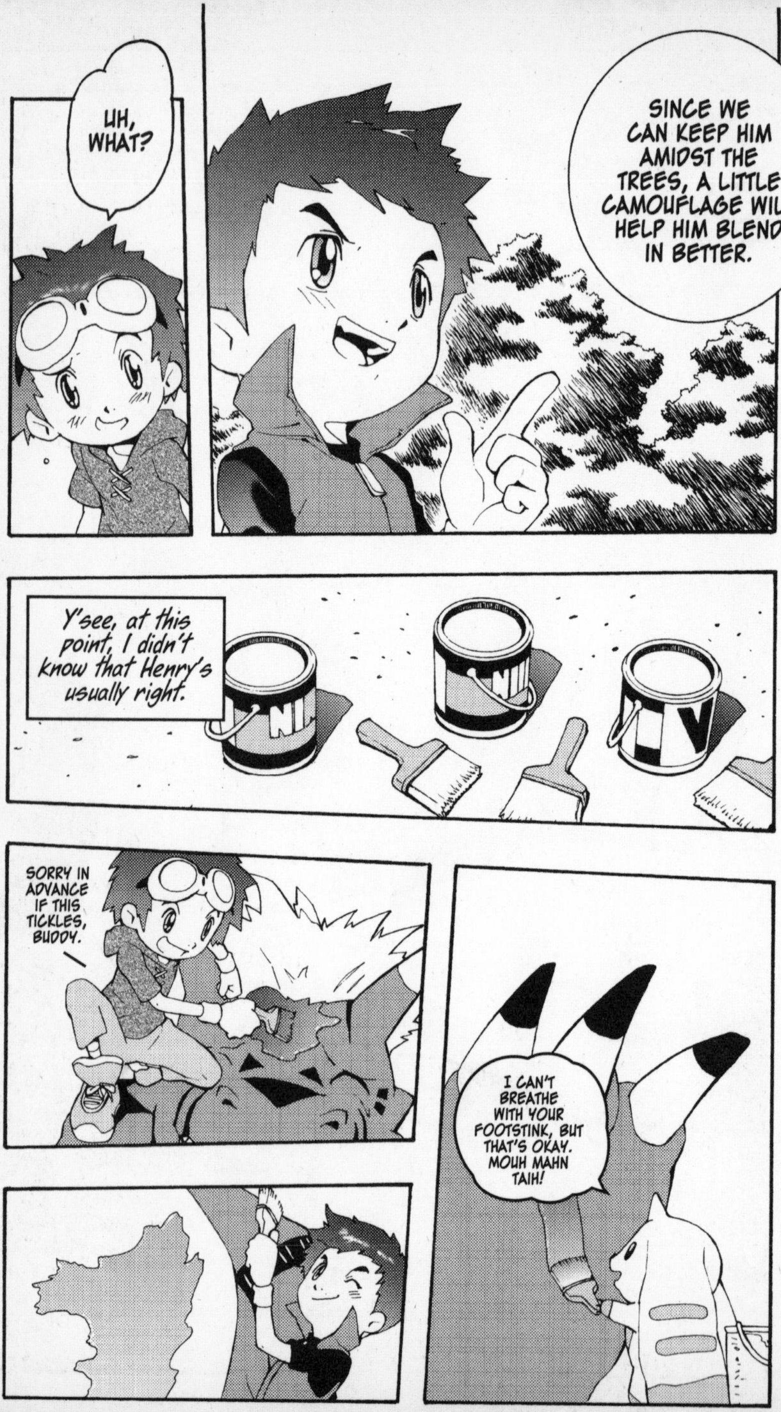
SINCE WE CAN KEEP HIM AMIDST THE TREES, A LITTLE CAMOUFLAGE WILL HELP HIM BLEND IN BETTER.
UH, WHAT?
Y'see, at this point, I didn't know that Henry's usually right.
I CAN'T BREATHE WITH YOUR FOOTSTINK, BUT THAT'S OKAY. MOUH MAHN TAIH!
SORRY IN ADVANCE IF THIS TICKLES, BUDDY.

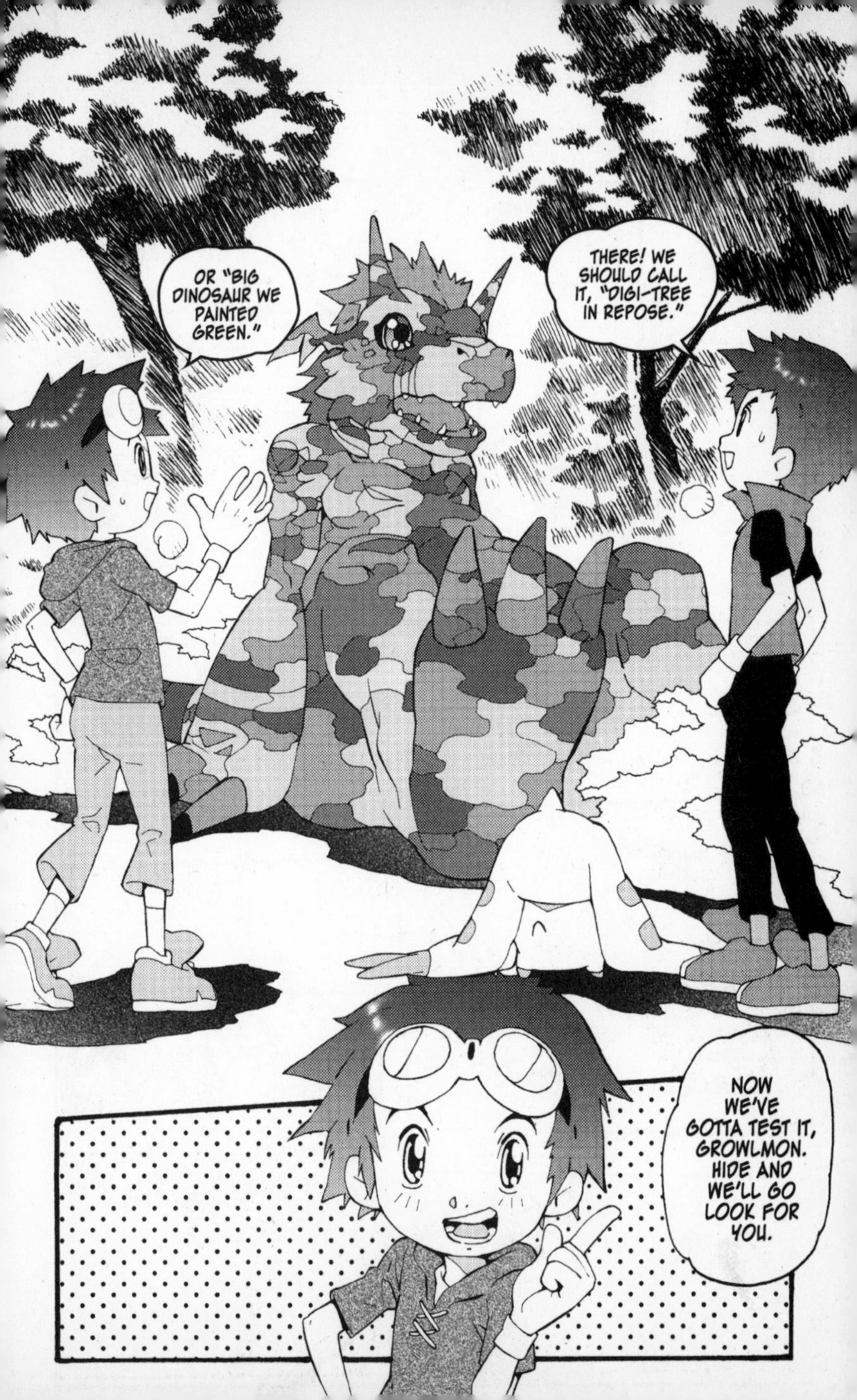
THERE! WE SHOULD CALL IT, "DIGI-TREE IN REPOSE."
OR "BIG DINOSAUR WE PAINTED GREEN."
NOW WE'VE GOTTA TEST IT, GROWLMON. HIDE AND WE'LL GO LOOK FOR YOU.

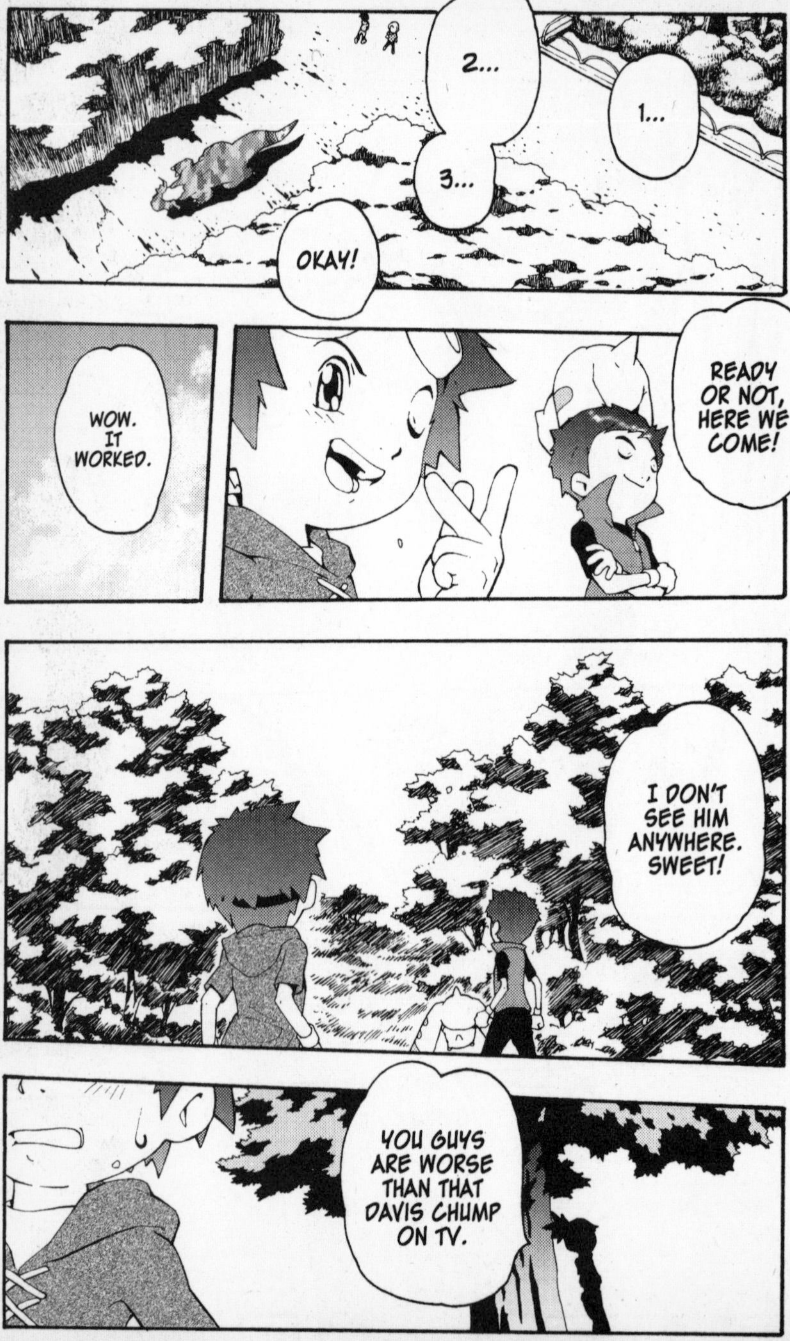
1...
2...
3...
OKAY!
READY OR NOT, HERE WE COME!
WOW. IT WORKED.
I DON'T SEE HIM ANYWHERE. SWEET!
YOU GUYS ARE WORSE THAN THAT DAVIS CHUMP ON TV.

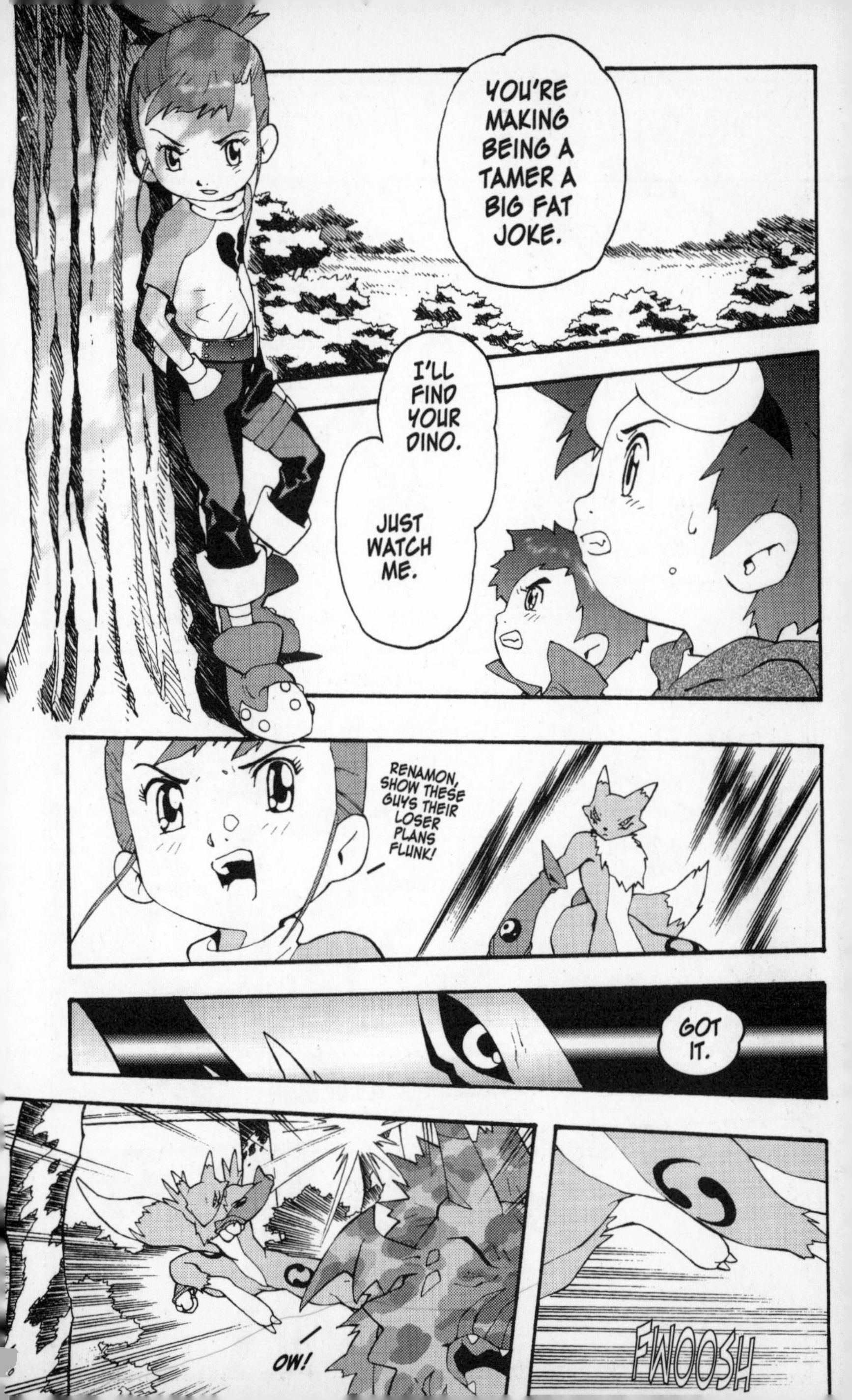
YOU'RE MAKING BEING A TAMER A BIG FAT JOKE.
I'LL FIND YOUR DINO.
JUST WATCH ME.
RENAMON, SHOW THESE GUYS THEIR LOSER PLANS FLUNK!
GOT IT.
FWOOSH
OW!

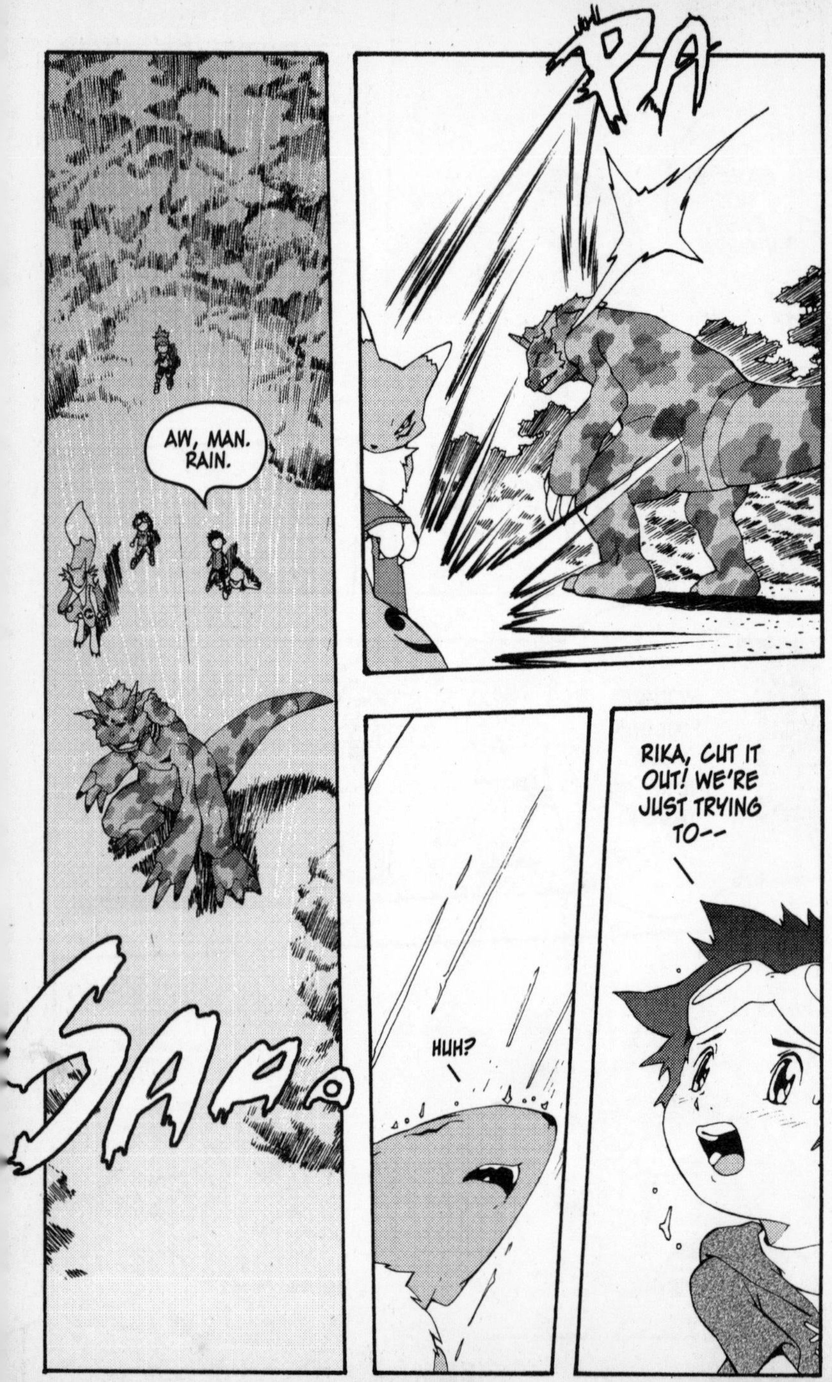
PA
RIKA, CUT IT OUT! WE'RE JUST TRYING TO--
HUH?
AW, MAN. RAIN.
SAAA

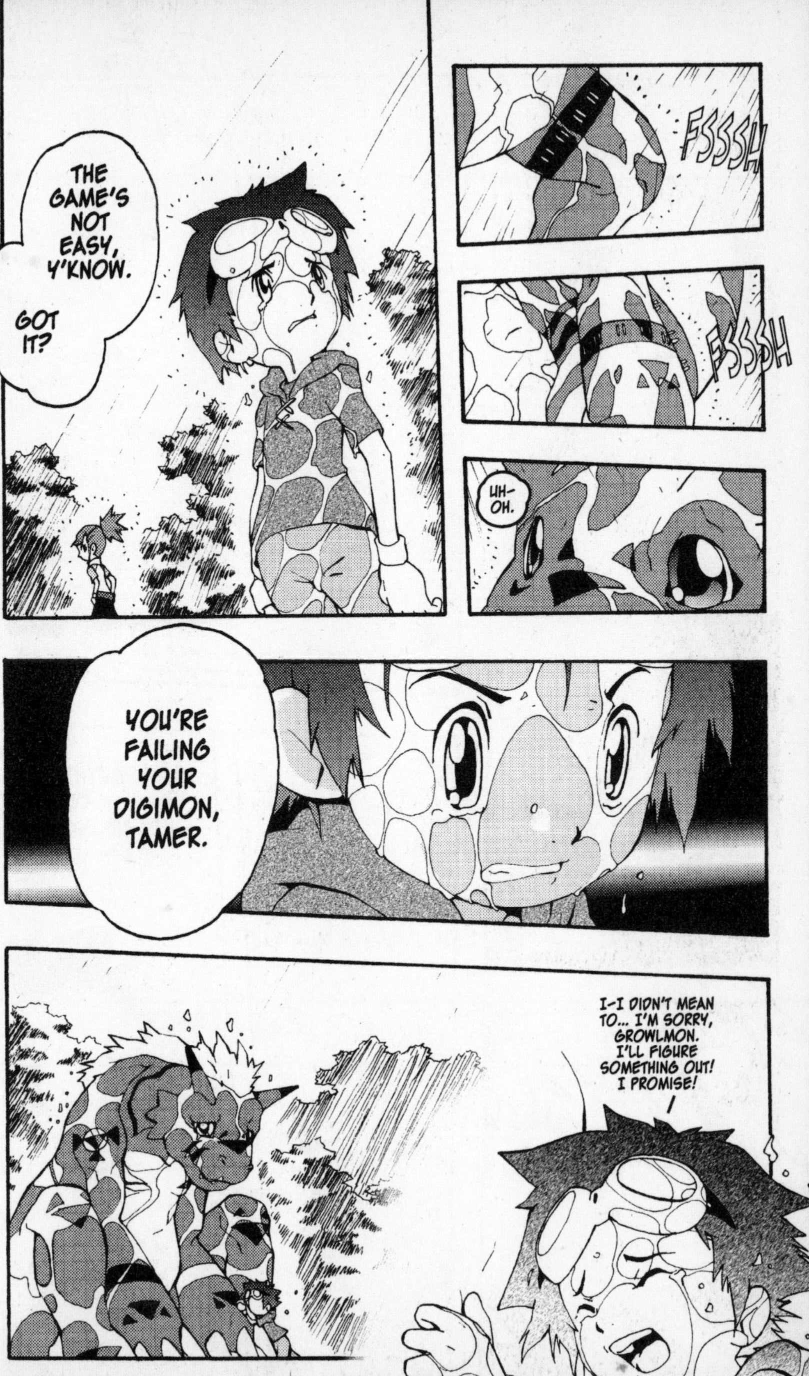

FSSSH
FSSSH
UH-OH.
THE GAME'S NOT EASY, Y'KNOW.
GOT IT?
YOU'RE FAILING YOUR DIGIMON, TAMER.
I-I DIDN'T MEAN TO... I'M SORRY, GROWLMON. I'LL FIGURE SOMETHING OUT! I PROMISE!

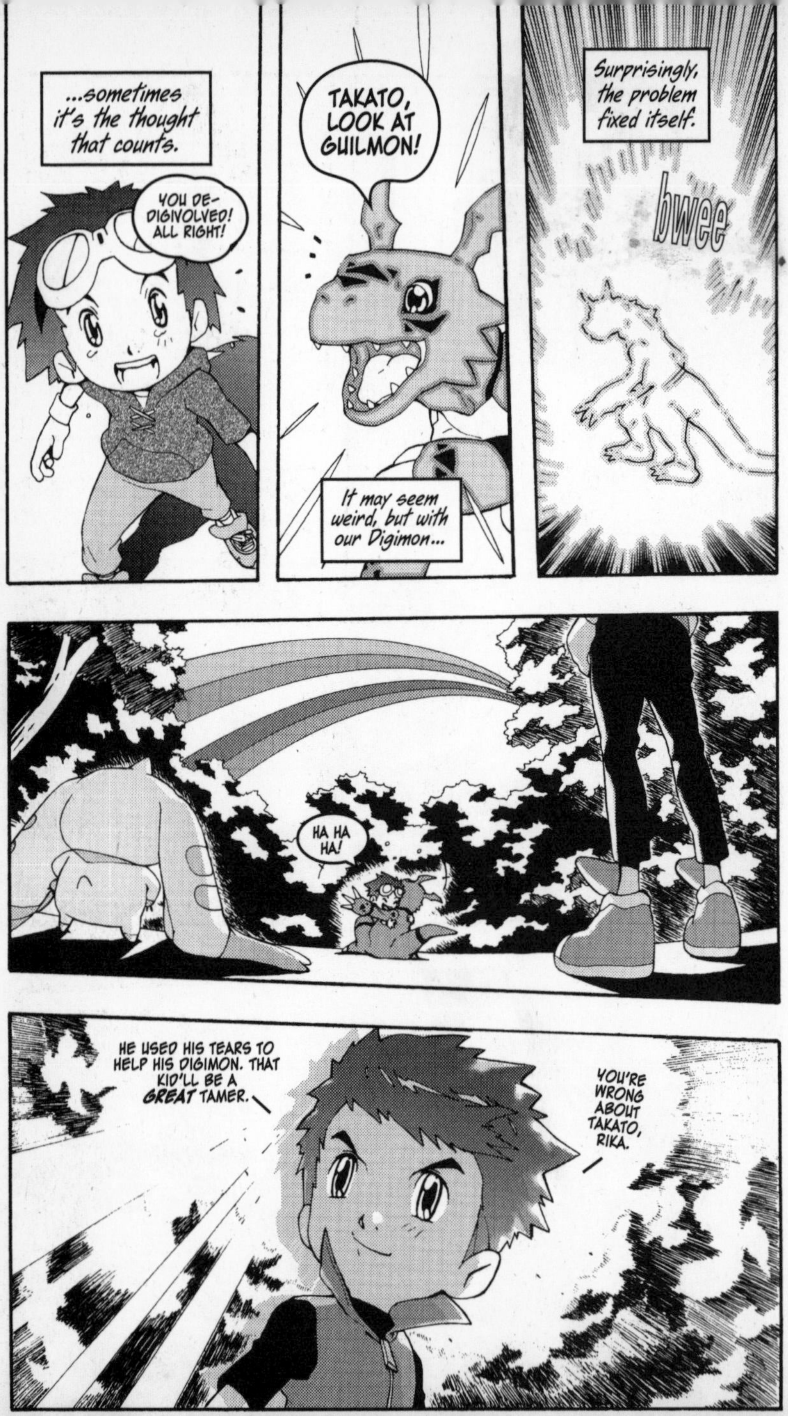
Surprisingly, the problem fixed itself.
bwee
TAKATO, LOOK AT GUILMON!
It may seem weird, but with our Digimon...
...sometimes it's the thought that counts.
YOU DE-DIGIVOLVED! ALL RIGHT!
HA HA HA!
YOU'RE WRONG ABOUT TAKATO, RIKA.
HE USED HIS TEARS TO HELP HIS DIGIMON. THAT KID'LL BE A GREAT TAMER.

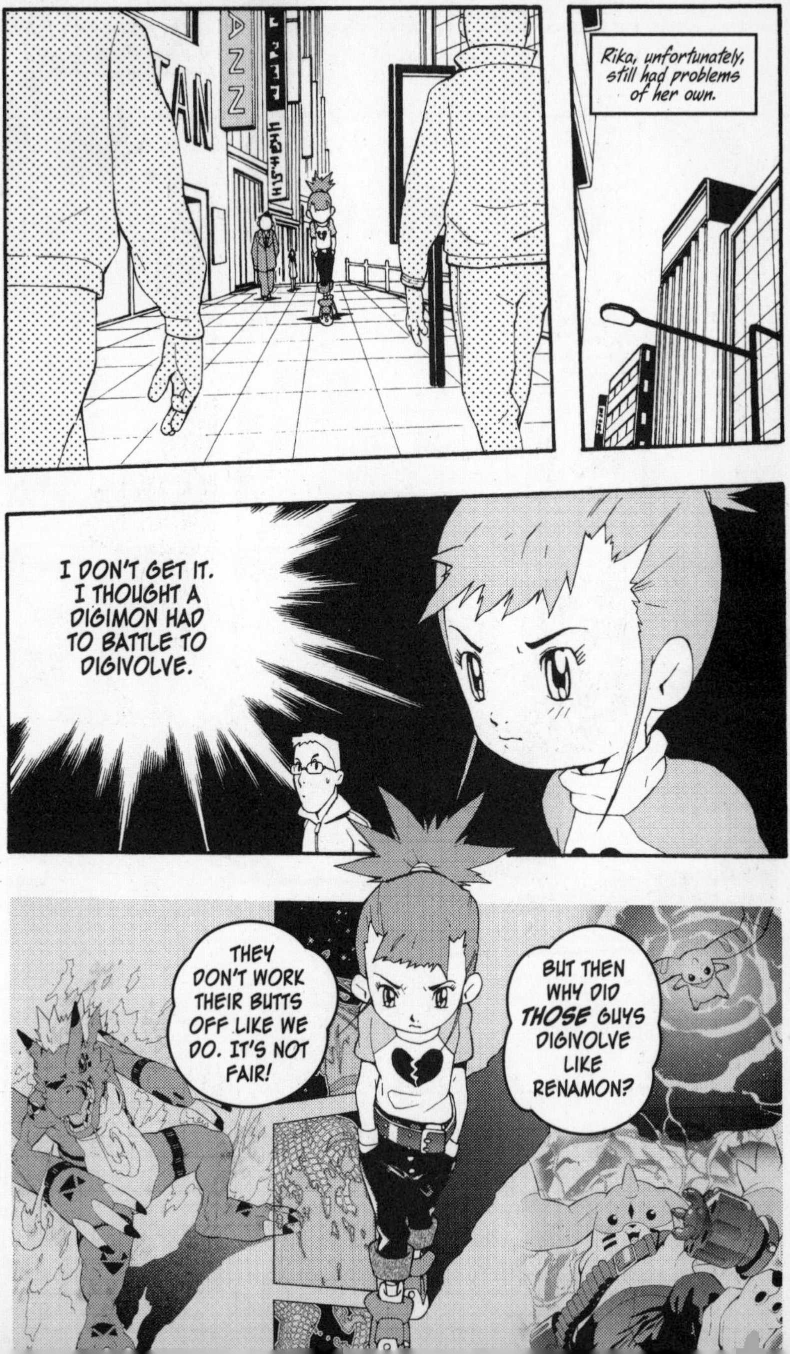
Rika, unfortunately, still had problems of her own.
I DON'T GET IT. I THOUGHT A DIGIMON HAD TO BATTLE TO DIGIVOLVE.
BUT THEN WHY DID THOSE GUYS DIGIVOLVE LIKE RENAMON?
THEY DON'T WORK THEIR BUTTS OFF LIKE WE DO. IT'S NOT FAIR!

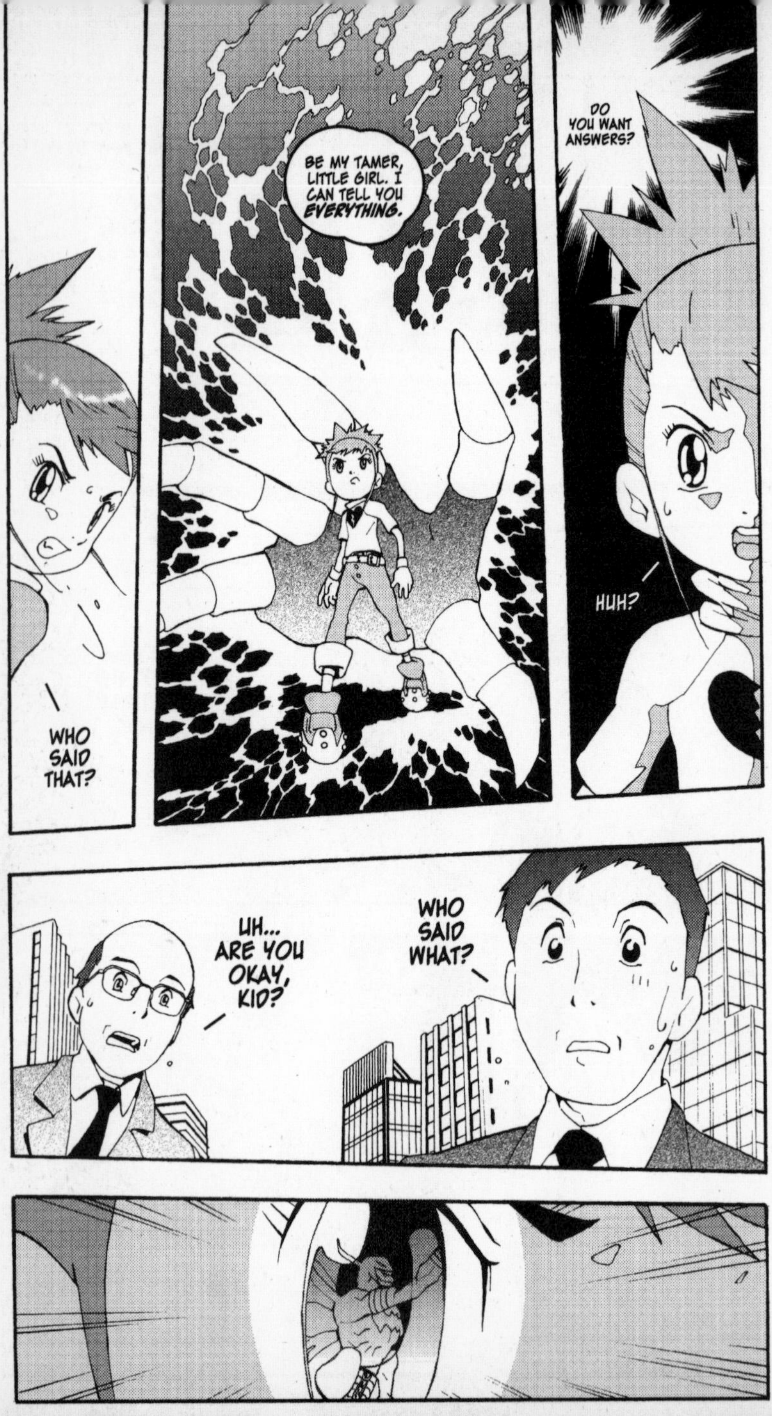
DO YOU WANT ANSWERS?
HUH?
BE MY TAMER, LITTLE GIRL. I CAN TELL YOU *EVERYTHING.*
WHO SAID THAT?
WHO SAID WHAT?
UH... ARE YOU OKAY, KID?

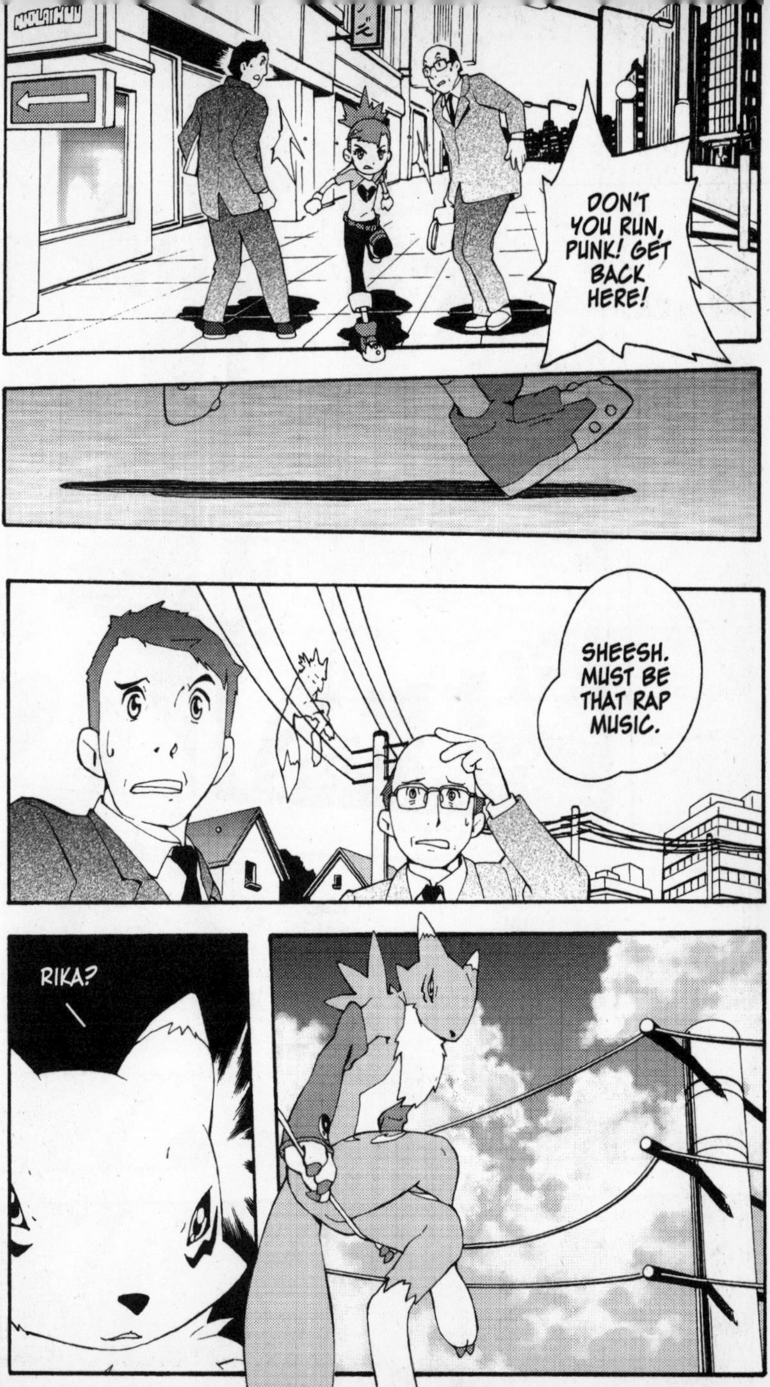
DON'T YOU RUN, PUNK! GET BACK HERE!
SHEESH. MUST BE THAT RAP MUSIC.
RIKA?

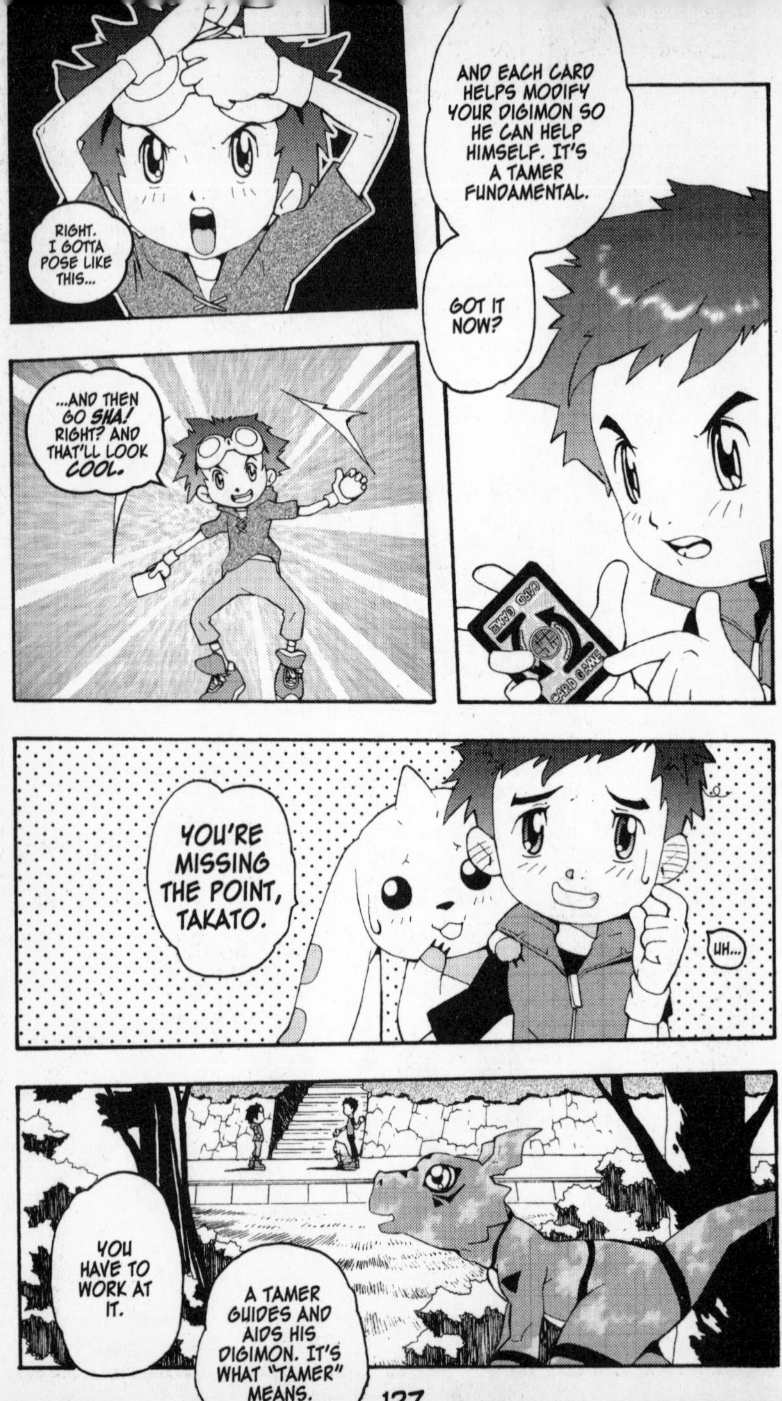
AND EACH CARD HELPS MODIFY YOUR DIGIMON SO HE CAN HELP HIMSELF. IT'S A TAMER FUNDAMENTAL.
GOT IT NOW?
RIGHT. I GOTTA POSE LIKE THIS...
...AND THEN GO *SHA!* RIGHT? AND THAT'LL LOOK *COOL.*
CARD GAME
YOU'RE MISSING THE POINT, TAKATO.
UH...
A TAMER GUIDES AND AIDS HIS DIGIMON. IT'S WHAT "TAMER" MEANS.
YOU HAVE TO WORK AT IT.

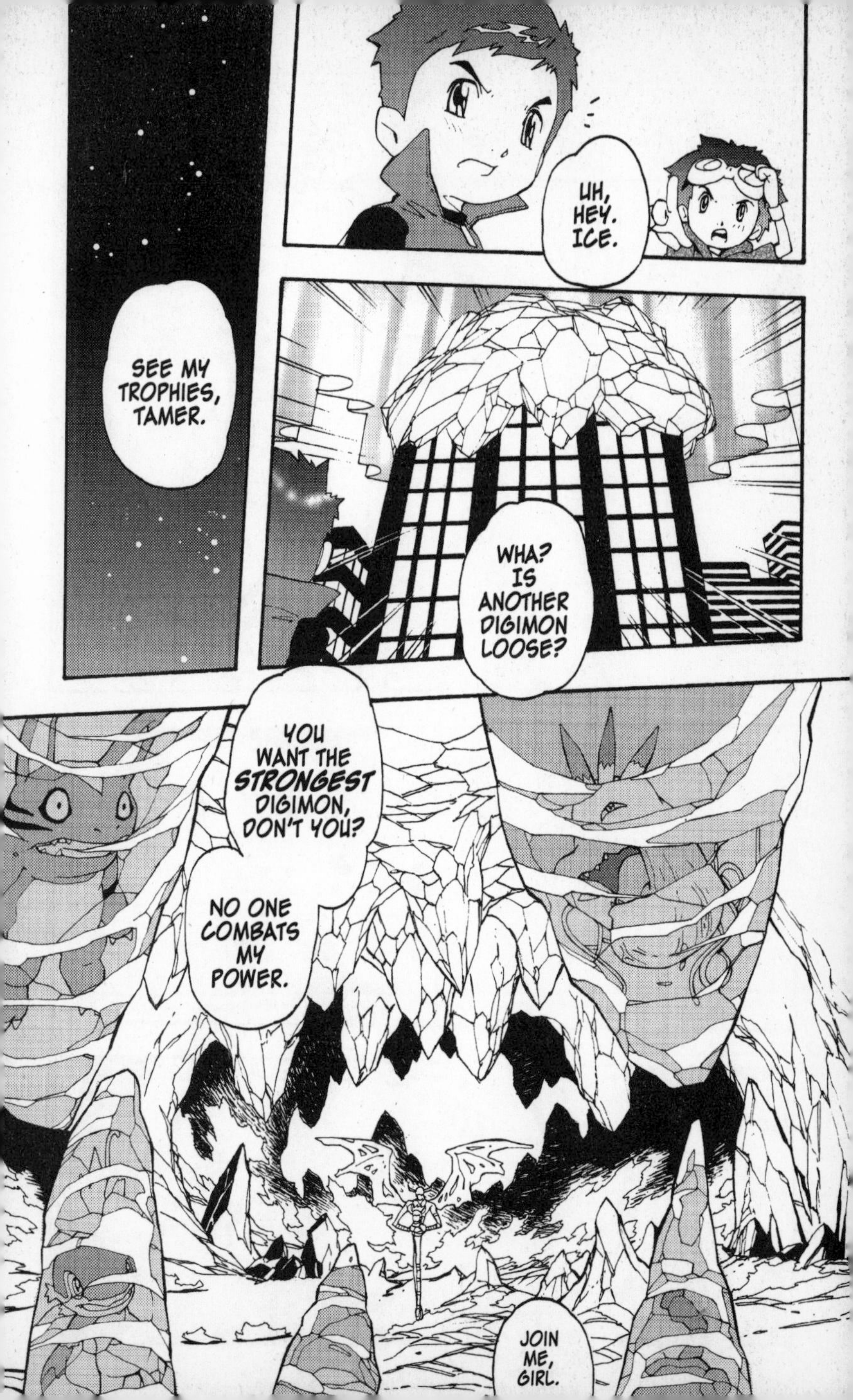
UH, HEY. ICE.
WHA? IS ANOTHER DIGIMON LOOSE?
SEE MY TROPHIES, TAMER.
YOU WANT THE STRONGEST DIGIMON, DON'T YOU?
NO ONE COMBATS MY POWER.
JOIN ME, GIRL.

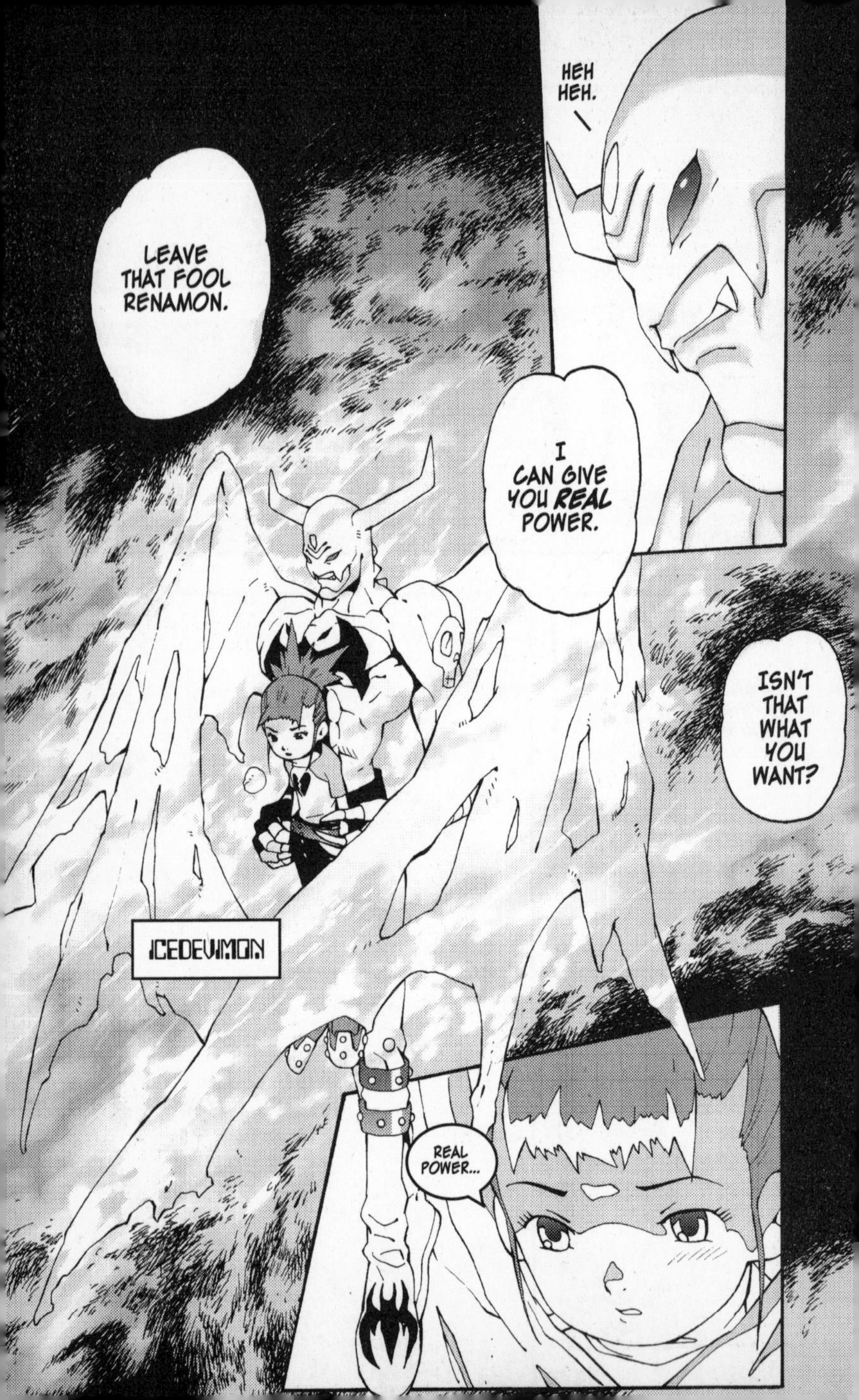
HEH HEH.
LEAVE THAT FOOL RENAMON.
I CAN GIVE YOU ***REAL*** POWER.
ISN'T THAT WHAT YOU WANT?
ICEDEVIMON
REAL POWER...

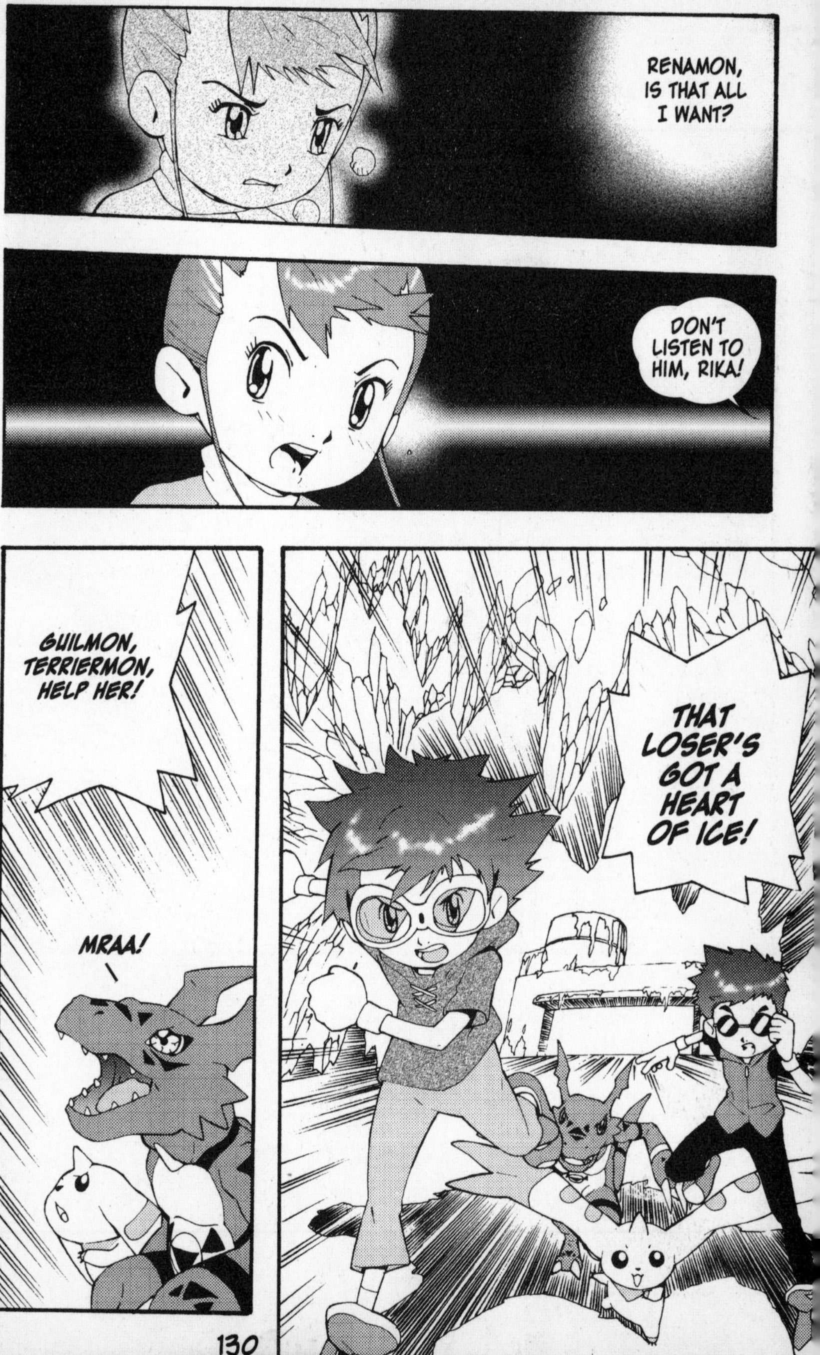
RENAMON, IS THAT ALL I WANT?
DON'T LISTEN TO HIM, RIKA!
THAT LOSER'S GOT A HEART OF ICE!
GUILMON, TERRIERMON, HELP HER!
MRAA!

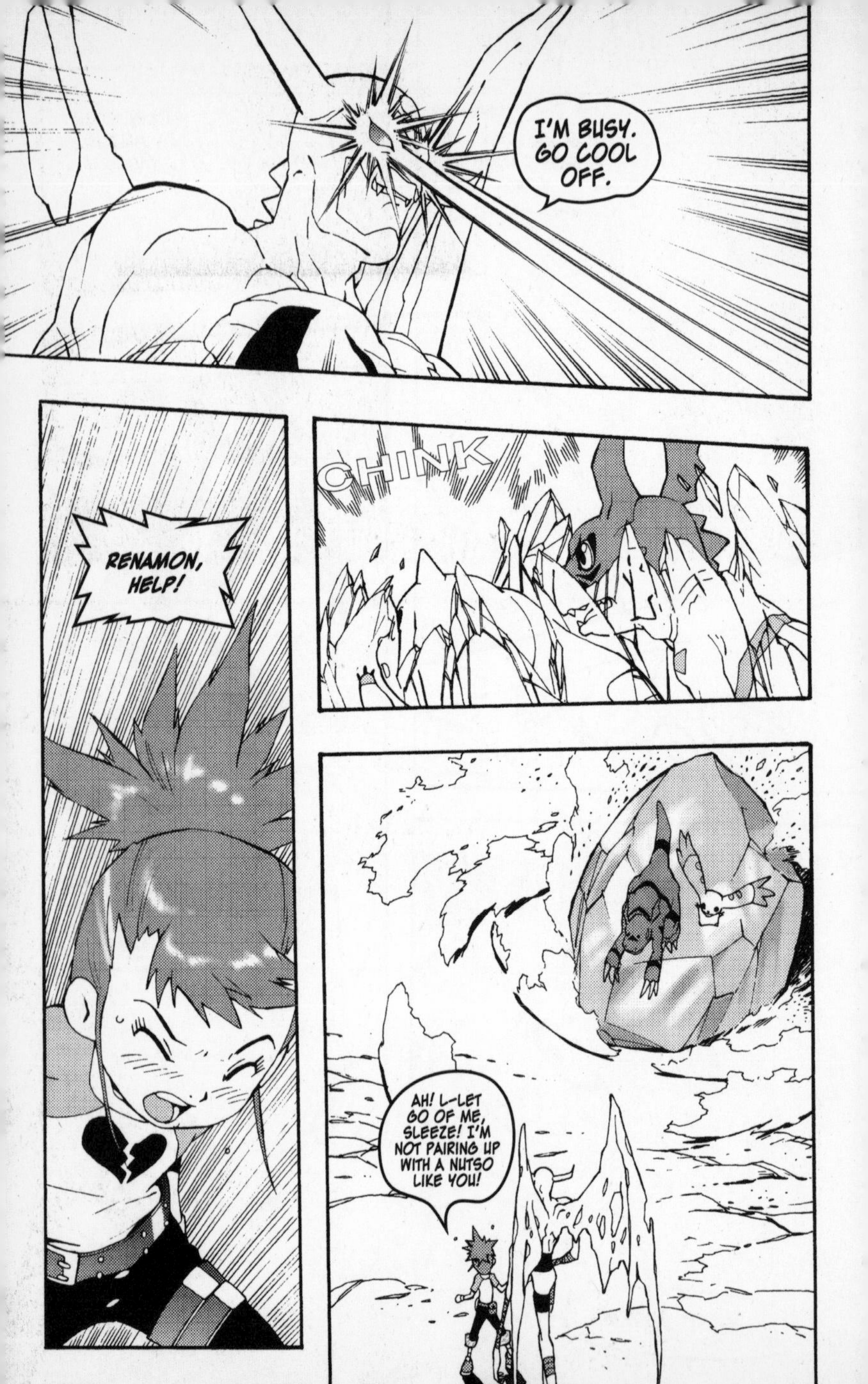
I'M BUSY. GO COOL OFF.
CHINK
AH! L-LET GO OF ME, SLEEZE! I'M NOT PAIRING UP WITH A NUTSO LIKE YOU!
RENAMON, HELP!

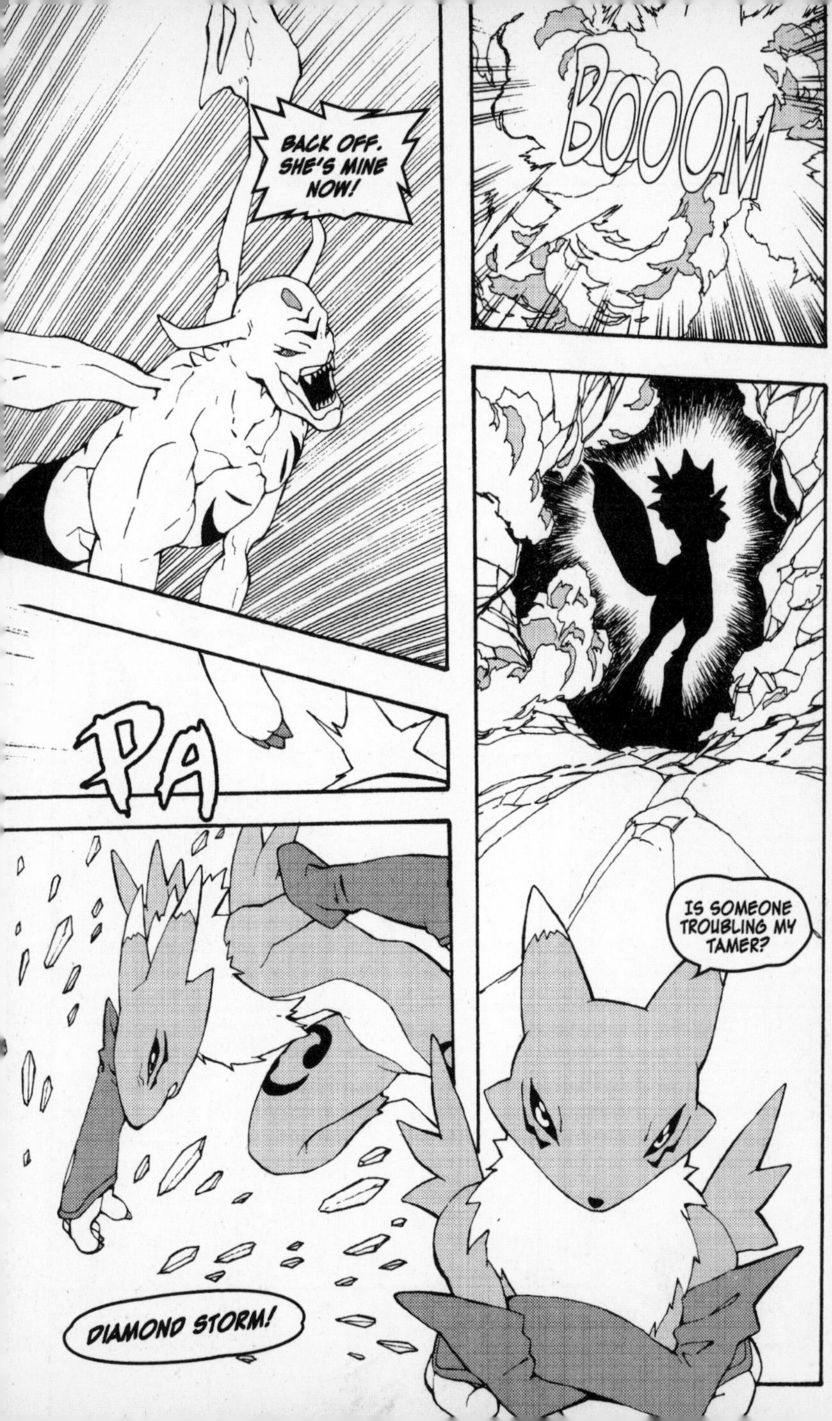
BOOOM
BACK OFF. SHE'S MINE NOW!
PA
IS SOMEONE TROUBLING MY TAMER?
DIAMOND STORM!

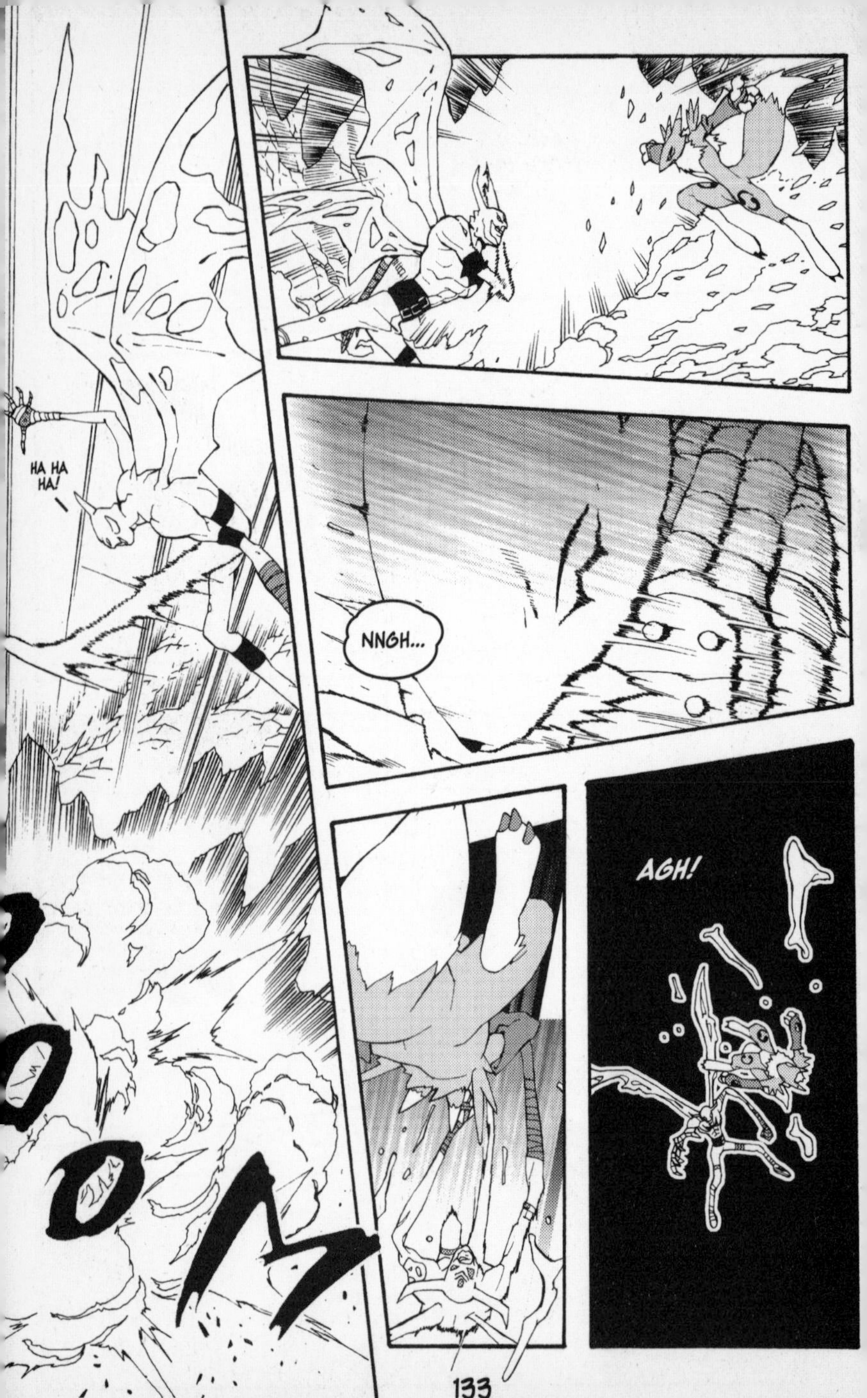
NNGH...
AGH!
HA HA HA!
BOOM

R-RIKA...

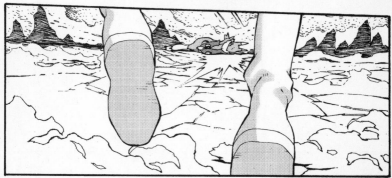

YOU'RE ALWAYS FALLING SHORT, RENAMON. THIS FAILURE IS YOUR LAST!

RENAMON! NO!

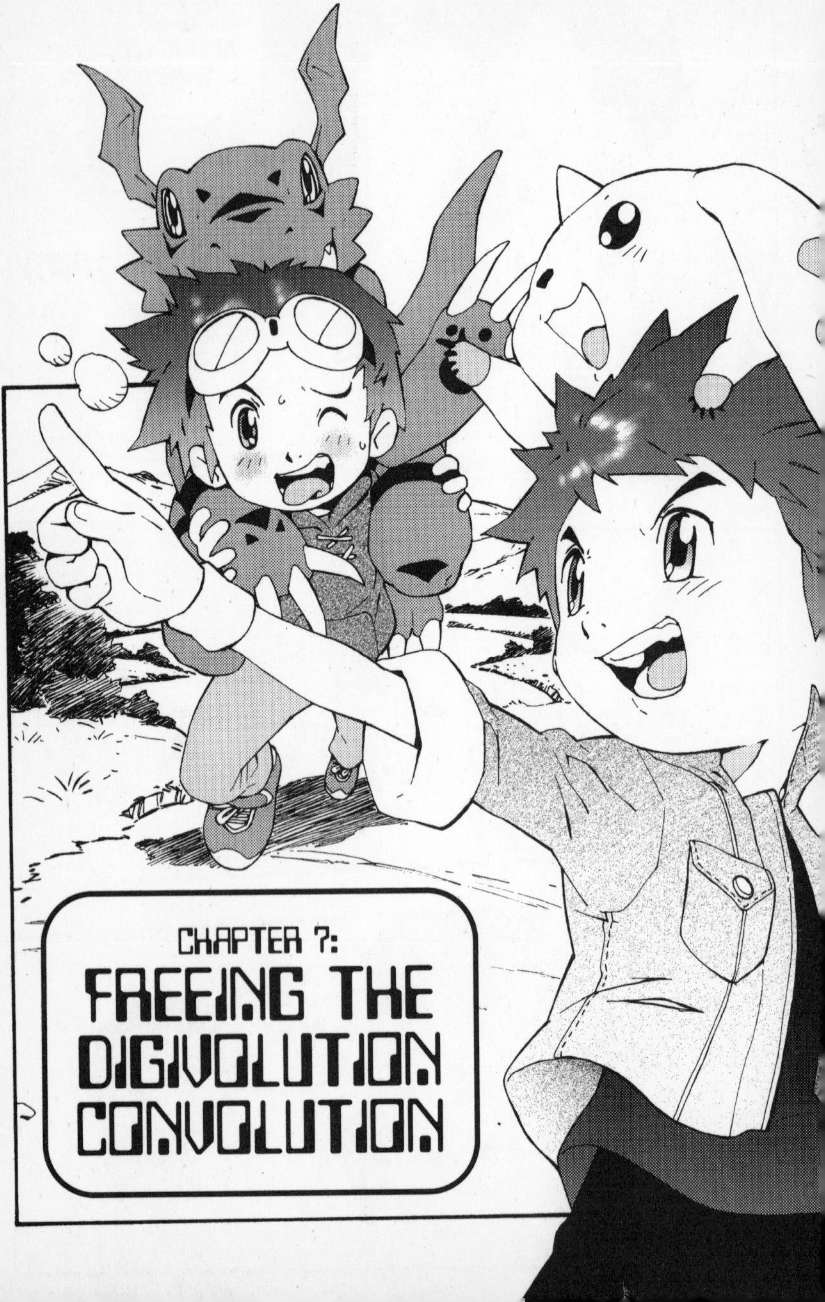
CHAPTER 7:
FREEING THE DIGIVOLUTION CONVOLUTION

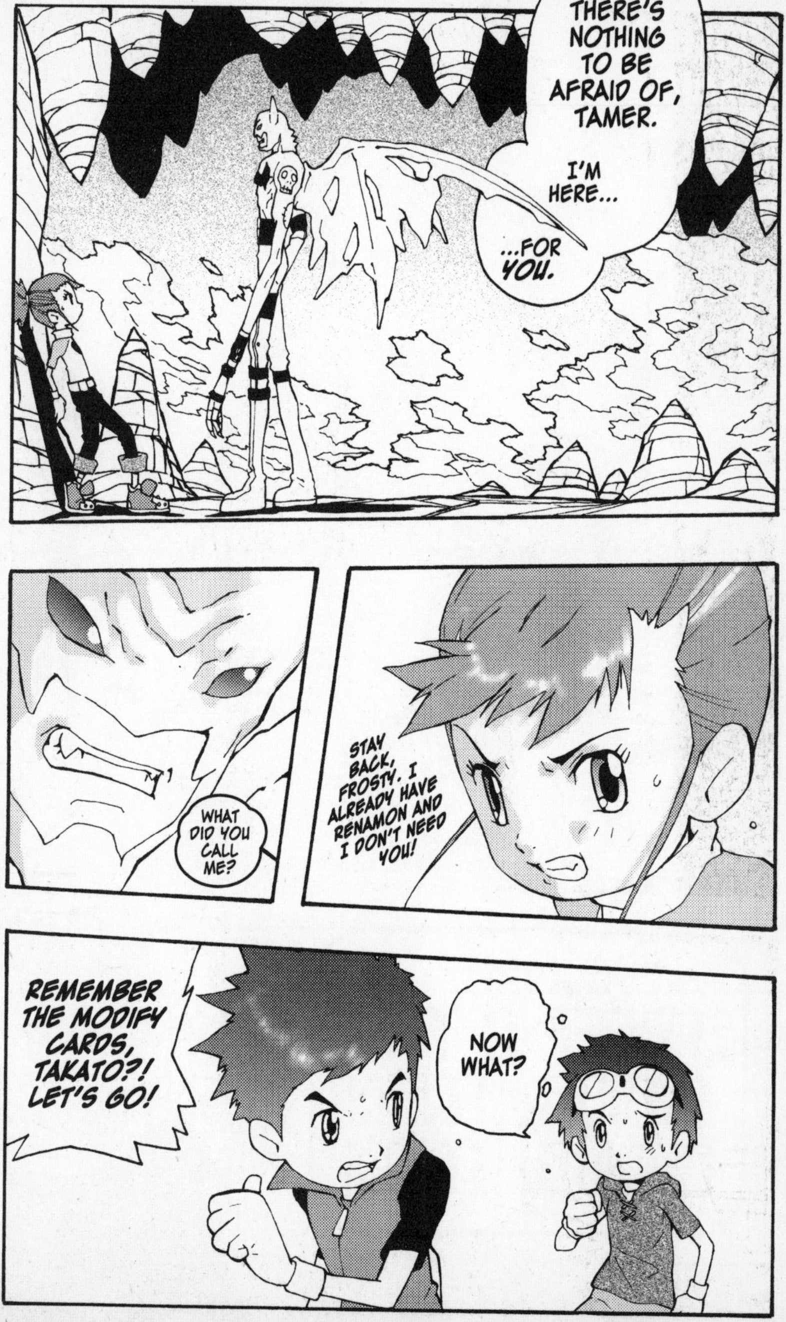
THERE'S NOTHING TO BE AFRAID OF, TAMER.
I'M HERE...
...FOR YOU.
STAY BACK, FROSTY. I ALREADY HAVE RENAMON AND I DON'T NEED YOU!
WHAT DID YOU CALL ME?
NOW WHAT?
REMEMBER THE MODIFY CARDS, TAKATO?! LET'S GO!

PWOOM

DIGI-MODIFY! EXPANSION ACTIVATE!

FOOSH

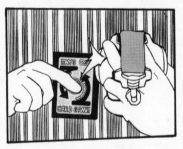

CARD GAME

CRACK

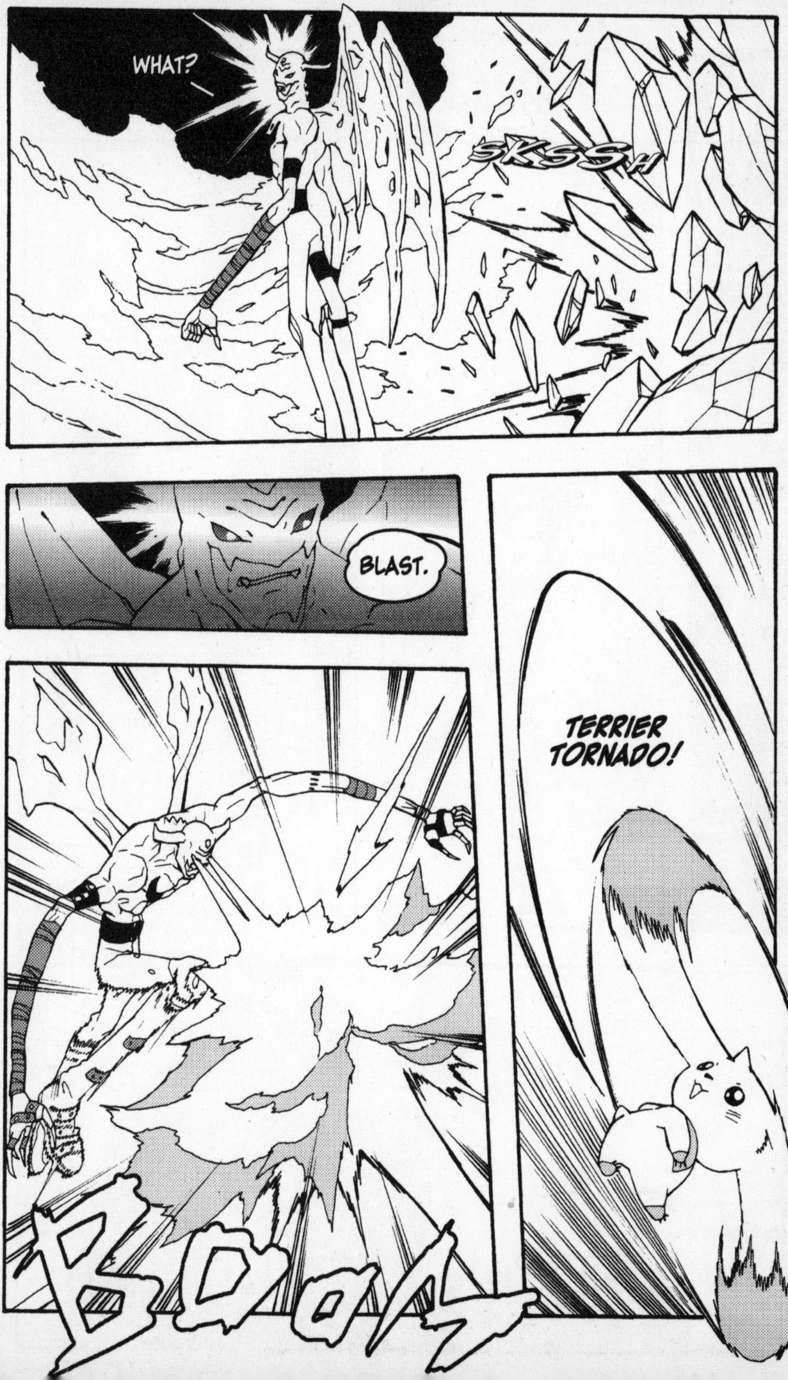
WHAT?
SKSSH
TERRIER TORNADO!
BLAST.
BOOM

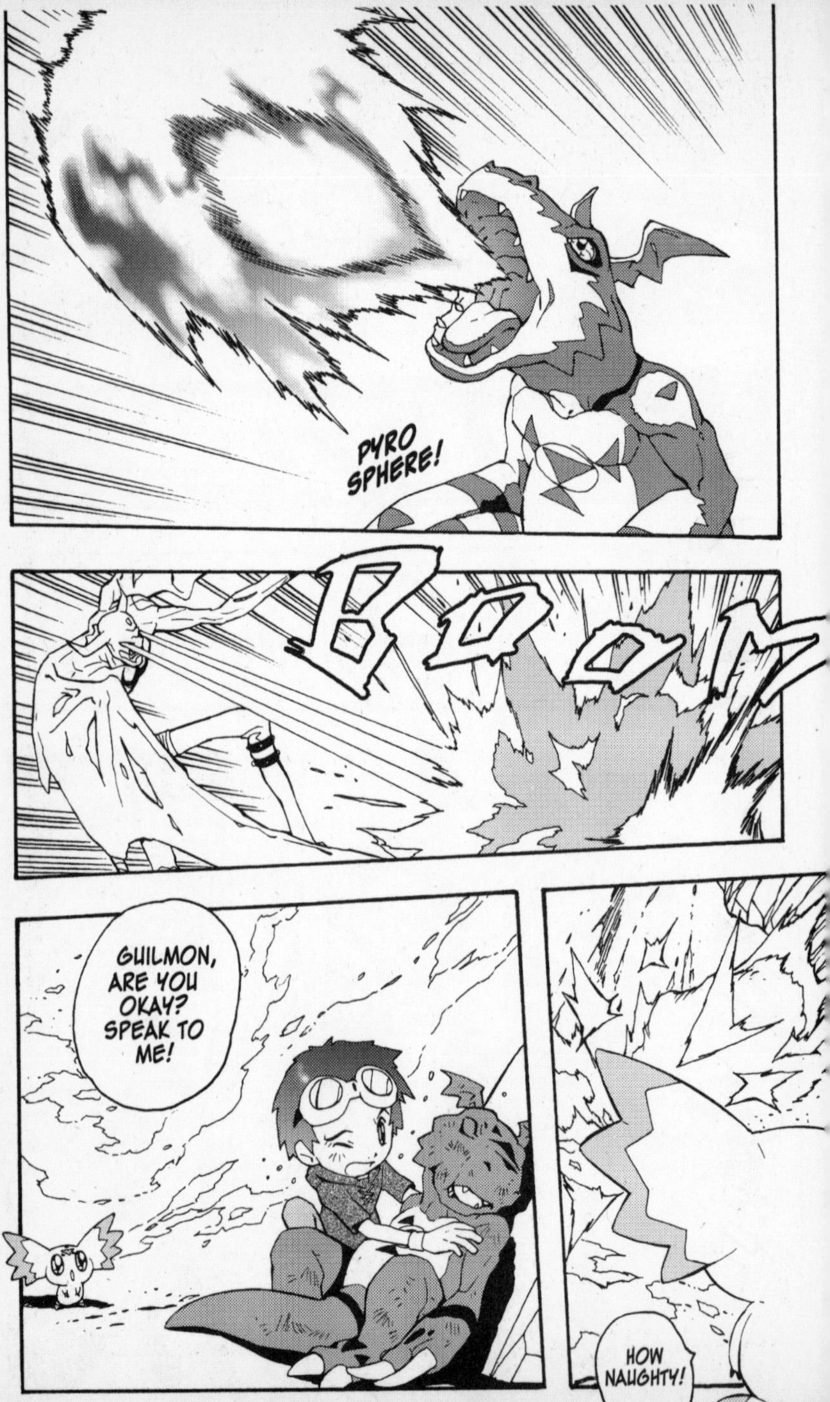
PYRO SPHERE!
BOOM
HOW NAUGHTY!
GUILMON, ARE YOU OKAY? SPEAK TO ME!

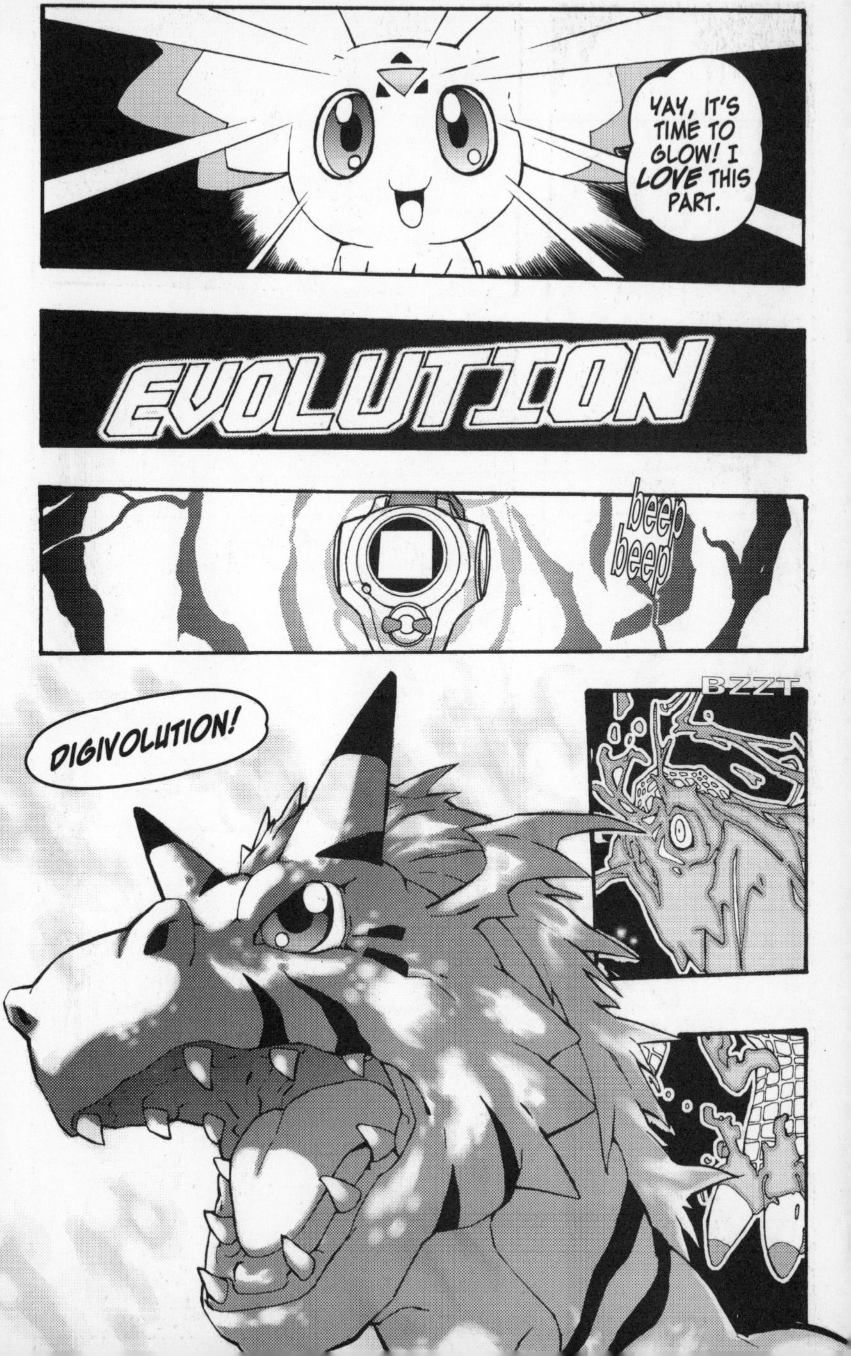
YAY, IT'S TIME TO GLOW! I LOVE THIS PART.
EVOLUTION
beep beep
BZZT
DIGIVOLUTION!

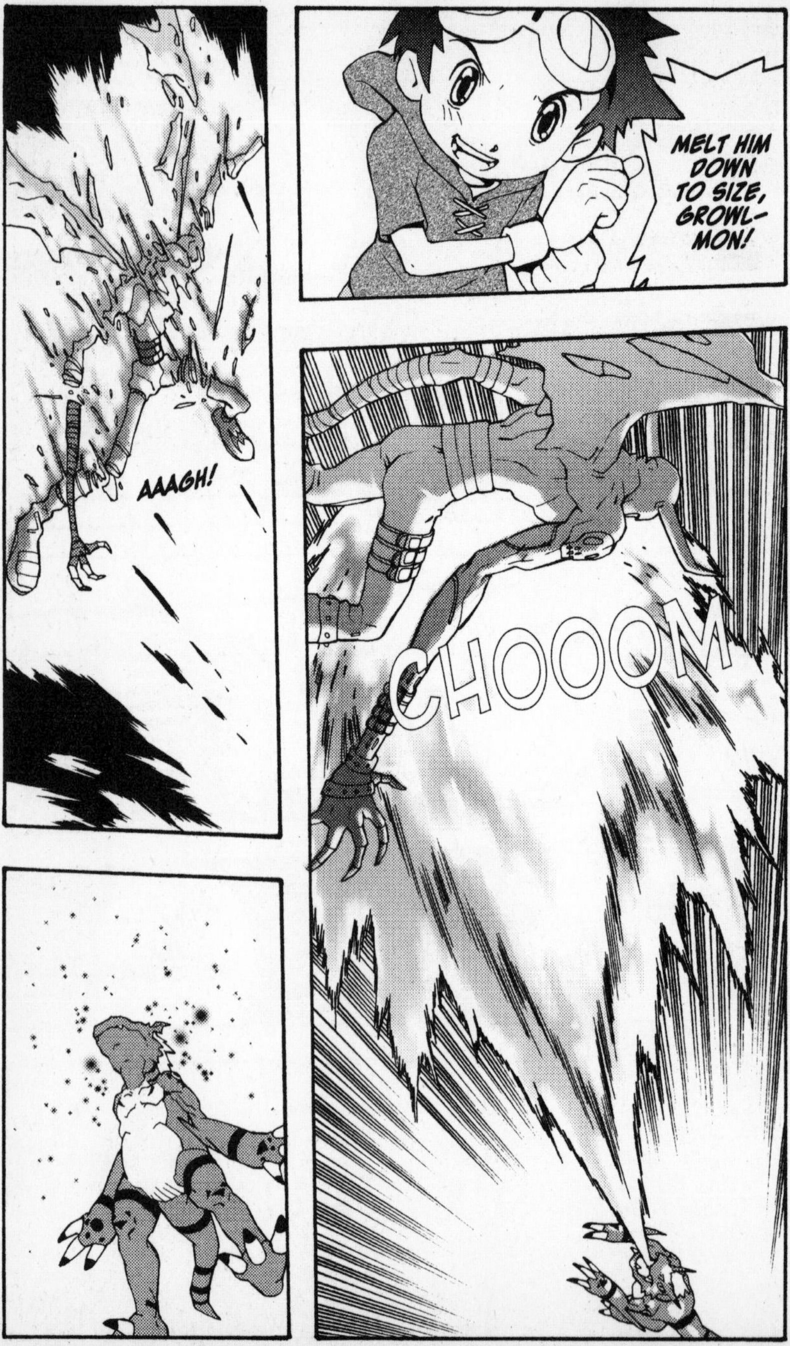
MELT HIM DOWN TO SIZE, GROWL-MON!
CHOOOM
AAAGH!

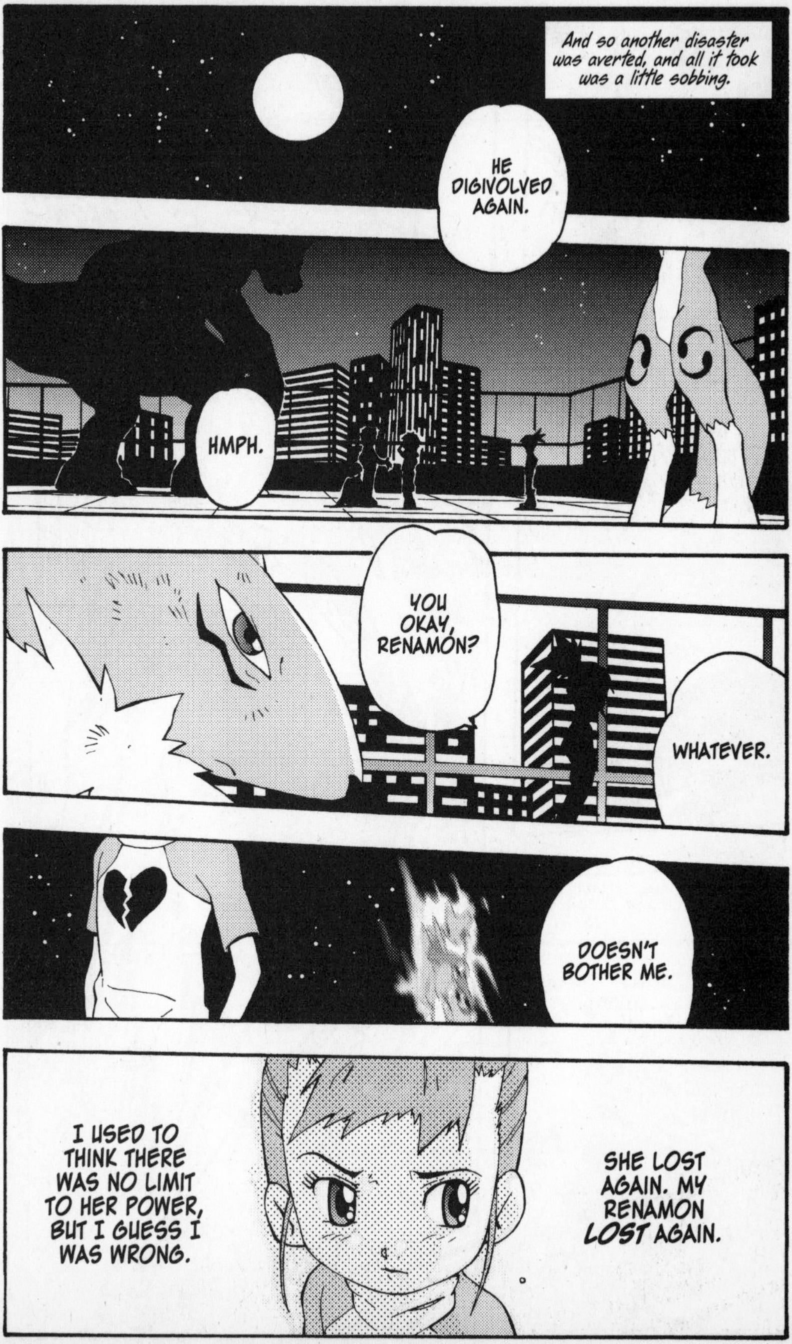
And so another disaster was averted, and all it took was a little sobbing.
HE DIGIVOLVED AGAIN.
HMPH.
YOU OKAY, RENAMON?
WHATEVER.
DOESN'T BOTHER ME.
SHE LOST AGAIN. MY RENAMON *LOST* AGAIN.
I USED TO THINK THERE WAS NO LIMIT TO HER POWER, BUT I GUESS I WAS WRONG.

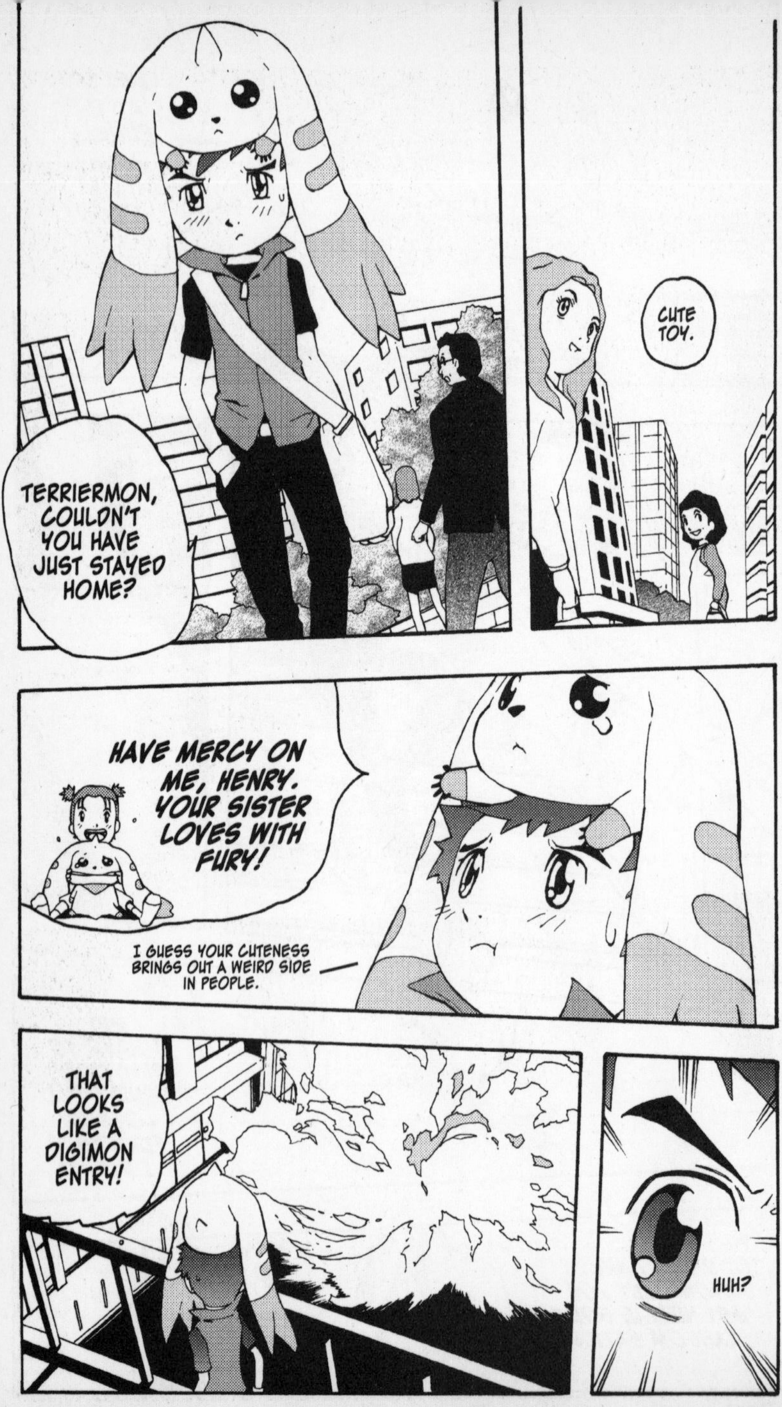
CUTE TOY.
TERRIERMON, COULDN'T YOU HAVE JUST STAYED HOME?
HAVE MERCY ON ME, HENRY. YOUR SISTER LOVES WITH FURY!
I GUESS YOUR CUTENESS BRINGS OUT A WEIRD SIDE IN PEOPLE.
HUH?
THAT LOOKS LIKE A DIGIMON ENTRY!

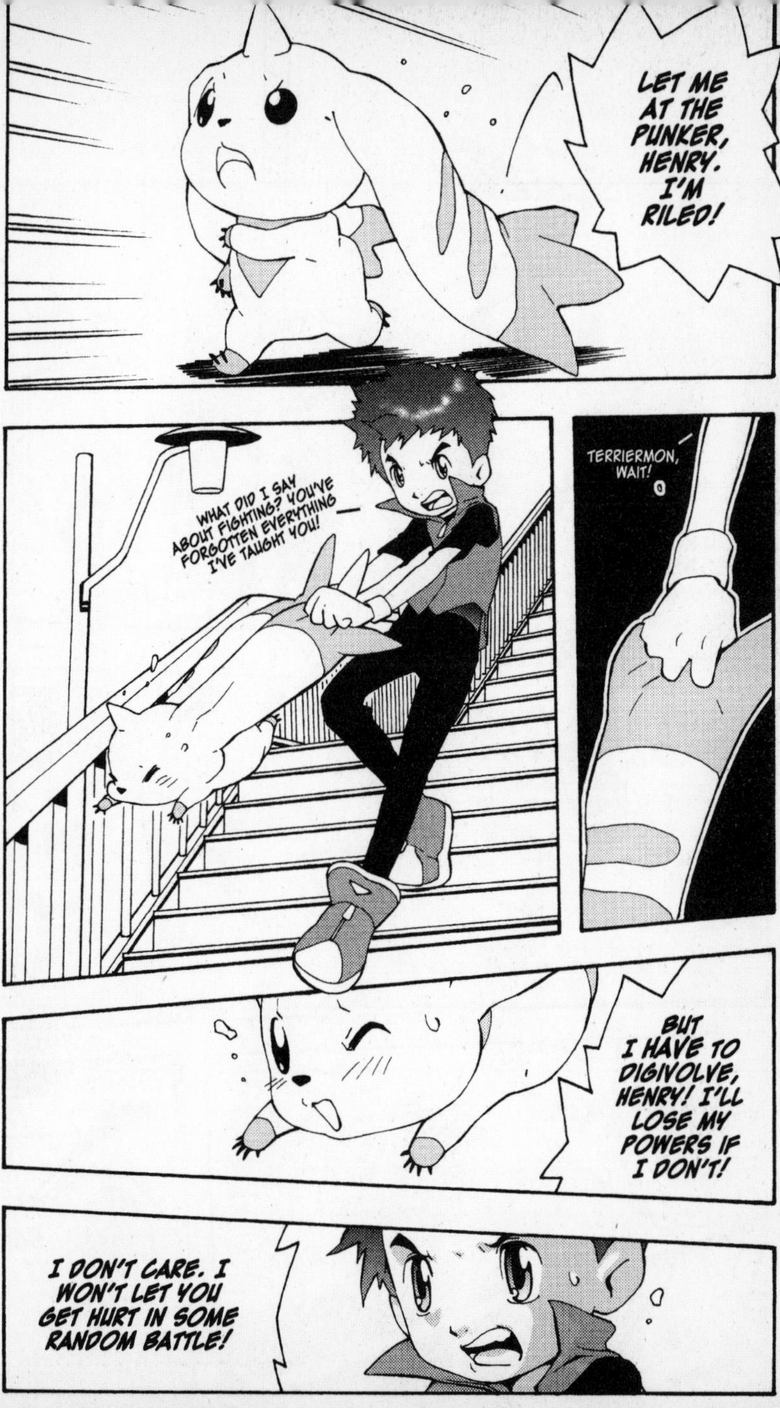
LET ME AT THE PUNKER, HENRY. I'M RILED!
TERRIERMON, WAIT!
WHAT DID I SAY ABOUT FIGHTING? YOU'VE FORGOTTEN EVERYTHING I'VE TAUGHT YOU!
BUT I HAVE TO DIGIVOLVE, HENRY! I'LL LOSE MY POWERS IF I DON'T!
I DON'T CARE. I WON'T LET YOU GET HURT IN SOME RANDOM BATTLE!

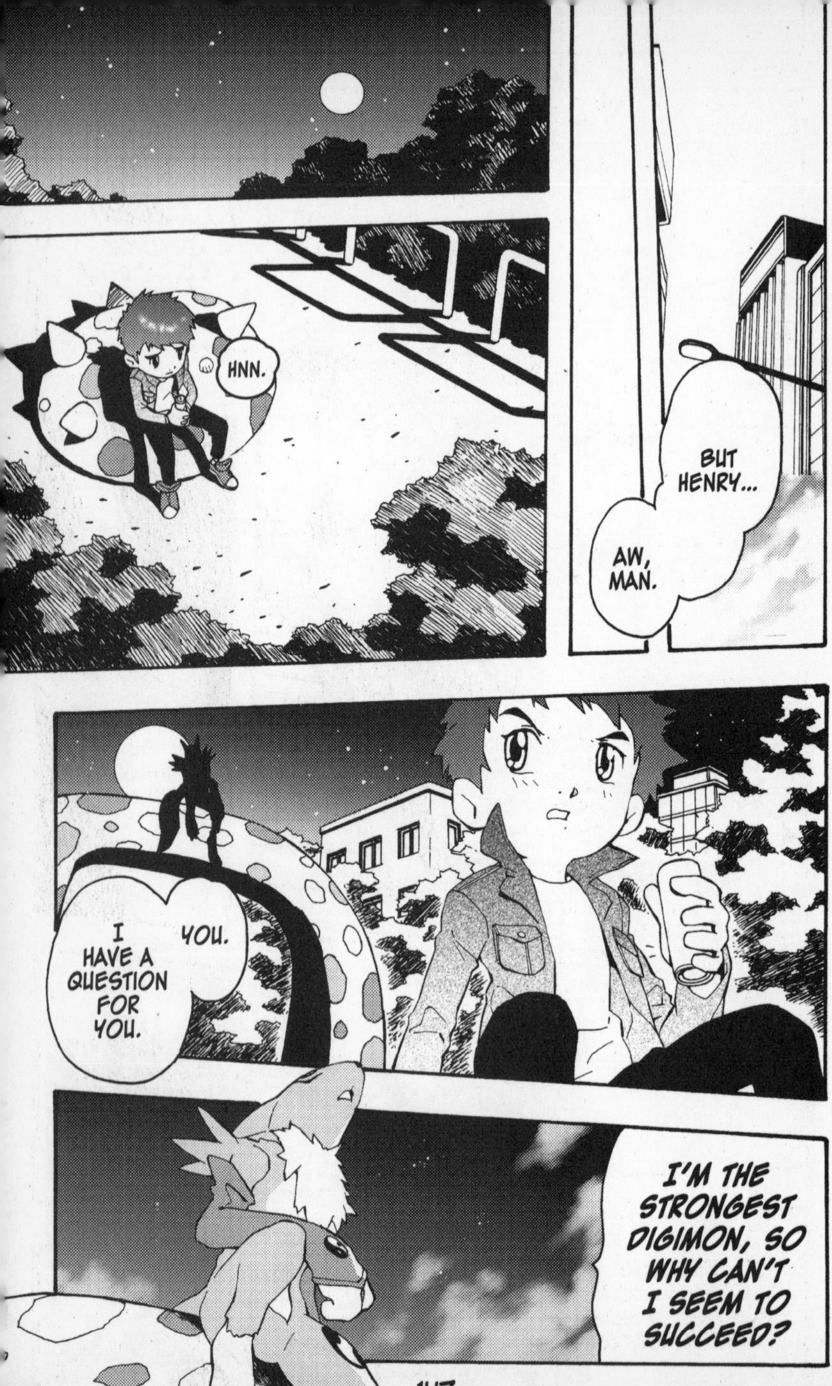
BUT HENRY...
AW, MAN.
HNN.
YOU.
I HAVE A QUESTION FOR YOU.
I'M THE STRONGEST DIGIMON, SO WHY CAN'T I SEEM TO SUCCEED?

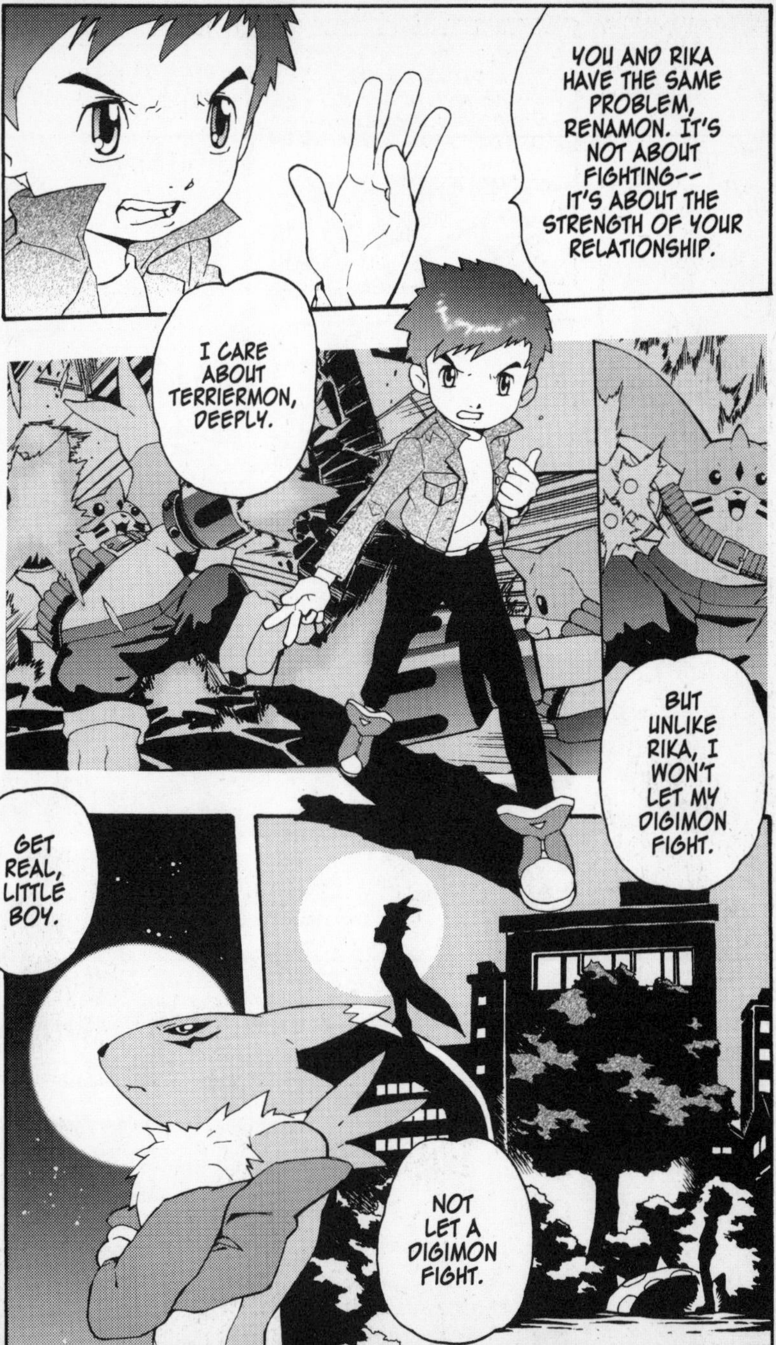

YOU AND RIKA HAVE THE SAME PROBLEM, RENAMON. IT'S NOT ABOUT FIGHTING-- IT'S ABOUT THE STRENGTH OF YOUR RELATIONSHIP.
I CARE ABOUT TERRIERMON, DEEPLY.
BUT UNLIKE RIKA, I WON'T LET MY DIGIMON FIGHT.
NOT LET A DIGIMON FIGHT.
GET REAL, LITTLE BOY.

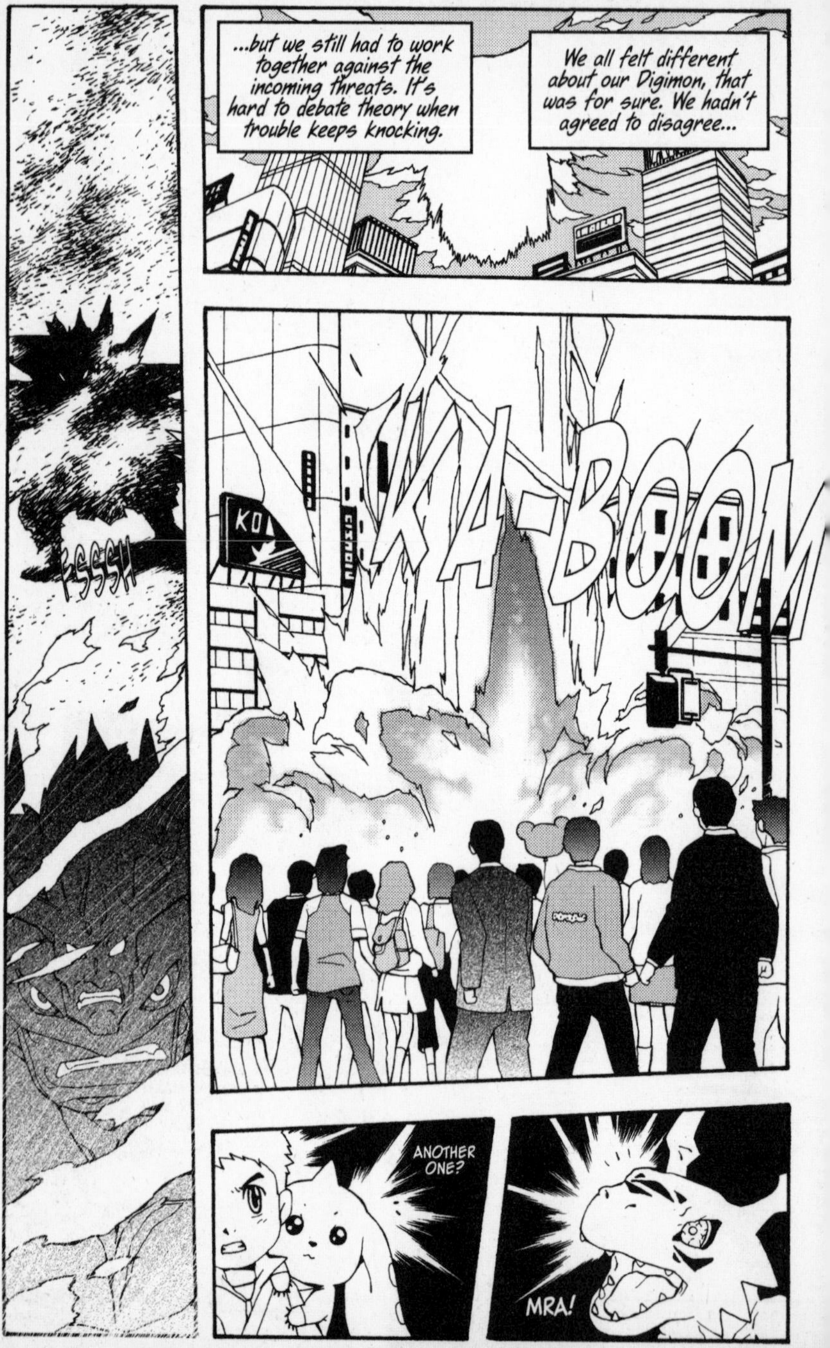
We all felt different about our Digimon, that was for sure. We hadn't agreed to disagree...
...but we still had to work together against the incoming threats. It's hard to debate theory when trouble keeps knocking.
KA-BOOM
MRA!
ANOTHER ONE?
FSSSH

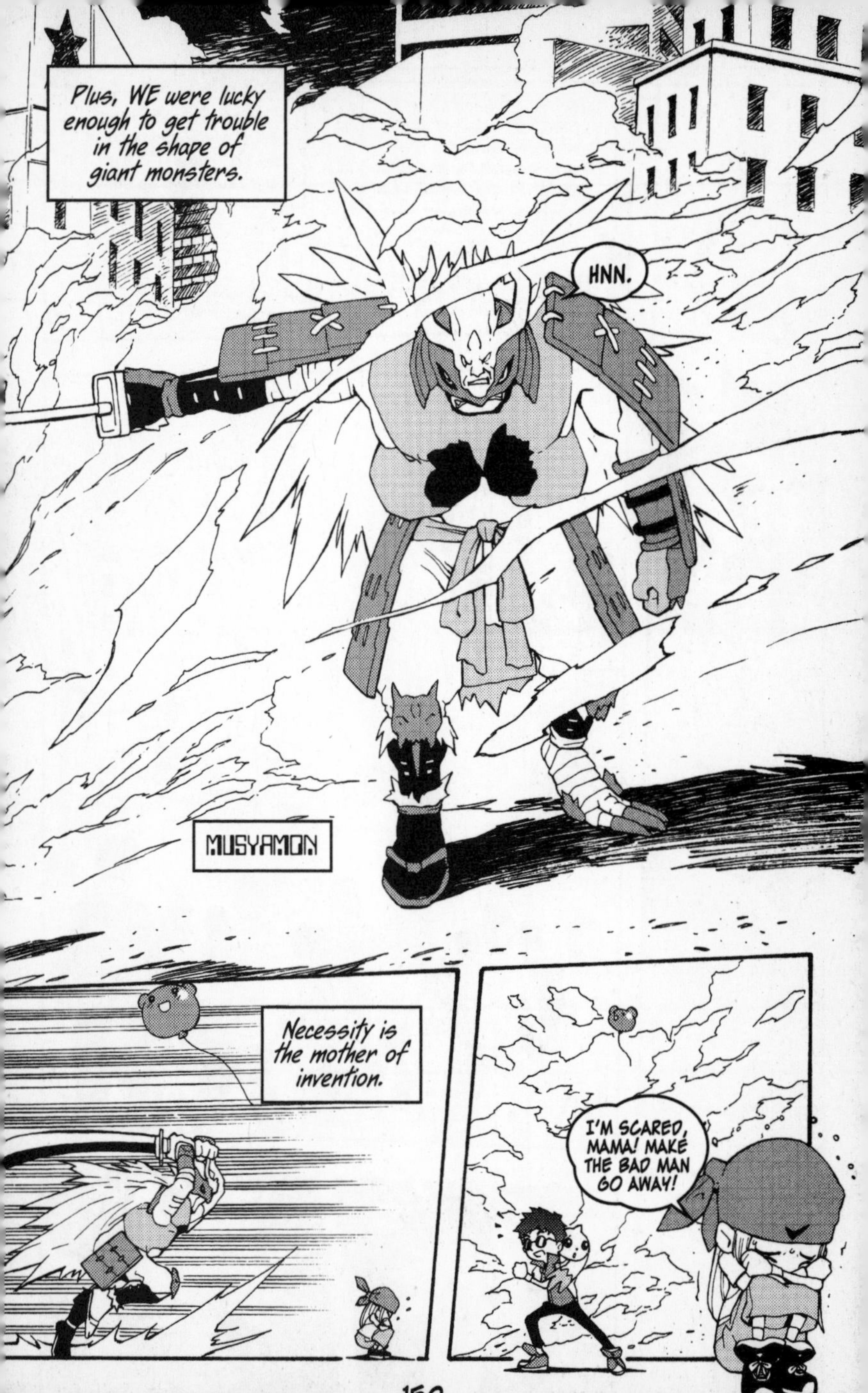
Plus, WE were lucky enough to get trouble in the shape of giant monsters.
HNN.
MUSYAMON
I'M SCARED, MAMA! MAKE THE BAD MAN GO AWAY!
Necessity is the mother of invention.

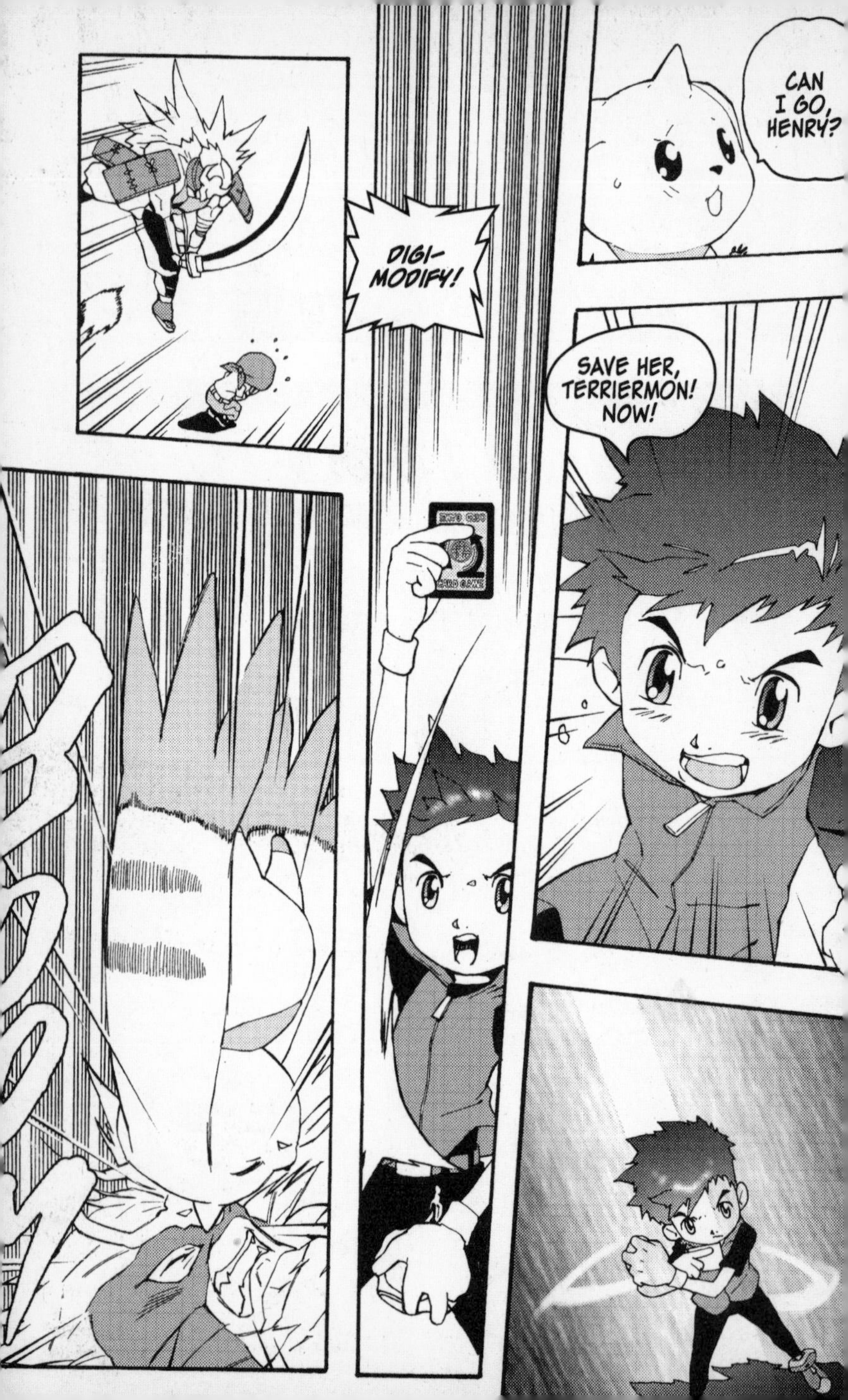
CAN I GO, HENRY?
SAVE HER, TERRIERMON! NOW!
DIGI-MODIFY!

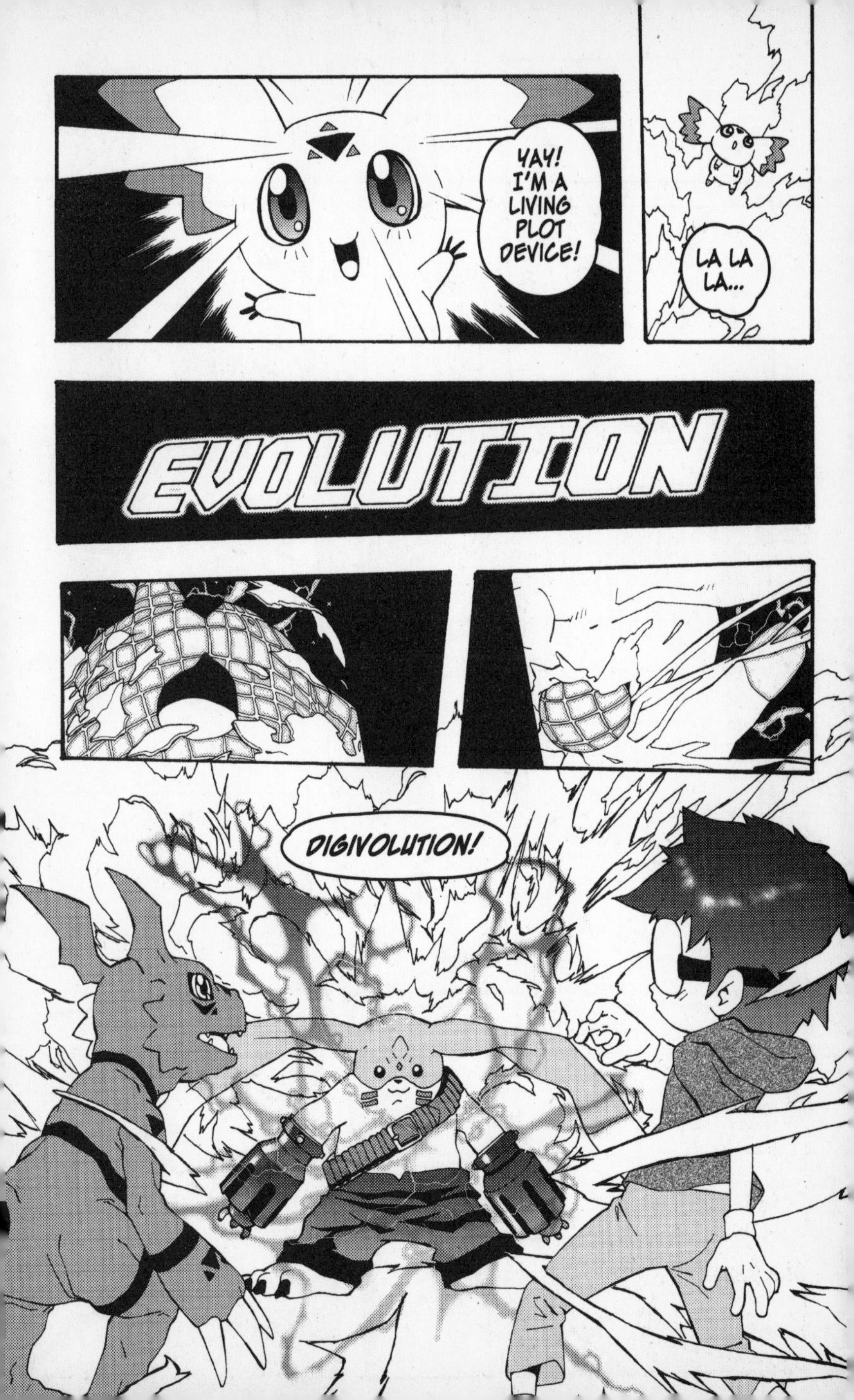
LA LA LA...
YAY! I'M A LIVING PLOT DEVICE!
EVOLUTION
DIGIVOLUTION!

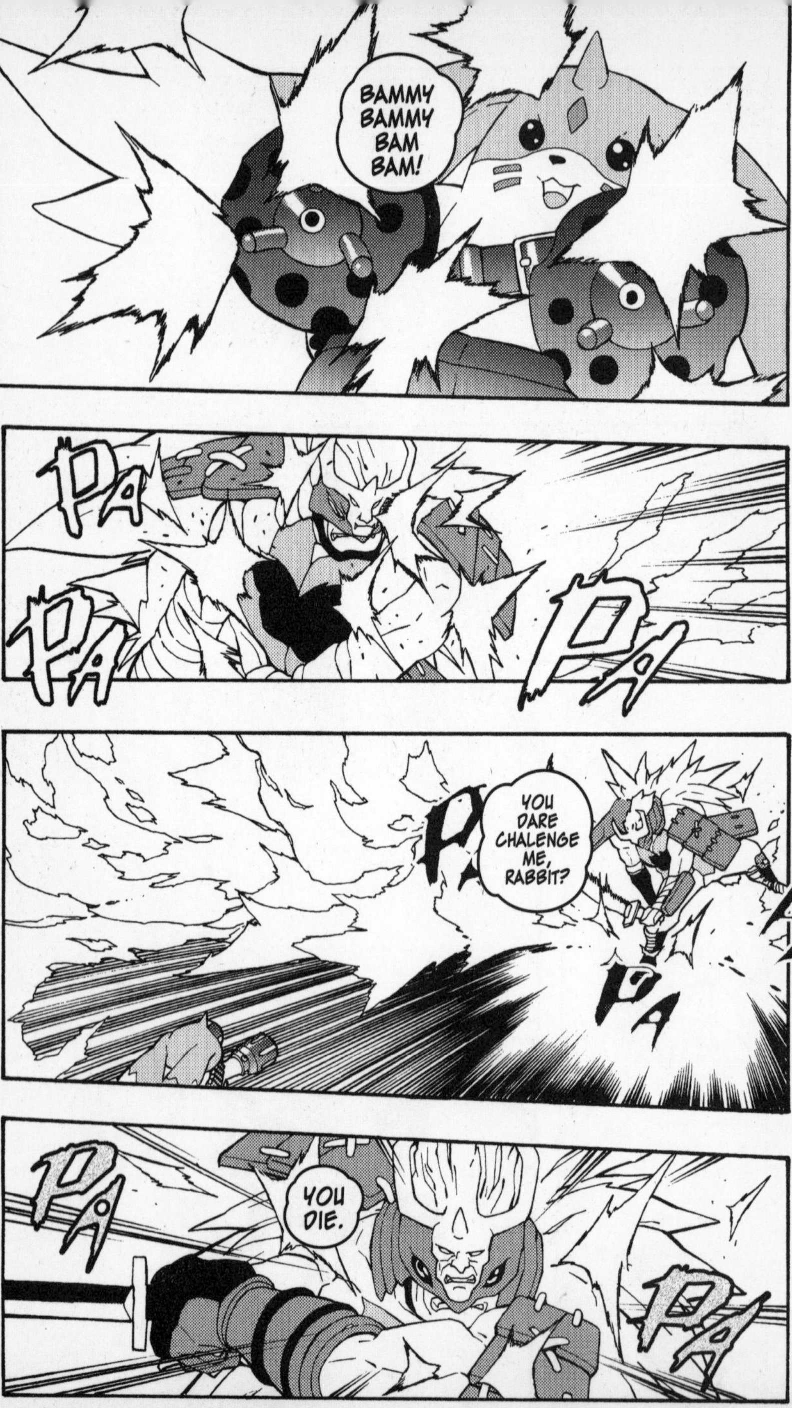
BAMMY BAMMY BAM BAM!
PA
PA PA
PA PA
PA
YOU DARE CHALENGE ME, RABBIT?
PA PA
PA PA
YOU DIE.
PA PA

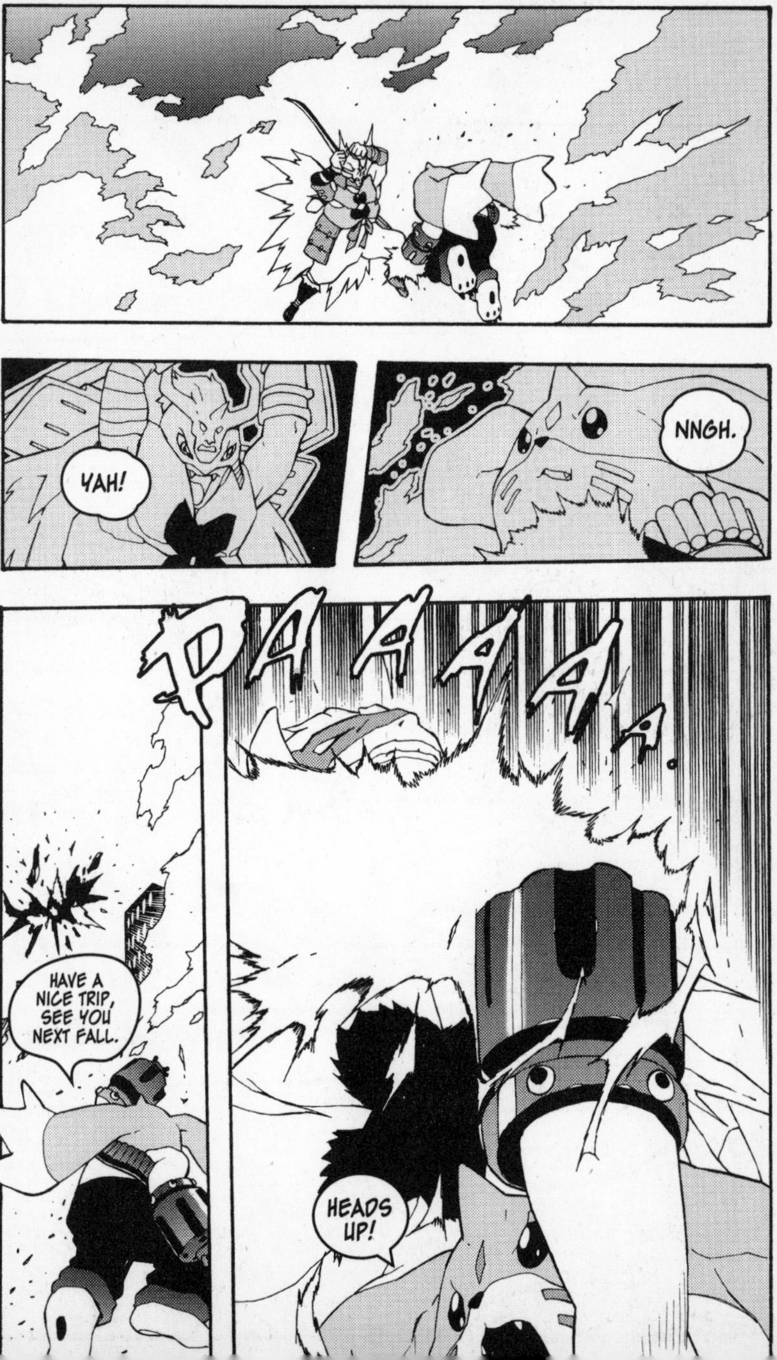
NNGH.
YAH!
PAAAAA
HEADS UP!
HAVE A NICE TRIP, SEE YOU NEXT FALL.

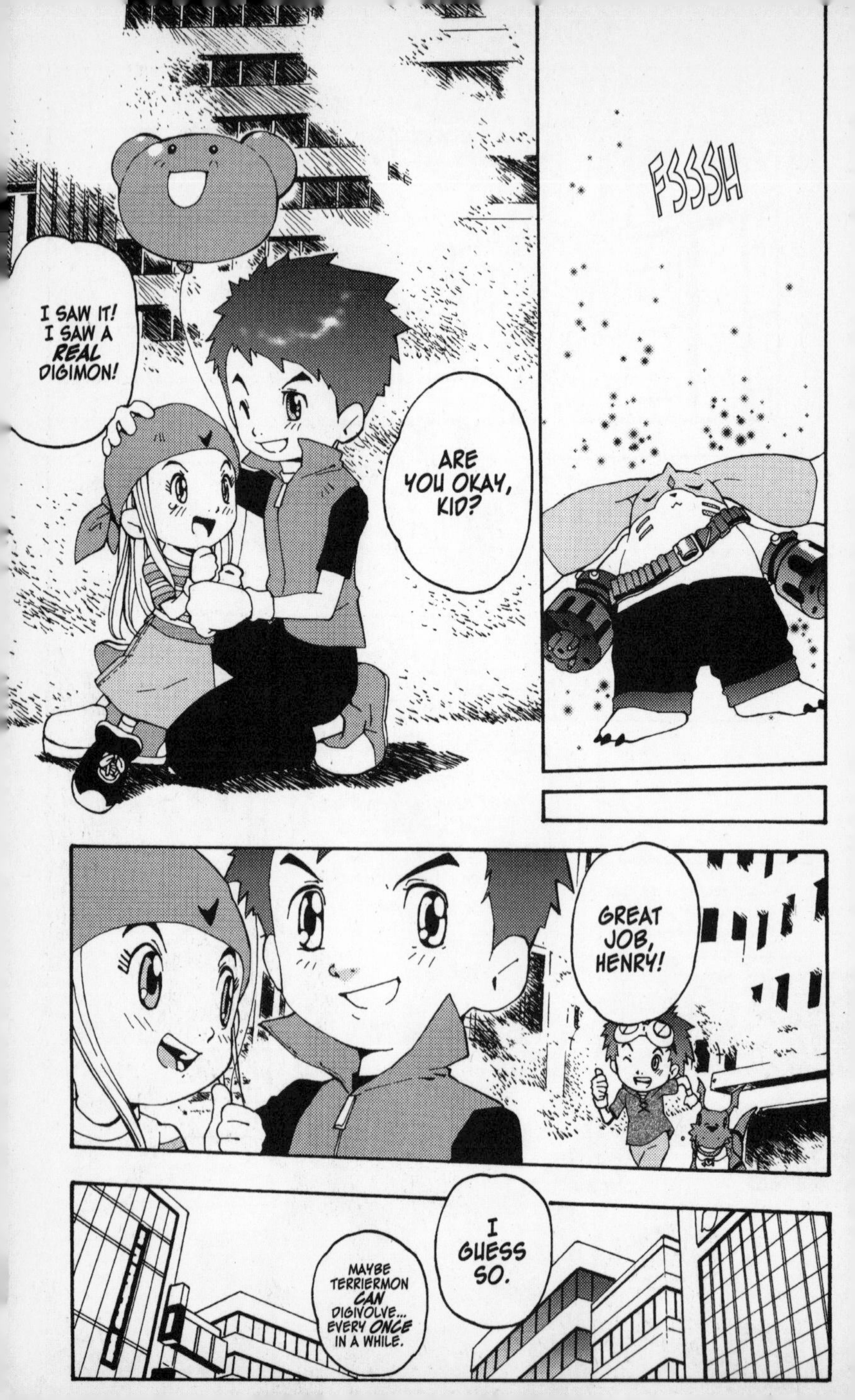
FSSSH
ARE YOU OKAY, KID?
I SAW IT! I SAW A REAL DIGIMON!
GREAT JOB, HENRY!
I GUESS SO.
MAYBE TERRIERMON CAN DIGIVOLVE... EVERY ONCE IN A WHILE.

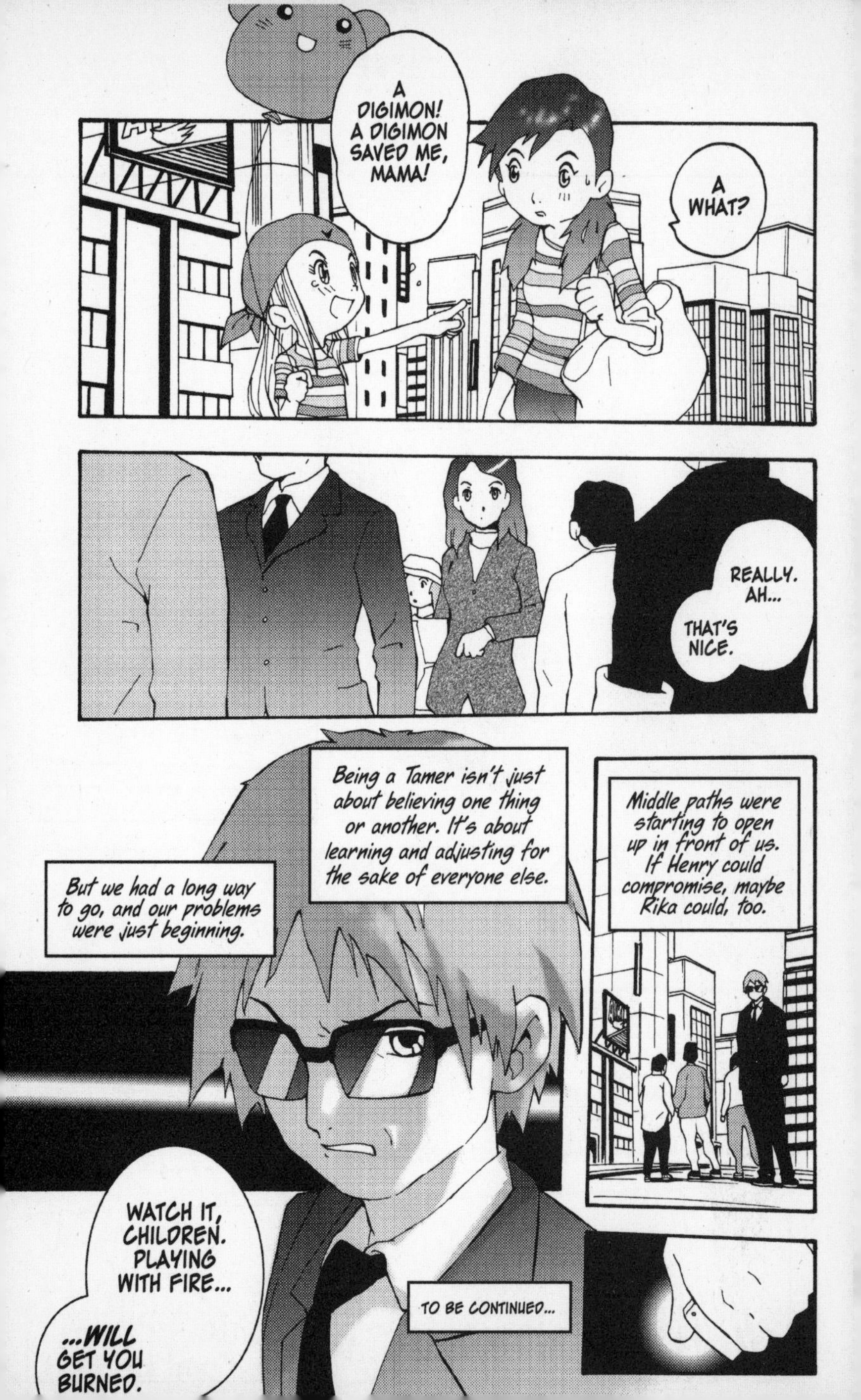
A DIGIMON! A DIGIMON SAVED ME, MAMA!
A WHAT?
REALLY. AH... THAT'S NICE.
Middle paths were starting to open up in front of us. If Henry could compromise, maybe Rika could, too.
Being a Tamer isn't just about believing one thing or another. It's about learning and adjusting for the sake of everyone else.
But we had a long way to go, and our problems were just beginning.
WATCH IT, CHILDREN. PLAYING WITH FIRE...
...WILL GET YOU BURNED.
TO BE CONTINUED...

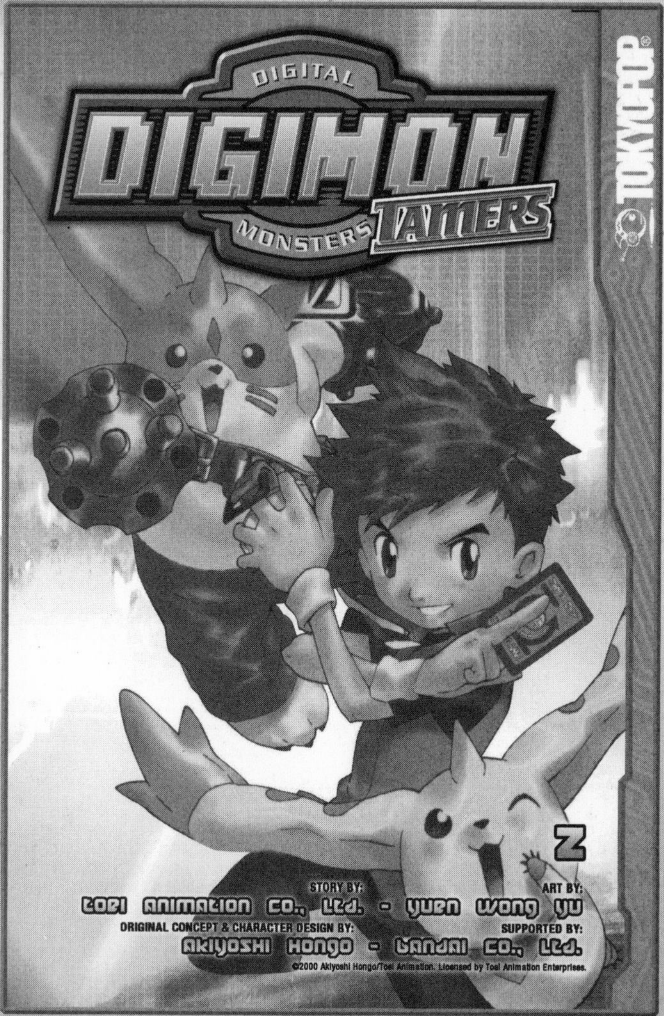

DIGITAL
DIGIMON
MONSTERS
TAMERS
TOKYOPOP
2
STORY BY:
TOEI ANIMATION CO., LTD.
ART BY:
YUEN WONG YU
ORIGINAL CONCEPT & CHARACTER DESIGN BY:
AKIYOSHI HONGO
SUPPORTED BY:
BANDAI CO., LTD.
©2000 Akiyoshi Hongo/Toei Animation. Licensed by Toei Animation Enterprises.

DIGITAL DIGIMON MONSTERS TAMERS™

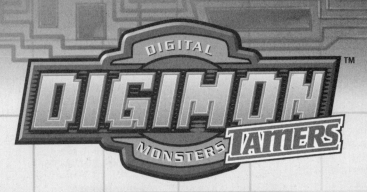

NEXT VOLUME

TWO WORLDS COLLIDE AS THE RIFT BETWEEN THE DIGITAL WORLD AND EARTH GROWS UNSTABLE. WHILE MORE AND MORE DIGIMON START MARKING THEIR TERRITORY ON EARTH, THE TECHNOLOGY INVESTIGATION BUREAU ENFORCES SOME BIG-BROTHERLY RULE (AND WE DON'T MEAN BROTHERLY LOVE). AS MORE SECRETS ABOUT THE REAL DIGIMON ARE REVEALED, THREE NEW PLAYERS GET PULLED INTO THE TAMER RING.

ALSO AVAILABLE FROM  TOKYOPOP®

SHUTTERBOX
SKULL MAN, THE
SUIKODEN III
SUKI
THREADS OF TIME
TOKYO MEW MEW
TREASURE CHESS
VAMPIRE GAME
WISH
WORLD OF HARTZ
ZODIAC P.I.

CINE-MANGA™

ALADDIN
ASTRO BOY
DUEL MASTERS
CARDCAPTORS
CONFESSIONS OF A TEENAGE DRAMA QUEEN
FAIRLY ODDPARENTS, THE
FAMILY GUY
FINDING NEMO
G.I. JOE SPY TROOPS
JACKIE CHAN ADVENTURES
JIMMY NEUTRON: BOY GENIUS, THE ADVENTURES OF
KIM POSSIBLE
LILO & STITCH
LIZZIE MCGUIRE
LIZZIE MCGUIRE MOVIE, THE
MALCOLM IN THE MIDDLE
POWER RANGERS: NINJA STORM
SHREK 2
SPONGEBOB SQUAREPANTS
SPY KIDS 2
SPY KIDS 3-D: GAME OVER
TEENAGE MUTANT NINJA TURTLES
THAT'S SO RAVEN
TRANSFORMERS: ARMADA
TRANSFORMERS: ENERGON

NOVELS

CLAMP SCHOOL PARANORMAL INVESTIGATORS
KARMA CLUB
SAILOR MOON
SLAYERS

ART BOOKS

ART OF CARDCAPTOR SAKURA
ART OF MAGIC KNIGHT RAYEARTH, THE
PEACH: MIWA UEDA ILLUSTRATIONS

ANIME GUIDES

COWBOY BEBOP
GUNDAM TECHNICAL MANUALS
SAILOR MOON SCOUT GUIDES

TOKYOPOP KIDS

STRAY SHEEP

**For more
information visit
www.TOKYOPOP.com**

02.03.04Y

ALSO AVAILABLE FROM TOKYOPOP®

MANGA

.HACK//LEGEND OF THE TWILIGHT
ANGELIC LAYER
BABY BIRTH
BRAIN POWERED
BRIGADOON
B'TX
CANDIDATE FOR GODDESS, THE
CARDCAPTOR SAKURA
CARDCAPTOR SAKURA - MASTER OF THE CLOW
CHRONICLES OF THE CURSED SWORD
CLAMP SCHOOL DETECTIVES
CLOVER
COMIC PARTY
CORRECTOR YUI
COWBOY BEBOP
COWBOY BEBOP: SHOOTING STAR
CRAZY LOVE STORY
CRESCENT MOON
CULDCEPT
CYBORG 009
D•N•ANGEL
DEMON DIARY
DEMON ORORON, THE
DIGIMON
DIGIMON TAMERS
DIGIMON ZERO TWO
DRAGON HUNTER
DRAGON KNIGHTS
DRAGON VOICE
DREAM SAGA
DUKLYON: CLAMP SCHOOL DEFENDERS
ET CETERA
ETERNITY
FAERIES' LANDING
FLCL
FORBIDDEN DANCE
FRUITS BASKET
G GUNDAM
GATEKEEPERS
GIRL GOT GAME
GUNDAM BLUE DESTINY
GUNDAM SEED ASTRAY
GUNDAM WING
GUNDAM WING: BATTLEFIELD OF PACIFISTS
GUNDAM WING: ENDLESS WALTZ
GUNDAM WING: THE LAST OUTPOST (G-UNIT)

HANDS OFF!
HARLEM BEAT
IMMORTAL RAIN
I.N.V.U.
INITIAL D
INSTANT TEEN: JUST ADD NUTS
JING: KING OF BANDITS
JING: KING OF BANDITS - TWILIGHT TALES
JULINE
KARE KANO
KILL ME, KISS ME
KINDAICHI CASE FILES, THE
KING OF HELL
KODOCHA: SANA'S STAGE
LEGEND OF CHUN HYANG, THE
MAGIC KNIGHT RAYEARTH I
MAGIC KNIGHT RAYEARTH II
MAN OF MANY FACES
MARMALADE BOY
MARS
MARS: HORSE WITH NO NAME
METROID
MINK
MIRACLE GIRLS
MODEL
ONE
ONE I LOVE, THE
PEACH GIRL
PEACH GIRL: CHANGE OF HEART
PITA-TEN
PLANET LADDER
PLANETES
PRINCESS AI
PSYCHIC ACADEMY
RAGNAROK
RAVE MASTER
REALITY CHECK
REBIRTH
REBOUND
RISING STARS OF MANGA
SAILOR MOON
SAINT TAIL
SAMURAI GIRL REAL BOUT HIGH SCHOOL
SEIKAI TRILOGY, THE
SGT. FROG
SHAOLIN SISTERS
SHIRAHIME-SYO: SNOW GODDESS TALES

02.03.04Y

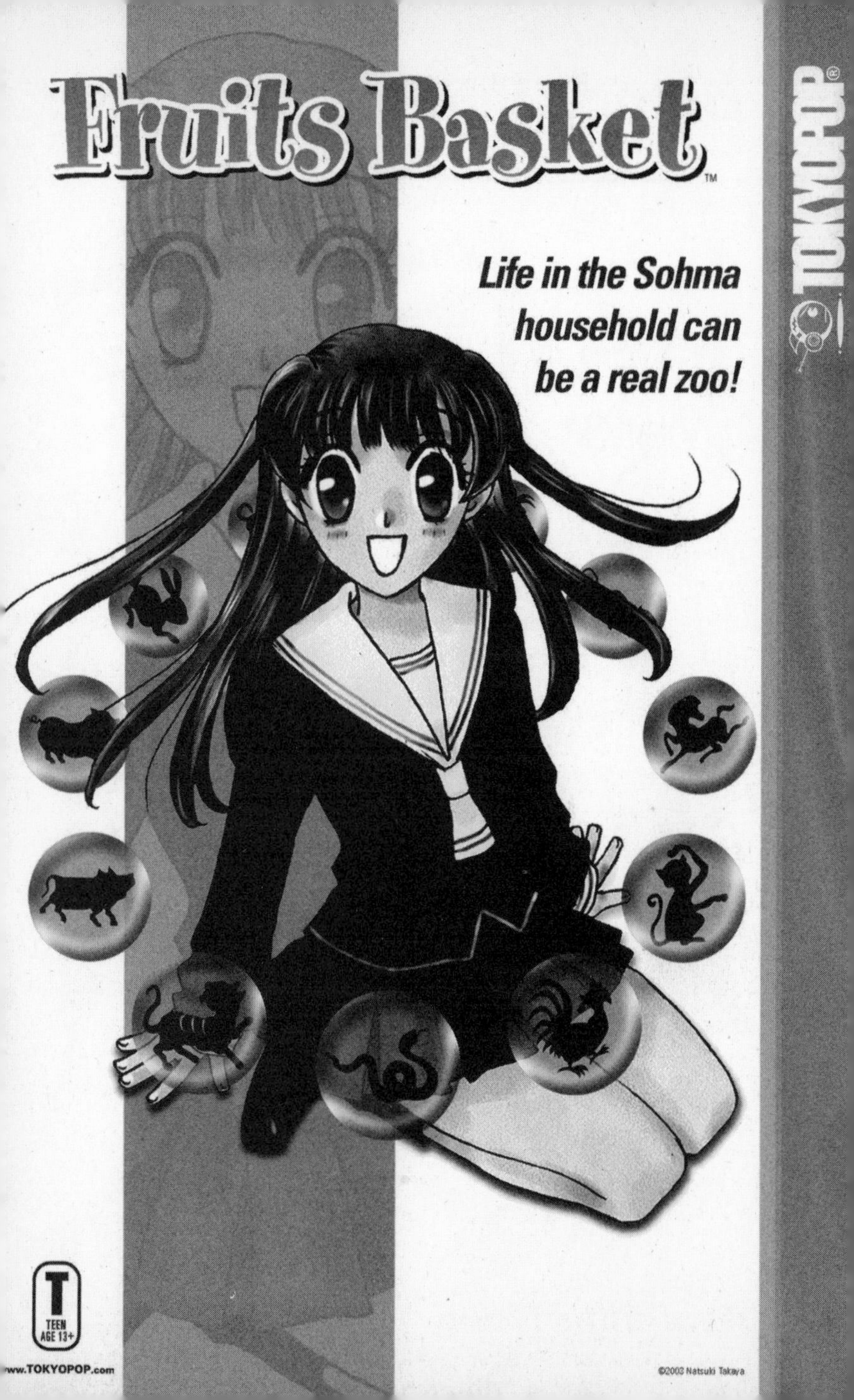

Fruits Basket™
TOKYOPOP®
Life in the Sohma household can be a real zoo!
T TEEN AGE 13+
www.TOKYOPOP.com
©2003 Natsuki Takaya

TOKYOPOP

GATE KEEPERS
ゲートキーパーズ

By:
Keiji Gotoh

Finding Time to Defend The Earth
Between School & Homework

GET GATEKEEPERS IN YOUR FAVORITE BOOK & COMIC STORES NOW!

www.TOKYOPOP.com

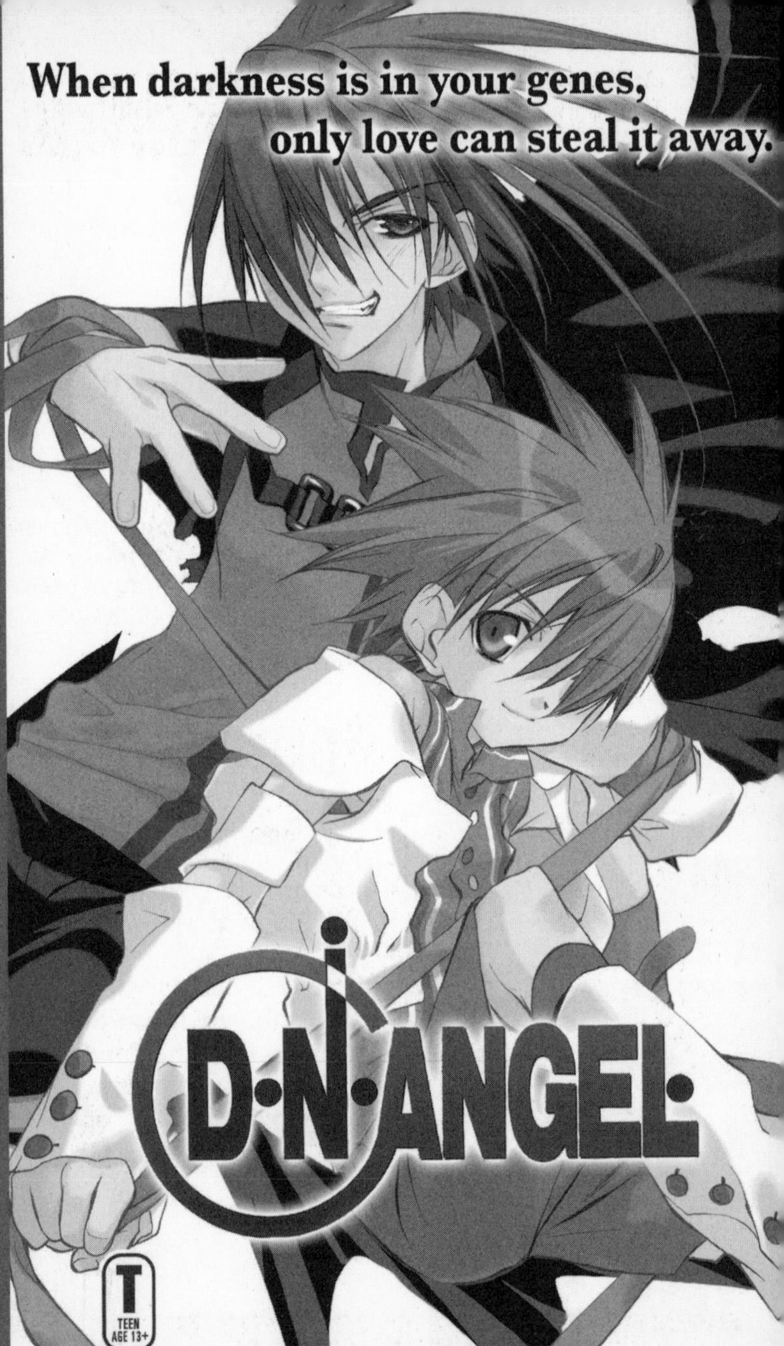
When darkness is in your genes,
only love can steal it away.
D•N•ANGEL
T
TEEN
AGE 13+

P9-BIZ-994

STOP!

This is the back of the book.
You wouldn't want to spoil a great ending!

This book is printed "manga-style," in the authentic Japanese right-to-left format. Since none of the artwork has been flipped or altered, readers get to experience the story just as the creator intended. You've been asking for it, so TOKYOPOP® delivered: authentic, hot-off-the-press, and far more fun!

DIRECTIONS

If this is your first time reading manga-style, here's a quick guide to help you understand how it works.

It's easy... just start in the top right panel and follow the numbers. Have fun, and look for more 100% authentic manga from TOKYOPOP®!